Transputers in
Real-Time Control

C³ INDUSTRIAL CONTROL, COMPUTERS AND COMMUNICATIONS SERIES

Series Editor: **Professor Derek R. Wilson**
University of Westminster, England

Transputers in Real-Time Control

Edited by

G. W. Irwin
The Queen's University of Belfast, UK

and

P. J. Fleming
University of Sheffield, UK

RESEARCH STUDIES PRESS LTD.
Taunton, Somerset, England

JOHN WILEY & SONS INC.
New York · Chichester · Toronto · Brisbane · Singapore

RESEARCH STUDIES PRESS LTD.
24 Belvedere Road, Taunton, Somerset, England TA1 1HD

Marketing and Distribution:

Australia and New Zealand:
Jacaranda Wiley Ltd.
GPO Box 859, Brisbane, Queensland 4001, Australia

Canada:
JOHN WILEY & SONS CANADA LIMITED
22 Worcester Road, Rexdale, Ontario, Canada

Europe, Africa, Middle East and Japan:
JOHN WILEY & SONS LIMITED
Baffins Lane, Chichester, West Sussex, England

North and South America:
JOHN WILEY & SONS INC.
605 Third Avenue, New York, NY 10158, USA

South East Asia:
JOHN WILEY & SONS (SEA) PTE LTD.
37 Jalan Pemimpin 05-04
Block B Union Industrial Building, Singapore 2057

Library of Congress Cataloging-in-Publication Data

Transputers in real-time control / edited by G.W. Irwin and P.J.
Fleming.
   p. cm. — (Industrial control, computers, and communications
series ; 8)
   Includes bibliographical references and index.
   ISBN 0-86380-140-4 (Research Studies Press). — ISBN 0-471-93738-X
(Wiley)
   1. Real-time control. 2. Transputers. I. Fleming, P. J. (Peter
J.) II. Series.
TJ217.7.T73 1992
629.8—dc20   92-25563
                                    CIP

British Library Cataloguing in Publication Data

A catalogue record for this book
is available from the British Library.

ISBN 0 86380 140 4 (Research Studies Press Ltd.)
ISBN 0 471 93738 X (John Wiley & Sons Inc.)

Printed in Great Britain by SRP Ltd., Exeter

Series Editor's Preface

It is a great pleasure to welcome the authors of the Chapters in this book to the Series in Industrial Control, Computers and Communications, and to thank the joint editors, Professors George Irwin and Peter Fleming, for their creativity in synthesising a book which demonstrates how transputers are being used in a wide range of real-time control applications. It is essential reading for all control and computer engineers.

The transputer is the only general purpose CPU that is currently in production in Europe. It was conceived as a transistor-computer that would contain, on one piece of silicon, the CPU, memory and I/O through the on-chip communication links; and therefore it provides a component for a scalable multiprocessor. Commercial products from European companies such as Parsys, Meiko, Parsytec and Quintek have utilised the transputer in their MIMD machines.

While such parallel computing machines have been well received, the worldwide revenue for all parallel computing machines is only of the order of £60 million at 1992 prices, which in worldwide computing values is the petty cash account! A general purpose CPU needs a mass market to generate the revenues to support the necessary future development that will take account of the improvements in silicon technology; at least ten million transistors per chip are predicted for 1995/96. The market for embedded systems and control is of crucial importance to the transputer. Consequently, a book on embedded real-time control is particularly timely and relevant. The authors have presented an exciting and stimulating range of applications, which clearly demonstrate the power and flexibility of the transputer in control.

The integration of computing has long been recognised as an essential feature of modern high performance equipment in which reliability, repeatability and safety are critical features. The complexity of many modern systems is now recognised as being beyond the capability of a human operator to control. There are many examples that can be cited to illustrate the fact that embedded control is an integral component of the total performance envelope - ranging from fly-by-wire in commercial aircraft as well as high-performance variable geometry, military aircraft to the stringent requirements of a nuclear power-station. The increase in embedded control in domestic equipment can be illustrated by the prediction that the cost of embedded control in a family car will increase in the next decade to 20% of the car's value. The particular examples chosen by the editors have brought together a comprehensive review of embedded control using the transputer. The book will prove a valuable and practical exposition of the subject for readers seeking to understand how they can implement transputer-based control systems, because commercial competition constantly demands that complex equipment meets the most stringent performance requirements, and that it is designed and delivered on time and within tight cost boundaries. This is particularly so in areas of the economy that have to react to the "peace dividend", in which new commercial challenges have to be surmounted.

There is a clear industrial and commercial need for expositions which show how new technology and techniques can be applied. The authors have satisfied this need and presented an excellent state-of-the-art review of a subject which is under continuous development.

Derek Wilson
London 1992

Preface

In some respects writing this preface has been the most pleasurable part of the whole exercise, not only because it represents the culmination of much hard work, but also because it provides an opportunity to look back and consider briefly the background of activity which led to this point.

Transputers are manufactured by Inmos Ltd, originally a UK government start-up company, now a member of SGS-Thompson Microelectronics NV. Inmos introduced the first member of the transputer family, the IMST414, in 1985. Since then the family has grown to include 16-bit and 32-bit processors, link adaptors and the C004 link switch. INMOS will soon bring to market the first members of a new series of transputer products, including the T9000 transputer and the C104 packet router. Embedded, distributed control applications were seen as an important market for the device right from the outset.

Our interest in the general area of parallel control grew alongside a series of events which were organised by the Institution of Electrical Engineers (IEE). The first Colloquium in the area of Control Engineering held in January 1987 was entitled, rather prophetically, "Parallel Processing - a New Direction for Control?". The success and obvious interest from both academia and industry prompted further Colloquia in 1988 and 1990 and the establishment of a series of Workshops in 1987-1989 on "Parallel Processing for Control - the Transputer and other Architectures". It is of satisfaction to note that these Workshops are now part of an IFAC series on

Algorithms and Architectures for Real-time Control (Bangor, UK 1991 and Seoul, Korea 1992).

The Science & Engineering Research Council/Department of Trade and Industry Initiative in Engineering Applications of Transputers has just been completed. The aim was to promote the development of transputer applications within the UK. As part of that process a Transputer Application Community Club in Real-time Control(CTACC) was established to co-ordinate and integrate both academic and industrial users of the new technology in the subject area of real-time control and some of the work described in this text initiated from that effort.

Given this background, and the imminent launch of the T9000 family, it is timely to produce a textbook which examines and reports on the use of transputers in real-time control across a spectrum of applications.

Our aim has been to showcase the potential of parallel processing for real-time control with the transputer as a unifying theme to provide a coherent and integrated text for the reader. The book will naturally be of use to control practitioners and researchers in the field. However, we have included an introductory Chapter to discuss more general issues associated with parallel processing for real-time control and to draw attention to the special features of this application area. It is anticipated that this will provide a useful pathway for newcomers to the subject.

In conclusion, we must pay tribute to the enthusiasm, energy and patience of our contributors and also thank our respective families for their support.

George Irwin   Peter Fleming
Belfast 1992   Sheffield 1992

Contents

List of Contributors

G M Asher
Department of Electrical and
Electronic Engineering
The University of Nottingham
University Park
Nottingham NG7 2RD
UK

A W P Bakkers
Control Laboratory
Electrical Engineering Faculty
University of Twente
PO Box 127
NL-7500 AE Enschede
Netherlands

R Cuyvers
Departement Elektrotechniek
Katholieke Universiteit Leuven-ESAT
Kardinaal Mercierlaan 94
B-3001 Heverlee
Belgium

P J Fleming
Department of Automatic Control and
Systems Engineering
University of Sheffield
PO Box 600
Mappin Street
Sheffield S1 4DU
UK

E Fraga
Department of Chemical Engineering
University of Edinburgh
The King's Buildings
Edinburgh EH9 3JL
UK

D F Garcia Nocetti
School of Electronic Engineering
Science
University College of North Wales
Dean Street
Bangor
Gwynedd LL57 1UT
UK

J O Gray
Department of Electronic and
Electrical Engineering
University of Salford
Salford M5 4WT
UK

S Hill
Department of Electronic and
Electrical Engineering
University of Salford
Salford M5 4WT
UK

D J Holding
Department of Electrical Engineering
and Applied Physics
Aston University
Aston Triangle
Birmingham B4 7ET
UK

G W Irwin
Department of Electrical and
Electronic Engineering
Queen's University
Belfast BT9 5AH
UK

R Lauwereins
Departement Elektrotechniek
Katholieke Universiteit Leuven-ESAT
Kardinaal Mercierlaan 94
B-3001 Heverlee
Belgium

L P Maguire
Department of Electrical and
Electronic Engineering
Queen's University
Belfast BT9 5AH
UK

R McKinnel
Department of Chemical Engineering
University of Edinburgh
The King's Buildings
Edinburgh EH9 3JL
UK

J Meijer
Control Laboratory
Electrical Engineering Faculty
University of Twente
PO Box 127
NL-7500 AE Enschede
Netherlands

J C Musters
Control Laboratory
Electrical Engineering Faculty
University of Twente
PO Box 127
NL-7500 AE Enschede
Netherlands

J W Ponton
Department of Chemical Engineering
University of Edinburgh
The King's Buildings
Edinburgh EH9 3JL
UK

J S Sagoo
Department of Electrical Engineering
and Applied Physics
Aston University
Aston Triangle
Birmingham B4 7ET
UK

N Skilling
Department of Chemical Engineering
University of Edinburgh
The King's Buildings
Edinburgh EH9 3JL
UK

M Sumner
Department of Electrical and
Electronic Engineering
The University of Nottingham
University Park
Nottingham NG7 2RD
UK

J M Tahir
Department of Automatic Control and
Systems Engineering
University of Sheffield
PO Box 600
Mappin Street
Sheffield S1 4DU
UK

H G Tillema
Control Laboratory
Electrical Engineering Faculty
University of Twente
PO Box 127
NL-7500 AE Enschede
Netherlands

G S Virk
Department of Electrical Engineering
University of Bradford
Bradford BD7 1DP
UK

Chapter 1
Introduction

PJ Fleming and GW Irwin

1.1 PRELIMINARIES

The aim of this introductory Chapter is to place the contents of the Research Monograph in context, by reviewing briefly how real-time control has developed to its present state and also, importantly, to explain why the research described in the following Chapters constitutes an exciting and significant future direction for the subject. Automatic control techniques are applied right across the spectrum of engineering, including electrical, aeronautical, chemical, mechanical, environmental and medical. Consequently the variety and scale of examples of control systems is equally wide, e.g. fly-by-wire aircraft, power station boilers, robots, greenhouse environments, electricity generators, domestic heating systems, insulin pumps and video recorders.

Typically a control system must function at a number of levels. *Loop control* generally involves the use of negative feedback, perhaps with dynamic compensation to produce a fast, accurate, well damped response which is resistant to external disturbances and robust to changes in the system being controlled. *Sequential control* is concerned with producing the sequence of operations which a system should perform, such as the timed program on a domestic washing machine. *Supervisory control* ensures that the overall or global objective of the control system is being achieved. At one level this may consist simply of a condition monitoring function, for safety and fault detection. In a chemical plant it may involve fusing data from several sensors to detect faults and assist the operator to recover from an unforeseen situation.

Not surprisingly perhaps, advances in automatic control over the past four decades have been greatly enhanced by corresponding developments in electronics, particularly digital computer technology. Process control, as used in the chemical industry, provides a good illustration of this linkage. Thus, in the 1950's, early digital computers were expensive, cumbersome and unreliable and were only employed for plant monitoring and the supervisory control of existing loops. The first use of a digital computer directly within a feedback loop did not come until 1962 when a Ferranti Argus 200 machine was installed at an ICI ammonia-soda plant to measure 224 variables and manipulate 129 valves directly. Direct digital control had arrived. More recently, the 1970s and 1980s saw rapidly developing microprocessor technology being widely used in the implementation of small-scale and inexpensive digital controllers, as described later, and the growth of distributed control systems with a single master computer supervising a number of slaves.

It is worth mentioning that computer technology has also influenced and stimulated research effort on theoretical aspects, such as adaptive control. Thus the concept of a self-organising control system, where the control law adapts to accommodate significant plant changes and hence maintain performance, was first put forward by Kalman [1.1] in 1958. Building on earlier theoretical progress in system identification and stimulated by the potential of microprocessors, adaptive control schemes like self-tuning and model reference adaptive control [1.2] have been advanced and refined in recent years.

1.2   THE CHALLENGE OF REAL-TIME CONTROL

Let us now look more specifically at real-time digital control where, amongst other functions, the calculation of the controller output must be performed, within the loop

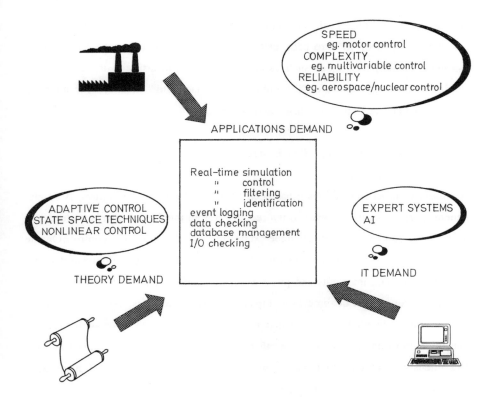

SPEED
  eg. motor control
COMPLEXITY
  eg. multivariable control
RELIABILITY
  eg. aerospace/nuclear control

APPLICATIONS DEMAND

ADAPTIVE CONTROL
STATE SPACE TECHNIQUES
NONLINEAR CONTROL

Real-time simulation
  "   control
  "   filtering
  "   identification
event logging
data checking
database management
I/O checking

EXPERT SYSTEMS
AI

THEORY DEMAND

IT DEMAND

Fig. 1.1 Real-Time Control Challenge

sample interval, on the basis of periodically sampled measurements. Despite the increasing computing power referred to above this can still be a problem in many cases. Thus a modern real-time control system (Fig. 1.1) might typically involve algorithms for control, simulation, optimisation, filtering and identification, in addition to simpler practical tasks such as event logging and data checking. Clearly, the more complex the algorithm, the more difficult the problem of performing the necessary calculations in real-time and it is arguable that the pull-through of advanced control theory into industrial applications is often hampered by the amount of computation required. In addition, different applications will place varying demands on a real-time controller. For example, the sample intervals for the control of electric motors will be short because of the small time constants involved. Multivariable systems will add complexity to the control calculations since several control signals must be calculated simultaneously and, in aerospace and nuclear control applications, reliability is essential. Finally, techniques such as expert systems and artificial intelligence are finding increasing application in control, as in "jacketing" software for adaptive controllers like the Expert 460 discussed below.

1.3   REAL-TIME HARDWARE SOLUTIONS

A variety of processor hardware has been employed for real-time control. A single, general-purpose *microprocessor* often requires a high number of interface chips and an external co-processor, or analogue processing, for fast real-time control. On the other hand, the *microcontroller* consists of a microprocessor with analogue and digital converters, timers, interrupts and pulse-width modulation (PWM) on-board the chip with a consequent low off-processor chip count. Microcontrollers, like the Intel MCS-96 and Motorola 68HC11, originated from microcomputer systems with program execution from on-chip ROM, rather than external RAM. They were introduced for I/O intensive, yet computationally simple, real-time applications and have been employed in cost-sensitive, consumer and commodity electronic products needing close-coupled, locally small-scale, real-time control using Boolean and analogue I/O, e.g. car electronics, video recorders and industrial instruments. Typical real-time control tasks which are performed on microcontrollers include data acquisition, digital filtering, closed-loop compensation, range clamping and parameter adaption.

A large number of new products, of ever increasing sophistication, for industrial process control have appeared on the market over the past decade. The progress made here can be best illustrated by considering the features of a microprocessor-based controller currently available in the market. The Expert 460 [1.3] claims automatic tuning of any plant which is open-loop stable. Three microprocessors support a one-shot tuner, an adaptive process estimator, a controller designer, the controller and an "expert system" overseer. As well as conventional PID control, the Expert 460 can provide two alternative adaptive control laws in the form of implicit control with a variable prediction horizon or a generalised explicit pole-placement controller.

Until recently the bandwidths of these processors were restricted with a consequential limited application to high bandwidth servomotor control. Microcontrollers have been successfully employed in automotive systems, both for non time-critical applications like the trip computer or the fuel gauge and, increasingly, for real-time engine management with outputs controlling gas ignition and fuel mixture and inputs associated with accelerator setpoint, air and engine temperature, engine revolutions etc. It is interesting to note that this application area has probably stimulated the rapid development of microcontrollers, rather than the smaller and more diverse industrial control market.

Application Specific Integrated Circuits or ASICS extend the microcontroller concept to minimise the off-processor chip count and on-chip silicon for a particular application.

Microcontrollers differ from *digital signal processors* (DSPs) in that the latter are not provided with sophisticated I/O facilities, nor the appropriate instruction sets, for real-time control. Rather, DSPs were conceived to implement the fast, repetitive, multiply-shift-add operations characteristic of signal processing.

New products are arising from the market for high performance microcontrollers, directed at the automobile and servomotor control sectors. In addition to the enhancement of existing microcontroller families, a new generation is evolving which incorporates the fast processing capabilities of the DSP, augmented with peripheral on-chip I/O facilities for real-time control. These are called *Digital Signal Controllers* (DSCs) and the first such device was the TMS320C14, introduced in 1988. This incorporated a hardware peripheral section, similar to 16-bit microcontrollers, an event manager, 4 independent timers and a parallel I/O port. The applications envisaged demand algorithmically intensive, real-time control on an instrument scale, e.g.

automotive (engine control, braking, and active suspension), disk drives (servomotor control of head position and spindle motor), robotics (multiple axis control), motor control (ac and dc industrial drives) and plotters (pen positioning).

1.4   PARALLEL PROCESSING

1.4.1   Background - Von Neumann Architecture

The conventional von Neumann architecture for the digital computer is illustrated by the schematic in Fig. 1.2. Essentially this structure implies a separation of the main memory (for storing data and instructions) from the central processing unit (CPU) which consists of a single arithmetic and logic unit (ALU) to execute the basic arithmetic and logic operations and a single control unit which decodes the program instructions and monitors their execution on the CPU.

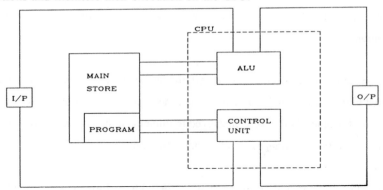

Fig. 1.2 Von Neumann Architecture

The performance of this computer architecture, as measured by the rate at which instructions are processed, is subject to two constraints: that imposed by the rate at which data can be delivered to the CPU and the speed of the CPU itself.

Improvements in the underlying integrated circuit technology have facilitated dramatic increases in CPU processing speeds through increased clock rates (from 1MHz in the early 1970's to 50 MHz for present day devices) and extended (8-, 16- and 32- bit) word lengths. Further performance improvements have accrued from exploiting low level parallelism within every component part of the von Neumann structure. Concurrent I/O (management of data while the CPU continues to compute), bit-parallel arithmetic, pipelining of instructions and the reduction of memory access time through parallelism are all examples of this approach.

1.4.2 Parallel Processing Architectures

The introduction of an increasing number of parallel processors [1.4], which offer an alternative to the von Neumann architecture is an exciting and practical alternative to the developments discussed above. Such devices include the BBN Butterfly, the WARP and IWARP array processors, the Intel Hypercube and of course the Inmos transputer which is the subject of this book. It is our thesis that parallel architectures will have a significant and long term impact on the future of control, not only in terms of implementation but also at the theoretical level.

A general parallel processing system is composed of several processing elements (PEs) which can operate concurrently, communicating with each other when necessary. Parallel architectures differ both in respect of the processing power of their PEs and the degree of interconnectivity between them. This leads to issues such as task granularity, which is a measure of the size of the tasks that can be effectively executed by the PEs of a specific architecture. PEs of fine-grain architectures are characterised by having limited functionality and a wide bandwidth for local data communication. On the other hand, PEs of coarse- or medium-grain architectures are more general-purpose and the interprocessor communication bandwidth is narrower.

Parallel architectures are classified according to a number of different criteria. One of the most widely used classification systems was introduced by Flynn [1.5], see Fig. 1.3, who considered the traditional sequential von Neumann model as a single stream of instructions operating on a single stream of data (SISD).

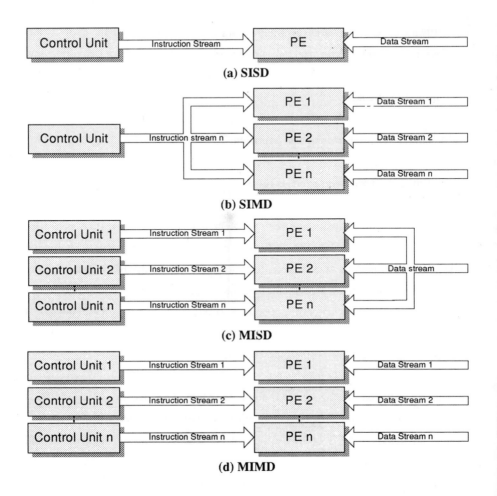

Fig. 1.3 Flynn's Classification

According to Flynn, parallel architectures may be classified as:

i) Single Instruction Stream, Multiple Data Stream (SIMD)

The same instruction is broadcast to all PEs which will execute this instruction simultaneously on different data. Array processors are an example of this architecture and are well suited for implementing regular algorithms involving matrix operations.

ii) Multiple Instruction Stream, Single Data Stream (MISD).

Several processors simultaneously execute different instructions on a single data stream. Few examples of this class exist and, indeed, it is held to be a somewhat impractical structure.

iii) Multiple Instruction Stream, Multiple Data Stream (MIMD).

This architecture consists of several independent processors, each capable of executing different instructions on different data. A variety of topologies exist for the interconnections. The transputer is an example of a MIMD architecture. Compared with SIMD architectures, MIMD machines can, in principle, deal with a wider range of problems but the designer must play a direct and fundamental rôle in successfully extracting the potential parallelism of the problem and in evaluating the trade-offs involved in parallel processing.

It should be noted that, while useful, this classification is by no means exhaustive: systolic arrays and neural networks are absent, for example.

In general, currently available SIMD architectures are fine-grained, with individual tasks consisting of a single operation, whilst MIMD architectures are usually medium- or coarse-grained.

The issues involved in the parallel implementation of an algorithm are directly dependent on the target architecture, the choice of which should itself be a function of the problem under consideration, as different problems display different levels of parallelism to be exploited. MIMD machines are deserving of special consideration due to their flexibility and ability to operate on unstructured and unpredictable operations and data. While they offer versatility to parallel computing they are also a difficult architecture class with which to work.

Performance benefits strongly depend on the compute/communicate ratio [1.6]. This ratio expresses how much communication overhead is associated with each computation. Clearly a high compute/communicate ratio is desirable. The concept of task granularity can be also viewed in terms of compute time per task. When large, the implementation is a coarse-grain task; when small, it is a fine-grain one. Although large grains may ignore potential parallelism, partitioning a problem into the finest possible granularity does not necessarily lead to the fastest solution, as maximum parallelism also incurs the maximum overhead, particularly due to increased communication requirements. Therefore, when partitioning the application across PEs, the designers must choose an algorithm granularity that balances useful parallel computation against communication and other overheads. Parallel algorithm approaches are discussed in Section 1.6.3.

1.5   TRANSPUTER AND OCCAM

1.5.1   Inmos Transputer - An Introduction

Attempts have been made to extend the simple von Neumann design to multi-processors for parallel operation using a single-bus for MIMD machines. However, a number of problems arise when using a single-bus multiprocessor. Adding more PEs to the data bus, after an initial improvement, causes a degradation in the overall performance due to the increased competition for use of the shared data bus (bus-contention). This results in extended "idle" times for each extra processor as they wait to gain access to the bus. Since in the von Neumann model only one processor may have access to the bus at any time, this condition is known as the von Neumann bottleneck [1.7]. The point-to-point configuration supported by the Inmos transputer, through four link interface units per PE, facilitates interprocessor communication and avoids the potential communication bottleneck of the single-bus system.

The Inmos transputer is a general purpose, single-chip, high speed microprocessor which is a member of the MIMD class of parallel architectures. Typical examples of this range are the T212 (16-bit processor), the T414 (32-bit processor) and the T800.

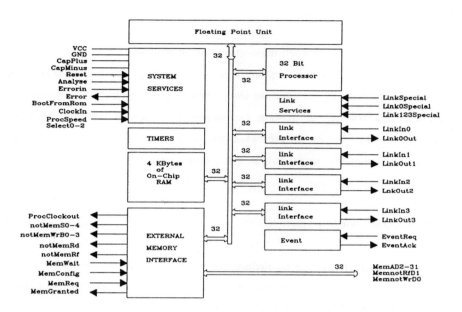

Fig. 1.4 Inmos T800-G20 Transputer Architecture

Fig. 1.4 illustrates the T800 architecture, which combines the 32-bit, 10 MIPS RISC processor with an on-board 64-bit floating point unit, memory and communications. Performance is quoted at an execution rate of 1.5 Mflops, at a processor speed of 20 MHz.

The key technical feature, which distinguishes the transputer from other high performance microprocessors, is the addition of four high-speed, duplex links. Bit-serial communication rates of 20 Mbits/sec are achieved via these interprocessor links. Serial/parallel data conversion is performed by the on-chip, link interface hardware. Most importantly, the links allow a single transputer to be used as a node among any number of similar devices to form a powerful parallel processing system. The transputer thus provides an important bridge between single chip, real-time control and general purpose real-time computer control systems, and, in effect, removes the current distinction between the two.

The normal method of program development using transputers would be to design, implement and test an occam program (typically) on a single transputer system, and then, when satisfied, to distribute the component processes to the transputers in the network. This requires configuring or mapping processes to the transputers by declaring which processes will execute on which transputer. The close association of the transputer and the occam language has produced efficient parallel processing systems.

1.5.2   Occam - An Introduction

A number of approaches to parallelism in software have been considered in the context of a multi-processor environment. Programming languages used for these systems are often extensions of existing sequential-mode languages (e.g. Parallel C, Parallel Fortran) for providing parallel programming features. Any program written for a multi-processor system must be partitioned across all the processors into self-contained sections which then will then run concurrently, communicating with each other when necessary. Conventional programming languages, however, were not initially designed to cope with these issues. A better solution is clearly a high-level programming language in which concurrency and efficient intercommunication are directly supported.

Occam model of parallelism

Occam is an abstract language that has the dual role of being an implementation language and a design formalism and is derived from the Communicating Sequential Processes model (CSP) of Hoare [1.8]. Employing the message passing paradigm, it has the ability to control and synchronise processes via channels on one or more processors. Occam programs which have been designed for a multi-processor environment can be written and tested on a single processor and then transferred to the multi-processor environment. Modula-2, Linda and Ada are other examples of concurrent languages. However their model of concurrency has not been implemented as efficiently as the occam model when executed in parallel [1.9].

When used on transputers, occam provides operational support for scheduling and process mapping with minimal overhead. Parallel processing using transputers programmed in occam thus offers a potentially cost effective solution when compared with alternative MIMD architectures and is especially suited to the support of parallel processing of real-time applications.

The basic units of occam programming are declarations and three primitive processes: assignment, input and output. Communication between processes is via point-to-point links known as "channels". Two important issues which must be addressed by a parallel programming language are those of synchronisation and the handling of shared variables. When several tasks are executing concurrently, they do so asynchronously, i.e. each task proceeds at its own speed. If the activities of these tasks are dependent on one another, then the programming language must provide a means of synchronisation to co-ordinate their activities. Further, when two or more tasks are accessing the same variable, control must be exercised to prevent data corruption arising from conflicting operations on that variable. Occam does not permit the use of shared variables. Instead, shared data is communicated to processes across the communication channels.

Synchronisation is handled in a natural way through the implementation of input and output commands. When an output command (denoted by "!") is encountered in a process, the process is halted until another process has executed the corresponding input command (denoted by "?"). Then the desired data communication takes place over the channel. Similarly, an input command cannot be executed until the corresponding output command is reached in another process. In this way communication cannot proceed until both processes are ready to perform the I/O transfer and synchronisation is thus secured.

Occam processes and constructs

Primitive processes are combined into conventional processes using constructors. These include a sequential constructor (SEQ), a parallel constructor (PAR) and a guarded communication statement (ALT). Typical constructors such as IF and WHILE are also supported.

The ALT construct is, perhaps, the most unfamiliar. Each guard consists of an input process, a Boolean expression and an input process, or a Boolean expression and a SKIP (which, in essence, reduces to a pure Boolean expression). ALT operates a "first-wins" procedure in which only the process associated with the first input to become ready is executed. In the following example if input.channel2 was the first to produce an input, then only process 2 would be executed and execution would proceed to the next construct:

```
ALT
      input.channel1 ? x
      ... process 1
      input.channel2 ? x
      ... process 2
      input.channel3 ? x
      ... process 3
```

Features of occam which are especially relevant to real-time implementation are reviewed in Section 1.6.4.

1.6   TRANSPUTER-BASED REAL-TIME CONTROL

1.6.1   Advantages of Parallel Processing

Increased computational speed is of course the primary benefit of parallel processing. This allows faster systems to be controlled and gives the control engineer the choice of added complexity in the control algorithm. Easy expansion, within a uniform hardware and software base, is another feature of concurrent control systems, since it is possible to add more processors as required. This has important implications for reducing the development and maintenance costs associated with real-time computer control.

Parallel processing also offers a closer relationship between the inherent parallelism expressed at the design stage, for example, between the block diagram representation of a system and its hardware implementation. This will be important in the development of tools for shortening the path from computer aided control system design (CACSD) to hardware implementation.

At first sight, a parallel processing system, consisting of a number of PEs, is likely to lead to reduced reliability. However, the flexibility of the system, its connectivity and ability to reconfigure, afford an opportunity for alternative system architecture designs to improve reliability. Thus, fault tolerance can be realised in a parallel processing system by organising computational operations in a distributed sense, so that an operational failure results in performance degradation rather than a complete breakdown of the controller.

1.6.2   Implementation Issues

Hitherto, we have referred to "processes" in connection with occam program construction and not to "processors". The latter term is the physical division of a task related to the target hardware while the former term is the logical division of the task. Occam provides a way to allocate these logical processes to actual hardware processors via PLACED PAR statements. The number of processors need not necessarily match the number of designated processes since it is possible to allocate several processes to one processor. It is good practice to decompose the problem to a greater, rather than lesser extent, creating more logical processes than physical processors. It is easier to group processes rather than sub-divide them once a design is established.

There are two main approaches to allocating tasks to processors: *statically* and *dynamically*. In static allocation, the association of a group of tasks with a processor is resolved before running time and remains fixed throughout the execution, whereas in dynamic allocation, tasks are allocated to processors at running time according to certain criteria, such as processor availability, intertask dependencies and task priorities. Whatever method is used, a clear appreciation is required of the overheads and parallelism/communication trade-offs already mentioned.

1.6.3   Parallelisation Methods

In order to fully utilise the computational potential of parallel processing hardware, it is essential to identify the concurrent features of the application. The most commonly occurring types of parallelism in engineering applications fall into four broad classes.

Functional Parallelism is a commonly applied method in which individual tasks are associated with the different control functions to be implemented. Sequential and parallel operations must be identified along with their interdependencies. This approach is susceptible to load balancing problems where unequal task sizes lead to an uneven distribution of computational load across the individual processors in the system.

Processor Farm architectures consist of a "farm" of processors receiving instructions from, and reporting back to, a controller. Each processor runs the same program (with data dependent branches) and has a complete, but different, set of data. There is limited communication between processors, although memory costs may be significant because large amounts of storage are required on each processor. Dynamic task allocation is required in this approach. The processor farm is analyzed in detail in Chapter 10 (along with other strategies), where it is found that there is a significant performance penalty associated with scheduling software overheads and increased communication requirements which may prove unacceptable in some real-time applications.

Many "physical" problems have an inherent regular geometrical structure which can be exploited to extract parallelism. This regularity allows data to be distributed uniformly across the processor array, each processor being responsible for a defined spatial area or volume. Neighbouring processors will have to exchange data at intervals. Compared with the Processor Farm, *Geometric Parallelism* requires only a fraction of the data on each processor but each has an essentially complete copy of the whole program.

Algorithmic Parallelism arises when each processor implements a part of the total control algorithm. In such a decomposition, data now flows between the processing elements, severely increasing the communication load on each element in the array and communication overheads can severely degrade performance unless care is taken. However, an advantage of this approach is that very little data space is required on each processor.

The techniques for parallelism described above involve distributing either the data or the computation across the processor array. While the resulting parallel structure will depend on the particular application, it is useful to define some useful measures of performance which characterise a parallel implementation.

The *speedup,* S, of an algorithm on N processors is defined as

$$S = \frac{\text{execution time on 1 processor}}{\text{execution time on N processors}} \times 100\% \qquad (1.1)$$

The *efficiency,* E, of a parallel implementation is given by

$$E = \frac{S}{N} \times 100\% \qquad (1.2)$$

It has already been noted in Section 1.4.2 that, in order to achieve good values for S and E, it is necessary to match the *granularity*, G, of the algorithm to that of the target hardware, where

$$G = \frac{\text{computation time}}{\text{communication time}}. \tag{1.3}$$

In summary, then,

> *Functional parallelism* is usually easily identified but may lead to a limited and unbalanced distribution of computational load;
>
> *Processor farm parallelism* is efficient and easy to use but each processor generally requires a large amount of memory and a significant operational overhead is incurred;
>
> *Geometrical parallelism* is efficient and easy to code but, for a fixed data size, the efficiency decreases as the number of processors increases; and
>
> *Algorithmic parallelism* has the finest granularity and its efficiency depends very much on balancing the loads on the individual processors, implying that the coding requires much thought and care.

1.6.4   Real-Time Features of Transputers and Occam

Control engineers view the transputer as a powerful processing element capable of easy implementation in an embedded parallel processing system. Its primary language, occam, is sufficiently high-level to permit clear expression of parallel software structures while retaining the efficiency of a low-level language. The facility whereby parallel software can be developed on a single processor and subsequently mapped onto a multiprocessor system is appealing for embedded system developers.

Real-time control involves execution of a set of cyclic processes along with other non-critical functions. Within this set of cyclic processes there will be a sub-set which are critical to the maintenance of control of the system. Strategies which ensure the integrity of the system, i.e. completion of the critical tasks within a pre-specified time interval, are still a subject of research.

Nonetheless, an attractive feature of the transputer for real-time implementation is its support for task scheduling and priority handling with low overhead. Current transputer hardware provides very fast pre-emptive scheduling for two static priority levels, with "round-robin" management within each level.

Bakkers et al. [1.10] suggest that the sampling process of a control system may be divided into three categories:-

    Time-bounded processes,
    Time-limited processes, and
    Background and alarm processes.

Time-bounded processes include sampling and actuation operations and must be scheduled at specific instants. Time-limited processes are actions which should be scheduled to meet their deadline, such as control signal calculations. Background and alarm processes involve operations of varying levels of priority such as alarms, condition monitoring and event logging.

A breakdown of these categories suggests a variety of levels of priority ranging from high priority, pre-emptive to a low level implemented by the transputer's low-priority, round-robin scheduler. These are not accommodated within the basic transputer-occam combination. A number of real-time kernels have been proposed such as Trans-RTXc [1.11]. In an attempt to retain efficiency, Welch [1.12] has proposed two schemes, implemented in occam with an acceptably low level of overhead, to realise multiple, fixed priority or multiple, dynamic priority scheduling on transputers.

The transputer handles interrupts on an event channel. However the interrupt handling facility available on the basic transputer-occam combination is too rudimentary for many applications and it is often necessary to extend this feature. Occam also contains a timer facility to support real-time programming.

The prioritization mechanism in occam is provided by means of its PRI PAR and PRI ALT constructs. The processes specified using PAR execute with equal priority and on any processor. Should any possible contention arise between parallel processes running on the same processor, the PRI PAR construct is able to assign priorities. PRI PAR can be used to specify that the first process has the highest priority, the second has next highest, and so on. The implementation of occam on the transputer, however, can only allocate high priority to the first process and low priority to the others.

The guards in an ALT constructor are evaluated in an undefined order. The PRI ALT constructor can be used to force the guards to be evaluated in the order in which they are textually listed. Again, however, its implementation on the transputer is restricted to two priority levels and only the first listed guard receives high priority attention.

1.7   OVERVIEW OF BOOK

Chapter 2 studies the application of transputers to the real-time simulation of process plant. The goal is to exploit the benefits of a faster model solution not only under steady-state conditions but also to include dynamic simulation. The latter employs complex nonlinear models typically consisting of a set of several thousand mixed differential and algebraic equations. Three different problem areas are described and it is interesting to note the approaches to parallelism in each case. For real-time simulation of a distillation column, *geometrical parallelism* is used to split the distillation column into sections and place each on its own transputer. In order to make the transition from serial simulation code to parallel as simple as possible, *a modelling toolkit* has been produced which runs on a 12-transputer Meiko surface connected to a Sun Sparcstation. Solution of the nonlinear algebraic equations is the key numerical problem and a new *algorithmic decomposition* technique, based on decomposing the equation set by "partitioning and tearing", is applied first to solving for the pressures and flows of an incompressible fluid in a pipe network consisting of 113 nodes, 123 pipes, with 59 unknown pressures. A number of solution strategies are compared for solving the system of linear equations and evaluating the function and the Jacobian, including *a master/slave paradigm*. The mapping technique is then extended to cover the dynamic case. The mapping problem is difficult for transputer arrays and the evaluation of a number of alternative mapping strategies for a particular application can be expensive and time consuming. It is interesting to note that Ponton and his co-workers have built a model of the parallel application as an extension to the Simula programming language which allows the user to construct a model of a parallel program executing on a parallel computer.

Chapter 3 contains a detailed technical treatment of hardware and software issues for real-time control of mechatronic systems using transputers, directed at a fast assembly robot application. The proposed architecture is described in terms of several layers. The first consists of the interface hardware and its matching real-time sampling software, The second layer contains the protection software which is essential for maintenance and fault diagnosis of the system during operation. The third layer contains the control algorithm and the necessary communication software for linking the layers together.

New hardware and software components, which have been developed at Twente University to realise this architecture are dealt with. These include the LINX backplane, based on VME standard specifications, and a real-time language called TASC (Transputer Application generator for Sampling applications in Control systems). The latter is an application generator allowing the control engineer to specify the sampling program in a high level language and permits independent control over all aspects of control processes such as timing, communication, control of interface hardware and error handling. Results measuring the performance of the new system are included.

Chapter 4 examines the problem of real-time, linear-quadratic optimal control of an advanced military aircraft with fast dynamics. The amount of computation involved in linearising the aircraft equations about the current state and control vectors has conventionally forced a number of simplifying assumptions like ignoring the cross-coupling between the longitudinal and lateral dynamics and assuming that the aircraft is time-invariant over small time intervals. Virk and Tahir formulate two optimal control problems for the linearised aircraft, corresponding to the lateral and longitudinal dynamics respectively. They account for the cross-coupling either explicitly, or implicitly in a modified control effort, and solve two decoupled sub-problems on a transputer network. The algorithm involves linearising the equations of motion, integrating Riccati equations in reverse time, computing the controls and updating the state vector. *Functional parallelism* is used, with one transputer responsible for the longitudinal computation and the other handling the lateral calculations. A number of methods of using a third processor for offloading some of the calculations onto a third processor are also investigated. The parallel autopilots are tested on a transputer-based C simulation of the aircraft and it is demonstrated that real-time control can be achieved with a fast linearisation update as required.

Chapter 5 is concerned with real-time adaptive control of the terminal voltage and speed of a generator using a self-tuning regulator (STR) to adjust the excitation. The existing controller, for a laboratory-scale turbogenerator, is implemented in C on an IBM PC-AT compatible machine with a numeric coprocessor. With a reduced form of the Generalised Minimum Variance algorithm, the fastest rate at which the control signal can be updated is 20ms. However, to meet industrial standards, this time must be at least halved. Timing results on an occam simulation of the turbogenerator system suggest that this target can be comfortably met with the controller implemented in occam on a single T800 processor. Indeed, the power of the transputer is such that the algorithm itself can be improved by employing a 9-parameter ARMA model which includes noise parameter estimation and a consequent improvement in performance. Further speedups accrue from applying parallel processing to the parameter estimator which accounts for some 60% of the computation. The Chapter describes two approaches: *heuristic partitioning,* with the aid of a Gantt chart, and *algorithmic decomposition,* based on a systolic array algorithm.

Chapter 6 deals with the real-time control of variable speed drives which find application in machine tool drives, traction, paper and steel mill rollers. The induction motor has practical advantages over the more commonly used dc motor but requires a more complex control structure since the voltage, current, torque and speed are all interdependent, leading to a highly coupled nonlinear control problem. A "vector" or "field orientated" control strategy is used in a three-level, motor control scheme. The lowest level consists of signal input, conditioning and actuator output for the power converter. The next level covers the drive's intelligence and memory. The highest level contains user I/O. *Functional partitioning* is employed for implementation of each level on a three-transputer array. The Chapter discusses practical features of occam for this real-time application and includes both practical results and useful discussion and comparisons with alternative hardware realisations.

Chapter 7 describes an interesting instrumentation application of transputers. The problem is real-time classification of faults in tubular metal samples using eddy current procedures. The probabilistic technique employed uses a set of Kalman filters corresponding to the set of likely fault conditions, implemented on separate processors, together with an appropriate probability update mechanism. The hardware system, which has been developed at Salford University, is discussed and results, from passing samples with known fault conditions through the coil system, included. It is shown that the instrument meets real-time performance requirements and, using the facility of the transputer architecture for easy expansion, it is indicated how the system might be extended to provide wider fault coverage.

The next two Chapters are concerned with hardware and software fault tolerance respectively.

Chapter 8 studies the possibilities and limitations offered by transputers for hardware fault tolerance. It is shown that the availability of multiple communication links and a hardware scheduler are attractive for this purpose. Fault tolerance for a single processor implementation of a controller is treated first, with transient and permanent fault detection and correction discussed for the CPU, memory and I/O in turn. The addition of a second or third processor in cold, warm, hot or active back-up configurations makes it possible to achieve high availability or high safety in the event of a transputer failure. More complex control algorithms are implemented on multiprocessor systems where the significantly increased probability of failure is offset by the availability of more processors to take over the tasks of the failed processor. While hardware fault tolerance is still based on the use of back-up, additional problems arise and recovery control is more complex. These issues are examined and a flexible multiprocessor fault-tolerant kernel, which has been developed at KU-Leuven, is described in detail.

Chapter 9 discusses software engineering methods for the design of real-time, concurrent software. Following an overview of formal methods, an integrated approach for the design of time-critical and system-critical software systems using Petri nets and temporal logic is described. Petri net models of the software constructs in occam are discussed together with the introduction of fault-tolerant techniques for ruggedising the implementation software. An application for which this research is intended is a new generation of flexible machinery in which mechanical complexity is traded for sophistication in control. Thus, mechanical transmissions used to synchronise actuator motions are replaced by sets of independent, electromechanical drives operating under software control. The Chapter concludes with a description of application of the methods to a high-speed manufacturing system.

Chapter 10 rounds off the book with a description of a suite of computer-aided design tools to automate the parallelisation of a class of algorithms and to permit on-line performance assessment. The tools form an environment known as EPICAS which integrates tools in the familiar CACSD package, MATLAB, with the Transputer

Development System. These tools enable the user to experiment with parallel mapping strategies and various hardware topologies and to analyze their performance on-line. Granularity issues, in particular, are explored in depth in this Chapter, while investigating a processor star and a processor farm arrangement using both T414 and T800 transputers. The importance of matching task granularity to processor granularity is stressed if the control engineer is to fully realise the speed-up potential of using transputer-based systems.

REFERENCES

[1.1]   Kalman RE: Design of a self-optimising control system, *Trans ASME*, pp468-478, 1958.
[1.2]   Astrom KJ and Wittenmark B: *Adaptive Control*, Addison Wesley, 1989.
[1.3]   Tinham B: A new era of multi-algorithm control?, *Control and Instrumentation*, Morgan-Grampian (Process Press) Ltd, pp127-130, 1990.
[1.4]   Trew A, Wilson, G (eds.): *Past, present and parallel- a survey of available parallel computing systems*, Springer-Verlag, 1991.
[1.5]   Flynn MF: Some computer organisations and their effectiveness, *IEEE Trans Comput*, **C-21**, pp948-960, 1972.
[1.6]   Stone HS: *High performance computer architectures*, Addison Wesley, 1987.
[1.7]   Dettmer R: Chip architectures for parallel processing, *Electronics and Power*, **31**, 3, pp227-231, 1985.
[1.8]   Hoare CAR: Communicating sequential processes "CSP", *Comm ACM*, **21**, pp666-677, 1978.
[1.9]   Burns A: *Concurrent programming in Ada*, Cambridge University Press, 1985.
[1.10] Bakkers AWP, van Rooij RMA and James L: Design of a real-time operating system (RTOS) for robot control, *Proceedings of the 7th Occam User Group*, IOS Press, pp318-327, 1987.
[1.11] Thielemans H and Verhulst E: Implementation issues of Trans-RTXc on the transputer, *Proc IFAC Workshop on Algorithms and Architectures for Real-Time Control*, Bangor, UK, 1991.
[1.12] Welch PH: Multi-priority schedulers for transputer-based real-time control, *Real-Time Systems with Transputers*, IOS Press, 1990.

Chapter 2

Simulation of Nonlinear Chemical Processes and Control Systems

JW Ponton, E Fraga, R McKinnel and N Skilling

2.1   INTRODUCTION

Chemical process plants are complex and expensive. Numerical simulation of their steady-state and dynamic behaviour has thus long been a tool in the development and evaluation of the design of the process and its associated control system.

In the past the emphasis has been on steady-state simulation: the evaluation of alternative stable operating points, often including economic criteria. Dynamic simulation has tended to be restricted to subsections of the plant, usually in connection with the design or analysis of parts of the control system, and often using highly simplified models. Dynamic simulation of complete processes using complex nonlinear models has long been recognised as desirable [2.1], but the effort required to construct, validate and solve such models has usually been seen as incommensurate with the expected benefit.

While the use of transputer hardware does not directly affect the problem of model construction or validation, it does offer the prospect of much faster model solution. This is obviously desirable for its own sake, but also will have, indirectly, beneficial effects on the two earlier phases. Much of the difficulty in model construction lies with the need to make simplifying assumptions to allow the model to run faster. With more powerful solution techniques the need for this simplification, and those steps in model validation associated with it, may be reduced or removed.

2.1.1   Steady-State and Dynamic Simulation

The dynamics of chemical processes are described by a mixed set of differential and algebraic equations, or d.a.e.s. These have a number of properties which distinguish them from sets of o.d.e.s [2.2]. Other points of note about this mixed equation set are as follows:

- Size. Typically several thousand equations are involved.
- Nonlinearity. Most of the algebraic equations are nonlinear, often highly so.
- Irreducibility. Because of the coupling between d.e.s and a.e.s and the nonlinearity of the latter, it is not in general possible to reduce the system to a set of state and output variables.
- Stiffness. The o.d.e.s are usually highly stiff.

Our interest is in the construction of comprehensive and robust dynamic models for complete processes, which we will wish to solve in "real time" or substantially faster. It transpires, however, that our difficulties are mainly associated with the solution of the *algebraic* equations which are more usually associated with steady-state simulations of the type, for which, as noted above, there already exists a substantial body of experience in the process engineering community. There are two reasons why algebraic equations dominate our dynamic simulations:

- The main source of nonlinearity lies in the algebraic subsystem of the d.a.e.s. Whatever solution strategy is adopted for the o.d.e.s, the algebraic subset will require iterative numerical solution at each time-step.
- Because the system is usually stiff, it will generally be necessary to use an implicit integration procedure to solve the o.d.e.s. This, in effect, turns them into a set of implicit algebraic equations by backward differencing.

In the three Case Studies which follow we will discuss a range of problems typical of different aspects of dynamic process simulation:

(a) A toolkit for dynamic problem solving applied to a typical system of moderate stiffness with embedded algebraic equations.
(b) A steady-state subproblem which frequently occurs at each step of a dynamic simulation.
(c) An equation solving technique suitable for both algebraic and mixed d.a.e. systems which makes use of particular properties of typical chemical process equations.

2.2   ALTERNATIVE PARALLELISATION STRATEGIES

The simplest way of identifying structure in any system is to look at its graphical representation on a flowsheet or circuit diagram. A simple but typical process flowsheet, Fig. 2.1, clearly shows blocks which correspond, depending on the level of system and model detail, to functional activities such as reaction or separation, or to actual items of physical plant equipment, or indeed to both. Some items of equipment may be further subdivided into subitems, as is the case with the distillation column, Fig. 2.2, which might represent one of the two separators in Fig. 2.1.

A system geometric approach to parallelisation takes a block and assigns it to a transputer. This is simple in concept and may often lead to minimum connectivity in terms of total number of interconnections. It does however have a number of flaws:

• Not all blocks will represent comparable computational load.
• Despite low connectivity, close coupling between certain blocks may lead to high local data rates. This is not apparent from geometry alone.
• The irregular structure of a typical flowsheet does not map readily onto available hardware network configurations.

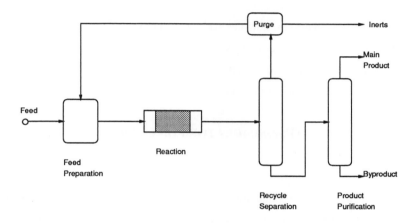

Fig. 2.1 A simple process flowsheet

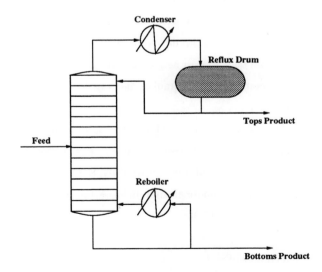

Fig. 2.2 A distillation column

Our use of this approach has been restricted to one particular type of process, namely distillation, which has a highly regular structure. This provides Case Study One which illustrates the approach and also our ideas about modelling tools and a modelling environment for complex dynamic process simulation.

The other two Case Studies eschew the explicit system structure and seek to exploit the structure of the equation solving task. In fact, one element of this has been found, or may be made, to dominate the solution time, and so our main efforts have been directed to the parallelisation of this task.

2.3   CASE STUDY ONE: A SIMULATOR FOR COMPLEX DISTILLATION PROCESSES

The geometric approach to simulation on a distributed memory parallel computer requires that the problem be partitionable into separate subproblems, where each subproblem can be solved essentially independently.

The distillation column, see Fig. 2.2, is an inherently modular piece of equipment. Its simulation involves the solution of a series of vapour/liquid equilibrium problems which transmit and receive data in the form of liquid and vapour flows and compositions to and from their nearest neighbours. It may have up to 250 individual stages, each involving complex tray hydraulics and vapour/liquid interactions.

The simulation method, which we have used, involves splitting the distillation column into sections and placing each on its own transputer. The sections are then solved separately. Each section requires information from its nearest neighbours, this being provided by the interprocessor communication links. A full description of this model and solution method is given in [2.3] .

As well as flow and composition data, there is a need for system communication. This is required to check for convergence in a given time-step, for interaction and for sending solutions to the outside world. Fig. 2.3 shows the general layout of the partitioning method.

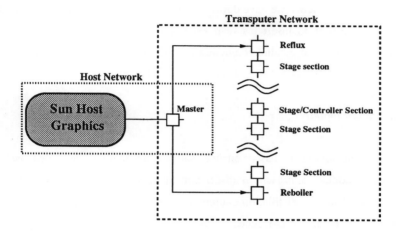

Fig. 2.3 Layout of the distillation network

Overall simulation control is performed by one of the stage processes, usually the middle one. System messages for convergence checking and simulation control are pipelined up and down the column structure. Locating the controller in the middle allows messages to be sent in two directions at once. This speeds up the control process and also halves the distance messages must be sent. The overall problem is set up by a master process on a separate processor which is responsible for collecting all solutions from the network. The processors themselves are linked linearly. This has proved to be the best configuration, [2.4], since all communication, except for solution transfer, is nearest neighbour.

2.3.1   Development of Simulation Tools

Once the problem has been partitioned there still remains the problem of developing the model. The main difficulty associated with developing a parallel model is that existing code requires some restructuring. For the user who wants to develop his simulation model quickly, without significant knowledge of parallel computing, this is likely to be a daunting task. To simplify this and to investigate techniques for the creation of future systems, we have developed a parallel distillation modelling toolkit. This allows the user to insert his own existing code with relative ease and with minimum knowledge of parallel computing beyond the way in which the problem is to be partitioned.

The simulation toolkit

The simulation toolkit is based on the partitioning method described and the "sequential modular" approach to distillation simulation. This approach involves starting at one end of a distillation column and then sequentially solving each stage in turn until the other end is reached.

There are four main tasks:

(a) Initialisation. At this step all the initial conditions required by the user's models are set up.
(b) The complete column is solved stage by stage.
(c) Convergence of the system is checked. If converged, then the simulation moves on to the next time-step.
(d) At the end of a time-step, any updates required are performed. These include controller model adjustment, manipulation of integration parameters or any other task that needs to be performed once per time-step.

The distillation toolkit developed follows this process almost exactly except that the complete sequence is performed on every processor. The format for the parallel version is:

(a) Each processor sets the initial values for its distillation stages.
(b) The set of stages on each processor is solved stage by stage. The code for this is the same as for a sequential program except that the number of stages is reduced. The boundary values at the top and bottom of the stage section are provided by the distillation toolkit's communications.
(c) Convergence of each processor's stage section is checked locally. The simulation will move on to the next time-step when the distillation toolkit decides that all the processors have converged.
(d) Any manipulation required once every time-step is performed as for the sequential version.

The idea is to make the transition from serial to parallel as simple as possible, with the distillation toolkit performing the additional tasks associated with the parallel network. The distillation toolkit has three main levels, see Fig. 2.4.

The first level is the parallel machine, here a 12-transputer Meiko Computing Surface. This is connected to the host computer, a Sun Sparcstation. On top of this is the toolkit. This software performs all of the parallelisation process, simulation management, convergence checking, solution transfer and user interaction. On the top level is the user interface which takes the form of four procedures, each corresponding to one of the items in the sequential modular task list. These are called by the simulation toolkit at the appropriate times. Inside them the user can insert code taken from an original sequential program.

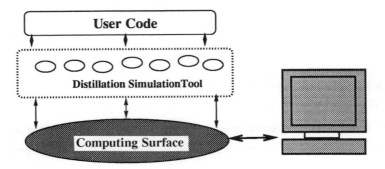

Fig. 2.4 Structure of the distillation toolkit

To allow the distillation system to interface neatly to the user's models, a large suite of variables is supplied to cover all likely simulation variables. The user can then map his original variables to those supplied by the system. An additional area of user-definable workspace is supplied for communication between processors for the simulation toolkit. This structure also allows different types of integration method, i.e. explicit and implicit, to be used.

Flexibility and interaction mechanisms

An important part of any simulation is user input and interaction. One aim of this column simulation toolkit is to demonstrate applications in process design and model based control, with a standard input scheme. The toolkit supports the use of different modelling methods and must therefore be able to handle the data required by all of these, for example different physical property estimation routines.

A data file scheme has been developed which allows both standard and user data to be input and distributed correctly between the simulation processors.

```
CONTROL_DATA_BEGIN
   {
   REFLUX_RATE default 1
      {
      controller1
         {
         description "Fixed Reflux Rate"
         type "Fixed rate controller"
         parameter1 "reflux rate" 7.0
         }
      controller2
         {
         description "Rate controlled by tops product
         composition"
         type "Proportional/integral controller"
         parameter1 "setpoint" 0.99
         parameter2 "controller gain" 4.0
         parameter3 "controller reset" 40.0
         }
      }
   TOPS_PRODUCT default 1
      {
      controller1
         {
         description "Tops rate controlled by level in tank"
         type "Prop/Integral level controller"
         parameter1 "reflux drum holdup" 5000.0
         parameter2 "setpoint" 2500.0
         parameter3 "controller gain" 4.0
         parameter4 "controller reset" 40.0
         }
      }
   etc...
```

Fig. 2.5 Data scheme for controllers

An important user-defined facility is the parameter setting of controllers on the column. Fig. 2.5 shows the model input scheme for controllers. In distillation there are four principal streams to be controlled: the tops product, the reflux rate, the bottoms product and the reboil rate. The input scheme allows a set of controllers to be described for each controllable stream by a description of the controller and controlled variables. The modeller must provide code in his models which can simulate these controllers, and the interface system can interact with the user in terms defined by the input scheme. Thus the user can manipulate variables and switch controller types while a simulation is running. Fig. 2.6 shows a diagram of how the controller interface appears to the user.

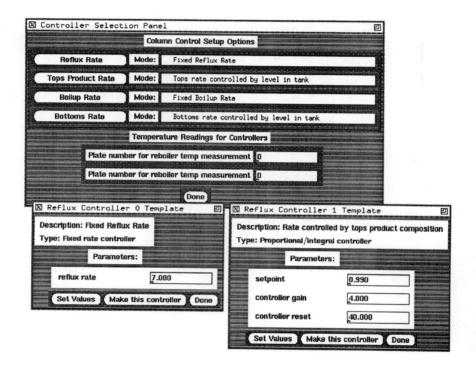

Fig. 2.6 Controller user interface

2.3.2 Test Results

Several studies have now been carried out with the distillation simulation toolkit and the general partitioning strategy. Models from different sources have been attached to the system with relative ease. All the information produced by a simulation can be displayed in either 2 or 3 dimensions using the graphics tool provided. Fig. 2.7 shows an example of how the simulation results are displayed to the user.

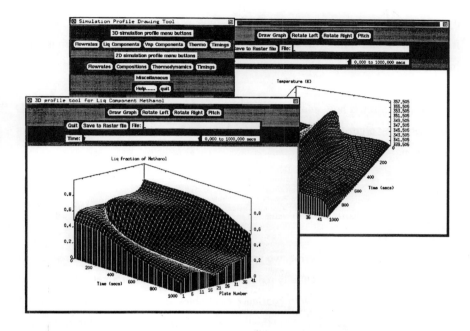

Fig. 2.7   Example of the graphics display system

2.4   PREAMBLE TO CASE STUDIES TWO AND THREE: NUMERICAL METHODS FOR ALGEBRAIC EQUATIONS ON MIMD COMPUTERS

The fundamentally different structure of the MIMD computer requires that most numerical software be completely redesigned for its optimal exploitation. There is no obvious route to automatic translation, and indeed, the serial single instruction concept is so ingrained in existing algorithms, as well as actual software, that redesign is probably desirable. This is the reason why many workers have chosen the system geometric approach, discussed above, in problems which might otherwise best be regarded as straightforward equation solving tasks.

Effective automatic translation of existing programs is difficult because static analysis alone cannot extract all the information required for such translation. To obtain this dynamic analysis of the program in actual runs will be required. Even then, the translated program is likely to be less than optimal if the underlying algorithm is serial in its conception.

We will now discuss how nonlinear equation solving may be carried out on a MIMD computer using algorithmic decomposition designed to take advantage of this type of parallelism.

2.4.1   Nonlinear Equation Solving

In the following we will describe two approaches to the solution of nonlinear algebraic equations. Because they essentially reduce to a series of nonlinear algebraic equations, both nonlinear optimisation with continuous variables and the solution of differential algebraic equations by implicit methods may be dealt with by similar techniques. O.d.e. integration by explicit methods is essentially a parallel task which can be parallelised trivially. Linear algebraic equations are a specific case. There is substantial literature on parallel methods for linear equations, see e.g.[2.5]. However, MIMD parallelism may well not be suited to solving very large linear systems, which are probably better handled on special vector processors. Case Study Two illustrates our experience which tends to confirm this view.

The philosophy of our approach derives from that widely used by process engineers, although less often taken by mathematicians, of equation set decomposition or "partitioning and tearing". In its classic form this is seen in the manipulation of process unit operation equations to reduce the solution for all the state variables of a flowsheet to a much smaller problem involving only those variables associated with recycle streams. Algorithms for such decomposition have been widely reported [2.6] and may be applied also to unsteady-state o.d.e systems [2.7].

The approach can be applied to general sets of equations and involves the following steps for a set of equations $f(x) = 0$.

(a) Determination of an "output set" for the equations $\tilde{x}$.

(b) Symbolic manipulation to rearrange the equation in terms of the output set, i.e.

$$\tilde{x} = \phi \ (x) \tag{2.1}$$

(c) Identification of partitions and minimum tear set $y \in \tilde{x}$ and a calculation sequence. The latter is a cyclic path through the directed graph of the equation set.

(d) Calculation along the above path such that for a given y a new set of values $y´$ is obtained.

(e) Repetition of the above step with adjusting of y at each iteration until $y \approx y´$ within a prespecified tolerance.

Since in effect $y´ = \phi \ (y)$, the last operation may be considered to be the solution for y of:

$$f \ (y) \equiv y´ - \phi \ (y) = 0 \tag{2.2}$$

by any convenient method. In the earliest examples of this approach simple repeated substitution, i.e. setting $y = y´$ at each iteration, was often used. This crude method is effective for process flowsheets since the property of conservation of mass and energy ensures that $\| \ d\phi/dy \ \| \leq 1$, the sufficient condition for such a scheme to converge.

An advantage of this approach is that in many problems a very substantial reduction in the number of variables may be obtained; a flowsheet involving several hundred state variables may reduce to less than ten recycle variables. The classic Theile-Geddes decomposition for distillation reduces the (number of trays times number of components) variables of a countercurrent cascade to just (number of components), typically a reduction of one or two orders of magnitude. The need to perform symbolic rearrangement might at one time have been considered a serious drawback to the general application of this approach, but now, given comprehensive symbolic processing packages, it no longer presents any real problem.

Once the analysis and symbolic operations have been completed the set of equations $f(y) = 0$ is solved numerically. This will be done by a Newton like method and this involves

(a) generation of the Jacobian J and of $f(y)$ and
(b) the solution of the linear system:

$$J \, \delta x = f_0 \, (y)$$

(2.3)

where δx is the correction to x.

The second task, because of the reduction in the number of variables, is the less significant, often by many orders of magnitude. Since in any case linear equation solving does not parallelise well on the MIMD configuration, we will carry out the step in a single machine, and concentrate on the parallelisation of Jacobian evaluation.

2.4.2   Jacobian Evaluation Strategies

In principle, if enough processors were available, we could assign one Jacobian element to each. This is unlikely to be sensible because communications would dominate the relatively small computational load of each element. Moreover, there will be common terms for each element whose evaluation it may be wasteful to duplicate.

We see the assignment process as being an exercise in matching the subdivision of the problem to what appears to be a sensible and affordable number of transputers. Reduction in the Jacobian size is thus a step in this direction. We are left with a Jacobian whose number of rows or columns, of the order of ten to a hundred, would appear to correspond to this reasonable number.

Two alternative strategies are thus suggested:

- Evaluate each Jacobian row, i.e. $\partial f_i / \partial y_j$ for all j on transputer i.

- Evaluate each Jacobian column, i.e. $\partial f_j / \partial y_i$ for all j on transputer i.

If we have insufficient processors we must obviously group several rows or columns together. As will be shown, both of these strategies have advantages. Although we discuss them in the particular context of modelling chemical processes, the approach can obviously be extended to other areas.

2.5   CASE STUDY TWO: FLOW NETWORKS, EVALUATION BY ROW

At each time-step of a dynamic simulation, we frequently require the solution for flows and pressures in a network of nonlinear resistances corresponding to a combination of pipes and valves carrying incompressible fluid. The solution of these nonlinear algebraic equations can be very time consuming and has been known to dominate the task of real-time simulation of, for example, LPG or oil handling systems.

The equations involved are of two types. Firstly, material flows

$$\sum_{i \in c_j} F_i = 0 \qquad (2.4)$$

for all nodes where c_j is the set of flows associated with the node j. Also, pressure flow equations

$$F_k - f (P_u , P_d) = 0 \qquad\qquad (2.5)$$

where P_u and P_d are the upstream and downstream pressures of nodes at each end of link k. Here $f(P_u, P_d)$ is a complex nonlinear function.

Following the solution strategy outlined above, we reduce the set of variables by symbolic manipulation to the pressures alone. This results in a set of equations

$$\mathbf{f} (P_i) = \mathbf{0}. \qquad\qquad (2.6)$$

This is typically less than half the size of the original equation set. The reduction is thus not as striking as for flowsheet problems such as Case Study Three. However, because only limited symbolic manipulation has been performed, it is quite straightforward to obtain analytical derivatives.

Row evaluation is particularly suitable where analytical derivatives are to be calculated. Determination of all partial derivatives of a function with respect to all variables, and the function evaluation itself, generally involves a number of common terms whose values can be stored to reduce the total workload. For simple expressions, symbolic derivatives may be generated, either by hand or by a symbolic mathematics package. It is worth noting however, that symbolic expansion can be avoided by the use of algorithms such as [2.8] or [2.9], both of which generate point values of functions and multiple derivatives economically without the need for explicit symbolic differentiation.

For the pipe network problem, the evaluation of the Jacobian uses both symbolic and numerical differentiation: if the flow through a pipe is laminar, symbolic differentiation is used; turbulent flows require numerical differentiation.

Three different implementations for solving this problem are discussed. All three implementations distribute the flow function and Jacobian calculations row-wise to the set of processors in the network, but differ in the implementation of the linear equations solver:

(a) a full linear solver on one processor,

(b) a distributed full linear solver, and

(c) a sparse solver on one processor.

All three methods were tested on a sample problem from industry, a pipe network consisting of 113 nodes, 123 pipes, with 59 unknown pressures. The result is a sparse Jacobian matrix with an average of 4 to 6 entries per row (in a matrix of rank 59).

2.5.1 Full Sequential Solver

The first approach involves using a master/slave paradigm. The master processor is responsible for the overall iterative process as well as finding the solution of the system of linear equations determined at each iteration. The slave processors are used to evaluate both the function and the Jacobian. Load balancing is achieved statically by evenly distributing all the rows over the set of slave processors. No attempt is made to determine the amount of effort each row would require, although the algorithm does not preclude the use any type of load balancing. The basic algorithm is shown below:

Master	*Slaves*
send **x** to slaves	get **x** from master
idle	compute **f** and **J**
get **f** and **J** from slaves	send **f** and **J** to
solve **J** δ**x** = **f**	idle
update **x**	idle

These steps are repeated until either δ**x** is small enough or δ**f** $\approx$ 0.

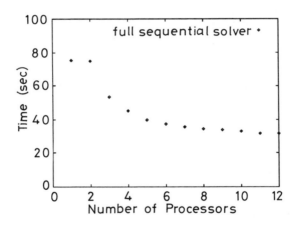

Fig. 2.8 Full sequential solver times

Figs. 2.8 and 2.9 show the behaviour of this method. Execution times initially improve as processors are added to the network. However, the improvements tail off faster than expected as the number of processors increases above 6. The breakdown of times shows that although the function and Jacobian evaluations are parallelised effectively (FUNCTION entry in the bar-graph, with number of slaves increasing from left to right), the overall speedup is limited by the amount of time spent in the linear solver (SOLVE entry).

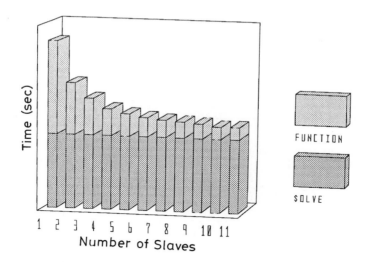

Fig. 2.9 Full sequential solver breakdown of times

2.5.2   Full Parallel Solver

The efficiency of the previous method was limited due to the amount of time spent by the master process in the linear system solver, since during the solution phase the slaves sit idle. The second approach to this problem therefore involves a parallel implementation of the linear solver. In this case, the processors are all treated equally, each processor being responsible for a particular set of rows. Each processor evaluates the function and the Jacobian and also performs the necessary Gaussian elimination steps on the rows allocated to it. Synchronisation amongst the processors is used at each iteration to determine whether the iterative procedure should terminate. As all processors are busy at all times, this method should be more efficient than the previous one, especially as the number of processors increases.

Fig. 2.10 shows that although the times have improved with respect to the full sequential solver method, the improvements are not significant. Although the solver is now done in parallel, the increase in communication has almost completely offset any savings in computation time. As the number of processors increases, the computation required by each processor decreases but the amount of computation stays essentially the same. The proportion of time spent communicating versus computing increases.

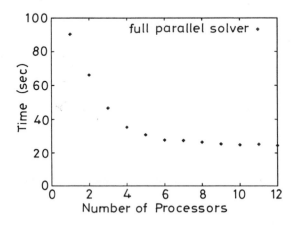

Fig. 2.10   Full parallel solver times

2.5.3   Sparse Sequential Solver

As neither a sequential nor a parallel solver gave good speedups for larger numbers of processors, an alternative approach was required. A typical pipe network consists of nodes that are only connected to a small number of other nodes. The result is a sparse set of linear equations. In the test problem, for example, most rows have an average of 4 to 6 entries, whereas the size of system is 59. In other words, the linear system is sparse, so the third approach consists of using a sparse sequential solver.

This approach is very similar to the first one: a master/slave paradigm is used in which the master coordinates the iterative procedure and solves the linear systems while the slaves are responsible for the function and Jacobian evaluations.

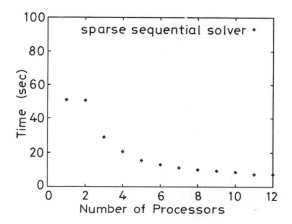

Fig. 2.11 Sparse sequential solver times

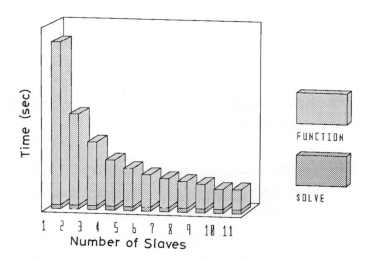

Fig. 2.12 Sparse sequential solver breakdown of times

The improvement achieved by using a sparse solver, even sequentially, is noticeable. Fig. 2.11 shows the new timings and Fig. 2.12 shows the breakdown of these times into the time taken to solve the linear systems and the time spent by the master processor for the function and Jacobian evaluations. The time spent in the solver is now a very small proportion of the overall time, thereby allowing reasonable speedups over the whole range of network sizes.

2.5.4   Conclusions

Reducing the amount of time any processor sits idle increases the efficiency of the overall algorithm. For the type of problem considered, the alternative that accomplishes this task best out of those considered is a sparse solver running sequentially with all function and Jacobian evaluations performed on a set of slave processors. For denser problems, it is likely that the second approach, a parallel full solver, would be a better approach.

Implementing a parallel sparse solver does not seem worthwhile for problems of the size considered here. The amount of time spent in the solver is negligible and the introduction of any communications overheads into a sparse solver would increase the amount of time taken to solve a system of equations.

2.6   CASE STUDY THREE: DYNAMIC FLOWSHEET SIMULATION, EVALUATION BY COLUMN

In this study we follow exactly the decomposition strategy of Section 2.4.1, but extend it to cover the dynamic case, using the techniques developed by Ponton and his co-workers [2.7],[2.10]. Briefly, this extension requires that our iteration variables y in eqn (2.1) are the "new time" tear variables $y(t+\delta t)$. In this case the preprocessing for step 2 in the algorithm requires that we obtain each output variable at $(t+\delta t)$ in terms of the corresponding input variable. For algebraic equations this means a solution of the form:

$$\bar{x}\ (t\ +\ \delta t)\ =\ \phi\ (\bar{x}\ (t\ +\ \delta t))$$

$$(2.7)$$

And for differential equations:

$$\bar{x}\ (t+\delta t) = \phi\ (\bar{x},\ \bar{x}\ (t+\delta t),\ t)$$

(2.8)

It was implied in the earlier discussion that **x** might thus be obtained analytically. This will not in general be the case and so numerical solution of these equations, both algebraic and differential, will be required for more complex systems. This has important consequences, as will be seen.

Given that the above step may be performed, solution of the complete system for the **y** is obtained by Newton's method, the Jacobian being evaluated in this case by column. It is not convenient to obtain analytical derivatives, (a) because of the extensive manipulation, and indeed sometimes numerical solution involved, and (b) because there are no obvious common terms between ϕ_j and ϕ_k or derivatives such as $\partial\phi_j\ /\partial x_i$ and $\partial\phi_k\ /\partial x_i$. We therefore use numerical differentiation by perturbation of each of the **y** . These perturbations are carried out in parallel, the overall strategy for *n* equations on *(n+1)* transputers being as shown below.

Processor 0	*Processor j=1 ... n*
send **y**	receive **y**; estimate perturbation δy_i
calculate $\phi(\mathbf{y})$	calculate $\phi^j(y^j)$, $\phi^j \equiv \phi(y^j)$,
	where $y^j \equiv \{y_1, y_2, ..., y_j + \delta y_j, ... y_n\}$
receive ϕ^i, i=1 ...	send ϕ^j
estimate **J** using:	idle
$\partial\phi_i\ /\partial y_j = (\phi_i - \phi^j_i)/\delta y_j$	
solve for new **y**	
check convergence	

Two disadvantages of this approach are:
• The numerical differentiation procedure.
• The idle period of the processors during the linear equation solution phase.

The first of these is a particular difficulty when coupled with the requirement for numerical solution of eqn. (2.2). This problem, which can lead to failure to converge the global solution procedure, was identified in early work on steady-state simulation [2.11] . One solution is to replace the rigorous forms of those equations which do not have analytical solutions by approximate equations, algebraic or differential, which do. This greatly improves the numerical differentiation by ensuring smooth and consistent behaviour of the perturbed system. This will of course yield only an approximate solution unless the approximate equations are refitted to rigorous forms. This can be done by exploiting the "idle" period of the processors to evaluate parameters for the approximate models using the rigorous equations, updating the former by simple Jacobi iteration. This approach has been very successful in serial computers [2.12] and appears to extend rather elegantly to the MIMD environment.

2.7   EVALUATION AND OPTIMISATION OF PARALLEL PROCESSING STRATEGIES

Underlying all MIMD developments there is the general problem of assigning computational tasks or processes to processors, known as the "mapping problem". In the Case Studies, assignment to processors was either made on an ad-hoc basis, or was guided by simple estimates of computational load, such as number of non zero elements in Case Study Two. In practice a number of factors have to be considered. It is desirable to map processes which communicate heavily with each other onto adjacent or identical processors; and to load all processors evenly. An exact algorithm for the mapping problem is not known, and so various heuristics have been proposed. Many different trial configurations or mappings of the parallel program may be necessary and testing of these can be very time consuming.

Our approach [2.13] to this problem involves building a model of the parallel application. Experiments to determine a good mapping can be performed on this model rather than on the real application. A simulation system has been developed to investigate different strategies.

The system is built as an extension to the Simula programming language and allows the user to construct a model of a parallel program executing on a parallel computer. The simulation language provides high level primitives to represent *computation*, represented simply as a time delay, and *communication* in a multi-process programming environment. The system allows rapid prototyping of various alternative parallel programming strategies, such as those discussed above. The model can also be developed alongside the real application [2.4]. We are presently using this technique to optimise allocation in the Case Studies described above.

2.8   CONCLUSIONS

We now have substantial experience of simulating chemical process plant using transputers. The major practical application we foresee for these simulation models falls in two areas:

- Highly realistic detailed simulation of processes to evaluate performance of plant, control systems and operating strategies, using graphic user interfaces such as that described in Case Study One.

- Fast and convenient steady- or unsteady-state simulation, or optimisation, applied at the design stage of the process, to enable design alternatives to be evaluated and compared.

Powerful and convenient simulations of this sort can greatly enhance the productivity of process and control engineers involved in the design and operation of chemical plants.

Another factor, which we have not stressed in our description of the case studies, is critical to any widespread use of these techniques. There is a large body of existing computer code, representing many man years of engineering knowledge and development, which we must avoid having to reprogram. Our experience suggests that, using MIMD computers and tools and techniques such as we have described, most of this important engineering content may be retained.

REFERENCES

[2.1]   Ponton JW, Johnson AI and Bobrow S: Application of a modular computer simulation system to the control of a reactor train, *Canadian J Chemical Engineering*, **50**, 2, pp275-280, 1972.

[2.2]   Petzold LR: Differential-algebraic equations are not ODEs, *SIAM J Sci Stat Comp*, **3**, pp367-384, 1982.

[2.3]   Ponton JW and McKinnel RC: Nonlinear process simulation and control using transputers, *IEE Proc D*, **137**, 4, pp189-196, 1990.

[2.4]   Candlin R, Luo Q and Skilling N: The investigation of communication patterns in occam programs, *Occam User Group Technical Meeting 11*, 1989.

[2.5]   Duff IS: Parallel implementation of multifrontal schemes, *Parallel Computing*, **3**, pp193-204, 1986.

[2.6]   Barkley RW and Motard RL, Decomposition of nets, *The Chemical Engineering Journal*, **3**, pp265-275, 1973.

[2.7]   Ponton JW: Dynamic process simulation using flowsheet structure, *Computers and Chemical Engineering*, **6**, 4, pp331-333, 1982.

[2.8]   Griewank A: On automatic differentiation, in *Mathematical Programming* **88,** Kluwer Academic Publishers, 1989.

[2.9]   Ponton JW: The numerical evaluation of analytical derivatives, *Computers and Chemical Engineering*, **6,** pp331-333, 1982.

[2.10] Alyott M and Lott DH: Development of a dynamic flowsheeting program, *I Chem E Symposium Series*, **92,** pp55-66, 1985.

[2.11] Johns WR: Mathematical Considerations in preparing general purpose computer programs for design or simulation of chemical processes, *EFCE Conference Proceedings*, Florence, 1970.

[2.12] Johns R and Vadhwana V: A dual-level flowsheeting system, *I Chem E Symposium Series*, **92,** p37.

[2.12] Candlin R and Skilling N, A modelling system for the investigation of parallel program performance, *Proc Fifth International Conference on Modelling Techniques and Tools for Computer Performance Evaluation*, Turin, 1991.

Chapter 3

Transputer-Based Control of Mechatronic Systems

AWP Bakkers, J Meijer, JC Musters and HG Tillema

3.1   INTRODUCTION

Recently the systematic application of advanced control algorithms to mechanical systems has been given the name "mechatronics." This term originates from Japan, where in 1989 the first International Conference on Advanced Mechatronics was organized by JSME [3.1]. In a mechatronical design it is continuously considered whether the desired properties can be better realized by changing the mechanical construction or by adding electronic control, rather than by adding the control system after completing the design of the construction. This enables the design of systems with superior performance. Typical examples of mechatronic systems are a compact disc player and an advanced photo camera with many electronic functions. Robotics can also be considered as part of mechatronics.

For the realization of a mechatronical system, advanced control algorithms and fast computer systems are needed. Because light mechanical systems have very fast dynamics, a high sampling frequency is essential. Conventional sequential computer systems are often too slow. By using parallel computing, the sampling frequency can be increased and more complex control algorithms can be realized. However, the use of parallel computing requires the total concept of the realization of a real-time digital controller to be reconsidered. This chapter gives a systematical analysis of the problems that are encountered when a real-time parallel computer system is to be set up and gives solutions to some of these problems.

Although the ideas presented are more generally applicable, the main emphasis will be on the use of transputers. The transputer was designed to be used as a building block for parallel computer systems. Simultaneously with the development of the transputer a parallel programming language has been developed: occam. Together they have properties which make them especially attractive for the realization of a real-time parallel computer system. It may be expected that the transputer and other future parallel processors will have a great impact on the realization of advanced control algorithms requiring high sampling rates.

In Section 3.2 the proposed layered system architecture will be introduced. The realization of the layered architecture requires an interconnection method for the transputers in the different layers. This necessitates the design of a transputer-link backplane which is described in Section 3.3. Besides hardware there is also a requirement for software that supports the layer concept. First there is the real-time sampling software described in Section 3.4, followed by the description of the necessary safety and fault detection software described in Section 3.5. The network software described in Section 3.6 interconnects the different software layers in a structured manner.

3.2   SYSTEM ARCHITECTURE

The use of transputers in a control system design necessitates the design of a transputer network that reflects the parallelism of the particular control system. There is no standard procedure to match a transputer topology to a corresponding control problem. Therefore the transputer topology should be tailored to the control problem. As a result of experience gained in the realization of several transputer-based control systems by Bakkers [3.2] and Stavenuiter [3.3], a layered architecture is proposed.

The basic idea is that there are several layers in a practical control system. The desired system can be described as a number of successive layers as illustrated in Fig. 3.1.

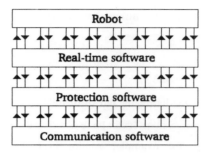

Fig. 3.1 System architecture

- The first layer called the hardware layer consists of the interface hardware and its matching *real-time sampling software*. The interface hardware of this layer contains A/D, D/A converters and digital interface circuitry.

- The second layer contains the *protection software*. It was originally designed to be used in the test phase of the control algorithms. However, it turned out to be a fundamental necessity after it had been completed. It should not only be considered a temporary convenience during the design of the equipment but an essential part in the maintenance and fault diagnosis of the system during operation.

- The third layer of a typical control system contains the software that calculates the actual control value. In this layer one soon requires a systematic way to communicate control variables to and from the different parts of the control algorithms. The *communication software* considered as the third layer provides the communication between the different parts of the controller software. This layer requires the use of parallel computing power, because more complex control algorithms have to be executed at higher sampling frequencies and thus in less time. The user or control engineer will only access the system via the communication layer. All other layers are transparent to the user and may therefore be called "system layer".

A more detailed description of the different layers is given below.

3.2.1   First Layer

The first layer consists of the hardware and software directly connected to the sensors and actuators of the control system. It can be realized as the first transputer layer. This interface layer includes for example: Analog-to-Digital, Digital-to-Analog and Resolver-to-Digital converters. Because these interfaces do not require more than 16 bits of data, the 16 bit transputer T222 can be used. The software of this layer performs primarily the sampling and control action and is further described in Section 3.4. This layer is also the right place to perform the necessary filtering of the measured data.

The processed measurements are available at the link interface input and outputs. Schematically the first layer and its interconnections to the second layer and the monitor and display may be represented as in Fig. 3.2.

3.2.2   Second Layer

The second layer consists of a transputer that executes the safety software which is further described in Section 3.5. This layer completely isolates the sensors and actuators from the rest of the control system.

Sensor data arrives here and may be compared with the actuator control signals to check whether the combination of the two may lead to a dangerous situation. If so, the safety software has priority and will set the control signals to a safe value. The topology of this layer could include one or more transputers, as illustrated in Fig. 3.2 where one T800 transputer is used.

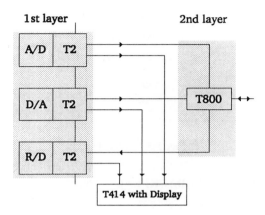

Fig. 3.2 Layers one and two

3.2.3   Third layer

The third layer typically contains the first calculation layer, which in robot terms could be the calculation of the robot dynamics. It is not very likely that this calculation can be performed in one transputer. Therefore, as an example, a transputer network of eight transputers is given in Fig. 3.3. This network consists of a central ring of T800 transputers where the majority of the (floating point) calculations are performed.

The T414 transputers on the input and output of this network perform the distribution and collection of data. For the distribution of the code over this topology the method based on list scheduling, see Hilhorst [3.4], or a technique known as Post-Game analysis, see Sunter [3.5] may be used.

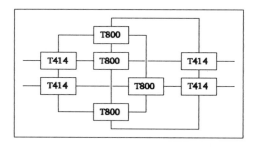

Fig. 3.3 Third layer

3.3   TRANSPUTER LINX BACKPLANE AND PROCESS INTERFACE

The Twente LINX backplane is a backplane for transputer links. When investigating the use of transputers in control applications, several configurations of transputer networks have to be considered. Therefore a reconfigurable transputer network is needed. Furthermore, it is necessary to be able to perform fast I/O to and from the network layer. The interconnection of the links should be realized by means of the Inmos C004 link switch chip in combination with a hardwired backplane.

The Twente LINX backplane has been designed as a solution for the cabling problem. The design of the backplane is based on the specifications of the VME standard. The LINX backplane is intended for use under severe environmental conditions. Therefore, a lot of attention was given to the electrical and mechanical robustness of the system, as closely following the VME specifications as possible. The design of the backplane was based on the following requirements:

- The backplane is primarily intended for real-time control systems with transputer based I/O.
- Both electrically and mechanically the backplane should be reliable.
- The backplane should be reconfigurable under software control.
- A modular design should provide a flexible, inexpensive system.

The requirements resulted in the following architecture. The backplane provides the user with eight slots for transputer boards and two linkswitch boards. Each of the linkswitch boards controls 32 links on the backplane and several links from the outside world. This adds up to a total of 64 links on the backplane, divided into two independent subsystems of 32 links each. From each slot, four links are connected to each subsystem. The switch cards placed on the left and the right of the transputer card slots perform the interconnections within each subsystem. The architecture of the LINX backplane is given in Fig. 3.4.

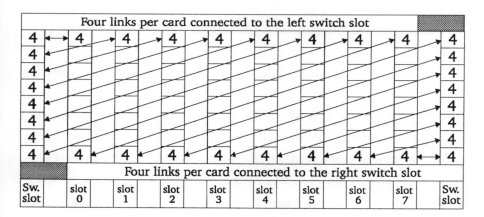

Fig. 3.4 Architecture of LINX backplane

The system is based on a VME rack size of 3 or 6 HE. A single backplane has a height of 3 HE. In a VME rack there is room for two backplanes, one for the top connector row and one for the bottom row. The Twente LINX backplane definition is flexible by demanding that either the bottom row or the top row or both contain a LINX backplane. In the first two cases the user can use 64 link interconnections, when two backplanes are used 128 link interconnections are possible. The LINX backplane may also be used in combination with a single Eurocard height system. Each backplane contains eight slots for transputer (I/O) cards and two slots for linkswitch cards.

3.4   THE REAL-TIME LANGUAGE TASC

In real-time control systems the timing of the different control actions is just as important as the correctness of the control action. This renders a correctly calculated control action which is executed too late incorrect. Real-time control systems consist of several tasks, which must be executed independently while carefully maintaining their proper timing relations. Traditionally programming of the control processes and their timing constraints had to be done manually. The resulting software, besides from being error-prone, is often hard to maintain. A solution to this problem is the use of the proposed real-time language TASC which is an acronym for "Transputer Application generator for Sampling applications in Control systems". The TASC language allows the specification of time-dependent tasks in a control system that are translated by the TASC compiler into executable code for execution on a transputer.

The TASC system is in fact an application generator that enables the control engineer to specify the sampling problem in a high level language. This real-time language permits independent control over all aspects of control processes such as: timing, communication, control of interface hardware and error handling. The TASC language provides simple language constructs to specify the interface hardware. With these constructs the TASC system can control the interface hardware in a nearly time optimal way. The control engineer does not have to be concerned with interface hardware details if the specification has been properly implemented by the interface hardware designer. The sampling applications generated by the TASC system may be used in a control environment that puts high demands on the sampling system.

Sampling frequencies of up to 5kHz can be realized. The TASC system was designed to operate in a control application as in Fig. 3.5, or in a similar environment. A fast assembly robot is controlled by a network consisting of T800 transputers. The interfacing of the network to the robot is performed by a front-end of dedicated 16-bit T222 transputers. The program for each such transputer forms a TASC application. To program a front-end, a coherent set of TASC applications must be generated.

In the fast assembly robot application, the T222 is interfaced to the robot in four different ways. All interfaces are memory-mapped.

1. Analog-to-Digital Converter board. The four converters have 4 to 1 multiplexers on the input. One 12-bit conversion takes 10 μs. Conversion can be triggered externally;

2. Digital to Analog Converter board. Four 12-bit converters are available;

3. Resolver to Digital Converter board. Two 16 bit angles can be measured.

4. Parallel interface. Two memory mapped 16-bit parallel inputs and two 16-bit parallel outputs are available.

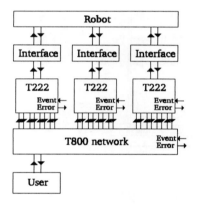

Fig. 3.5 The TASC target application

3.4.1 The TASC application

The TASC application is discussed as an implementation based on the TASC system. Fig. 3.6 shows the processes that need to be implemented in the model. The sampling nucleus performs all sampling actions and other programmed functionality generated by the TASC compiler. The GetLink processes handle input data packet reception, and PutLink processes perform the transmission of output data packets. A sampling event starts with the execution of the sampling nucleus, followed by the transmission of the output packets by the PutLink processes. Reception is asynchronous. All inter-process communication is performed using shared memory. The sampling nucleus is generated by the TASC-L compiler. The real-time behaviour of the system is optimized for high I/O loads.

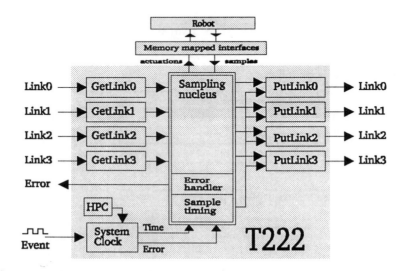

Fig. 3.6   Active TASC processes in the control mode

Link communication

Each of the four available links can autonomously transfer a packet to or from the transputer memory. The processor has to supply a pointer to the packet buffer and the number of bytes to transfer when using an in or out instruction. Links operate concurrently, so every link input and output requires its own dedicated handler, as shown in Fig. 3.6. Both GetLink and PutLink communicate only with the sample nucleus. Shared variables are used for inter-process communication.

The sampling nucleus

The sampling nucleus performs all sample actions, system control functions and error detection. It is completely constructed by the TASC system. The sample nucleus performs the following functions to support the TASC framework:

1. Increment the system clock "SystemTime", set up the next wake-up and check that the corresponding event-pin pulse has arrived on-time. If not, generate a jitter error, and set the safety condition "Park" to true. These functions must be performed before any other action can be performed;

2. Update the loop status variables "loop.InTime";

3. Update the input data packets. If input data packets missed their deadline, default data is used for the update instead. If Park is true, the park mode alternative enter data packet is used in the update, otherwise the alternative data of the control mode is used;

4. Update the loop status variable "Loop.OutTime";

5. At the end of each sampling event, check if ErrorFlag was set. If so, set the transputer error flag.

GetLink/PutLink process priority

The real-time performance is heavily influenced by the priority at which GetLink and PutLink run. PutLink must run on high priority, because any delay would immediately add to the turnaround time. Also transmission must end before the next sampling event begins. GetLink processes can wait a while, but any delay suffered near the start of the sampling event effectively adds to the turnaround time. Since there normally are no high priority processes near the moment of actuation, GetLink can be run at low priority, but a guarantee must be given that when actuation moments are near, there are no other processes on the Low Priority (LP) queue. In the target application, the GetLink processes will be the only LP processes. The priorities at which the different processes run are:

Priority	Routine	Function
High	Event	Watches the event pin period
High	SystemClock	Increments System time
High	SampleNucleus	Performs the sample actions
High	PutLink	Transmits measurement packets
Low	GetLink	Receives actuation packets

System clock distribution

As indicated before, every TASC application must access the system clock. The system clock tick determines the sample resolution with a maximum sampling frequency of 5000 Hz and, therefore, a system clock tick of 200 µs or less must be supported. Any uncertainty about the system time adds to the turnaround time. The system clock can be distributed to individual processors by making use of the transputer High Priority Counter (HPC) and the event input pin. The event pin is asserted with the signal shown in Fig. 3.7. The event pin is always monitored for positive going edges, with two consecutive edges making up a period. When, in initialize mode, four identical periods have been detected, at t_m, the system clock tick is assumed to be $T_t = T_i/4$. After t_m the event pin period is checked for a change in the period. When a change occurs at t_c, the control mode is entered. The new period must be equal to T_t. If it differs too much, as at t_p, a jitter error is detected and the system enters park mode. Small errors occur constantly due to the fact that the event pin clock and the transputer clock are not fully synchronised. Whenever the accumulated error rises above one HPC tick, it is adjusted in the opposite direction. This will occur infrequently, therefore its effect on jitter performance is negligible. The error does increase the turnaround time, though. In park mode, the event pin is ignored and the system time is no longer synchronized between processors. All sample processors will continue to operate, but their internal copy of the system time will show an increasing error. This will lead to a totally unsynchronized system within a few seconds! The system must achieve a parked state within this period.

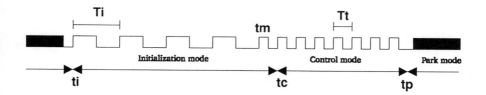

Fig. 3.7 Timing signals on the event pin

3.4.2 The Interface Model

The interface model is a set of assumptions about the actual behaviour of the interface hardware, given a formal specification of the interface hardware. The formal specification allows language constructs to be developed using the interface model. The TASC system can figure out which actions the processor must perform on the interface hardware in order to implement the sampling of the specified actions. The advantage is twofold:

• Separation of responsibilities between the interface hardware design engineer, and the control engineer. The control engineer specifies the desired sampling actions, the hardware design engineer provides a formal specification of the interface hardware. The TASC system uses the interface model to implement the sampling actions on the specified interface hardware.

• With the interface hardware specified, the TASC system can take advantage of hardware parallelism. Sampling actions can be implemented as efficiently as possible.

The interface model enables the TASC system to autonomously implement sampling actions. Sampling actions often require just a single processor read or write. Such actions are referred to as simple actions. However, more complex devices exist, which require several processor reads and writes to implement a single sampling action. Such actions are referred to as complex actions.

Symbolic representation of the interface world

The TASC system should be able to generate an optimal sequence of simple actions that implements all sampling actions specified in the sampling program. This sequence is referred to as an I/O-schedule. The generation of this schedule is the task of the action scheduler. A guarantee must be given that all sampling actions have been implemented correctly. As stated before, an interface model is a set of assumptions about the actual behaviour of the interface hardware, given a formal specification of the interface hardware. This formal specification includes the following areas:

- **Sampling**: In a control environment sampling is the transformation of a continuous signal into a digital data stream, or vice versa. The signal is digitized such that each datum in the data stream is a sample that corresponds to a signal level at a terminal, an input or an output, at a specified moment in time.
- **Symbols**: A sample is a symbol. It symbolizes a physical entity in the physical process. Symbols are named in the sampling program, and are located within the interface hardware. Such a location is referred to as a device. Symbols are said to originate at a device. Actually the symbol value originates at the device. Both the signal level and the datum are occurrences of the same symbol.
- **Actions**: The sampling processor is capable of performing actions on the interface hardware. Any action is a symbol transfer to or from a device. The symbol is said to be inserted or extracted at the device. An action can be described by the symbol transferred, the direction of the transfer and by device accessed. An action must preserve the integrity of the sampling symbol, otherwise the purpose of the action is lost.
- **Devices**: Devices are implicitly defined by actions. An action transfers a symbol to or from a device. The symbol is assumed to be preserved at the device. A device is a limited resource, as it can represent a single symbol only. The actual

representation of the symbol value is irrelevant. Typical devices are interface registers and terminals. The symbol value is typically represented as a signal level at a terminal, or as data stored in an interface register. Devices can be located within the interface hardware. Their location permits three classes of devices to be distinguished:

1) Terminal devices connect the control system to its environment, the physical process.

2) Bus devices connect to the sampling processor.

3) Hidden devices are the remaining devices within the interface hardware. They connect only to other devices, not to the sampling processor or the physical process.

The symbolic representation of a typical interface model is illustrated in Fig. 3.8.

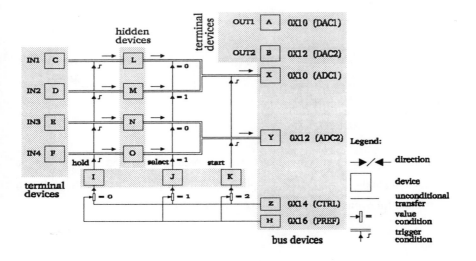

Fig. 3.8 Symbolic representation of interface network

The TASC interface model is an ad hoc implementation, designed to permit access to a wide range of interface hardware. It was designed with the objectives of easy specification of simple and complex device accesses, so that its functioning can be predicted by the programmer efficiently. The characteristics of the TASC interface model may be understood from their specification in the TASC device statement. Refer to Fig. 3.8 and assume that hold, select and start are bus devices. In addition to a 1 µs delay, to allow the sample and hold to settle, a 10 µs delay is introduced for the conversion to take place.

```
device hold        @0x14;   /* sample and hold */
device select      @0x16;   /* multiplexer */
device start       @0x18;   /* start conversion register */
device ADC1 (hold [1 µs], select, start [10 µs] ) @0x10;
device ADC2 (hold [1 µs], select, start [10 µs] ) @0x12;
```

The inputs IN1, IN2, IN3 and IN4 can be accessed through the above device statements. For example, to access IN1 in a sample program, the implicit actuations must be given the correct values as:

```
x_angle = ADC1(1, 0, 1);
```

A mini sample program which specifies a measurement of all four inputs, could be the following:

```
x_angle<N> = ADC1(1,0,1);
x_vel<N>   = ADC1(1,1,1);
y_angle<N> = ADC2(1,0,1);
y_vel<N>   = ADC2(1,1,1);
```

The action scheduler will now detect that the both x_angle and y_angle can be performed in parallel, because their implicit actuation sequence matches fully. It will suggests the following operations to access these values:

```
@0x14 = 1;                       /* Sample and hold */
[wait 1 µs]                      /* wait minimum of 1 µs */
@0x16 = 0;                       /* Set multiplexer to channel0 */
@0x18 = 1;                       /* Start conversion */
[wait 10 µs]                     /* wait minimum of 10 µs */
x_angle<N>=<N>@0x10;  /* Read ADC1 */
y_angle<N>=<N>@0x12;  /* Read ADC2 */
```

The scheduler will detect the same parallelism for x_vel and y_vel, but also that this pair matches part of the access path of x_angle and y_angle. Therefore only the following additional operations need to be generated to access x_vel and y_vel:

```
@0x16 = 1;        /* Set multiplexer to channel1 */
@0x18 = 1;        /* Start conversion */
[wait 10 μs]      /* wait minimum of 10 μs */
x_vel = @0x10;    /* Read ADC1 */
y_vel = @0x12;    /* Read ADC2 */
```

The TASC action scheduler looks for matching device names in the implicit actuation sequence, from the beginning of either sequence. Therefore if the two sequences are identical, they can be fully parallelized.

3.4.3   The TASC language (TASC-L)

The TASC language (TASC-L) is a dedicated real-time language to specify sampling problems. As such it has a special set of statements to support programming of sampling processes of the TASC system. A number of major design decisions had to be made in order to realize the TASC system. The TASC-L statements are not discussed explicitly here, but some examples are given. The major design rules consider:

- how to give the user access to TASC data
- how to perform error handling
- how to model the interface hardware

The following rules have been used to guide the design of TASC-L:

1. TASC-L must have primitives that allow the definition of input and output data packets, loops and sampling actions.

2. Error handling and system control must be supported. The way the TASC system heaps sample actions simplifies error handling and system control to a

large extent. These functions can be performed because each sampling process has global access to all loops.

3. Programming of actions of the sampling loop must be independent. The TASC system does not enforce independent programming, as all sample actions can be heaped together. Clarity is improved if independent loop programming is encouraged by the syntax.

4. Ideally the TASC system should support a division between the responsibilities of the hardware and software engineers. The hardware engineer should be able to describe the interface hardware accurately. The software engineer should be able to symbolically access the interface hardware. The TASC system should relate the two.

5. In a real-time environment, time must be managed. Any language constructs that cause the real-time behaviour to be unpredictable or slow must be excluded.

6. The TASC system performs tasks that can be difficult to debug. Therefore the TASC system should perform as many checks as possible in order to detect oversights or inconsistencies from the part of the user.

The sampling action process has to perform several functions such as: actuation, measurement , error handling and system control. The sampling actions must access several resources i.e. input and output data packets, devices, communication control (enabled/disabled), loop timing (sample interval, moment of measurement, etc.), system status (error flag, operating mode, system clock) and error status. The possible operations are given in Table 3.1.

operator symbol	operation	comment
()	priority	Nesting
?:	conditional expr.	Optimized
~	logical NOT	
!	boolean NOT	true int 1, false int 0
<<	Shift left	Logical shift
>>	Shift right	Logical shift
&	logical AND	
/	logical OR	
^	logical EXOR	
*	signed multiply	
+	add	
-	subtract	Both unary and dyadic

Table 3.1 TASC-L operators

A sample program illustrating the use of two WITH loops is provided in Table 3.2.

```
with elbow {
    timed sample_cnt = 0;   /* init sample counter */
    DAC1 = (in.motor & 0x7fff) << 1; /* actuate motor */
    out.angle = ADC1(1,0,1);   /* read ADC1,channel0 */
    out.speed = ADC1(1,1,1);   /* read ADC1,channel1 */
    out.deadline = elbow.InTime;   /* get deadline */
    out.cnt = sample_cnt = sample_cnt +1;/*count samples*/
};
with {
    /* global access to packet variable */
    motor_direction = (elbow.in.motor & 0x8000) >> 15;
}
```

Table 3.2 Sample program

In the sample program listed above, the sampling actions for the loop "elbow" are specified. A D/A converter is actuated and two A/D converter inputs are measured. The results are stored in output data packet "elbow.out". The measured data in elbow.out is complemented with a deadline and a sample count. The sample counter is constructed through the use of a timed variable "elbow.sample_cnt". It is incremented each time elbow is measuring. A second "with" statement is added to show how multiple statements can be added, and how loop data can still be accessed in this untimed "with" statement. The "with" statement only suggests but does not enforce a partitioning of the sampling application on a per loop basis. Note that all data is globally accessible.

3.4.4   The Sample Action Scheduler

The TASC system must optimize the turnaround time. As mentioned previously the sampling actions must be scheduled in order to take advantage of the parallelism in the interface hardware. The time gaps that the schedule will contain should be used to perform calculations.

Scheduling constraints

The TASC scheduler constructs a search tree. The search tree is often small enough to permit an exhaustive tree search in order to find the optimal sequence. The optimal schedule is selected from the possible schedules using an evaluation function. The function used is the estimated total time needed to perform the sampling actions in the sequence specified by the schedule. The number of possible schedules is limited by the following constraints:

1. A complex device must be accessed as a sequence of implicit actuations, followed by the main actuation or measurement. All sampling actions performed in this sequence must be spaced in time according to the delays specified in the "device" statement. These delays are taken to be minimum values.

2. An actuation can only be performed if the actuated value is available at that moment in time. The actuation has to be delayed until the measurements have been performed that make this value available.

3. Transfer parallelism must be exploited. The TASC device model with only actuation conditions permits a simple algorithm to extract transfer parallelism.

The first two constraints can be easily modelled in a graph that consists of all sample actions that must be performed to access all complex devices. Associated with such a graph is a set of ready actions. Only ready actions can be scheduled. When such an action is scheduled, subsequent actions are enabled, which in turn become ready if all incoming actions have been scheduled. The third constraint is implemented using some heuristic seeding of the initial search condition.

3.4.5   Transputer Suitability for TASC Model Implementation

The suitability of an implementation of the TASC system on a transputer is influenced by:

Variable execution times

    The main transputer deficiency is its lack of constant execution times. The resulting jitter problem can be solved by inserting extra timer syncs in the sample nucleus, at those locations where jitter would otherwise become too high.

External vs. internal memory

    Transputer programs execute fastest from internal RAM. Since it is unlikely that the TASC program can run completely from internal RAM, only the most time critical processes will be placed in internal RAM. The sample nucleus must run from internal RAM, since it is most time-critical in all aspects. If there is still enough space, then the code for PutLink and GetLink is placed there too. All data is kept in internal RAM, except for static data, like the enter packet descriptor tables GetLink uses. Differences in timing should be taken into account when forecasting the real-time performance.

Link communication

    The main transputer feature is its autonomous link interface. A link allows a packet to be transmitted without processor assistance when the data is in consecutive memory locations. The TASC system employs buffers for both incoming and outgoing data. For incoming data the TASC system employs two buffers, which are alternately used for storing incoming data. During the sample action, actuation data is read from the other buffer. To access the actuation data the transputer must index the buffer. The extra cost involved with indexing is low because the transputer can access local data more quickly.

3.4.6   Real-time Performance of the TASC System

This paragraph discusses briefly how the use of the TASC system affects the real-time performance of the sampling application. The TASC implementation has been outlined above. It is compared with the situation where sampling actions are executed as a string of independently executed sample processes. A wake-up list consisting of a list of all timed actions could serve as the basis for such an implementation. The TASC system heaps the sampling actions into one process, the sampling nucleus, which is executed each system clock tick. The sampling nucleus can be optimized well, which results in a performance increase. Although the processor now performs many more sampling actions than necessary, worst case performance is affected favourably. If sampling actions were executed separately, many more timer syncs would have been necessary. This saving is offset by the double buffering required by the TASC system. Heaping all sampling into one process results in a minimum of sequence errors. Sequence errors increase linearly with the total time taken to perform all sample processes. Sequence errors are low because:

- only one timer sync is necessary
- sequence errors increase less than proportionally with the number of sample processes
- sample data can be shared, so fewer accesses to slow interfaces are needed
- parallelism can be exploited better.

It can be concluded that the TASC model helps to achieve a highly stable real-time performance that is well suited to the distributed sampling environment.

A generated schedule of a sample application is illustrated in Fig. 3.9. This TASC application serves two control loops each with a protection backup loop over link 2. The timing has been calculated on the compiler generated code for the following data: Four actuation data packets, of 4 words each; four measurement data packets 8 words each; two A/D converters with conversion time of 10 µs, with two samples are taken per ADC; two D/A converters and a system clock tick 200 µs.

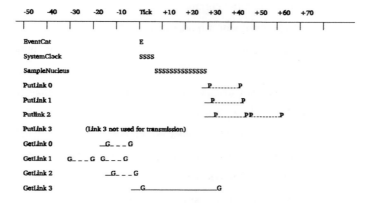

Fig. 3.9 Schedule of TASC application

3.5   THE PROTECTION LAYER

The purpose of the protection layer is to protect the system from hazardous situations. These hazardous situations may occur during normal action or during failures. During normal operation one can distinguish two types of hazardous situation, namely situations concerning the angles of the robot links and situations concerning the position of the gripper and other parts of the robot. Depending on the situation the protection acts on the angle or on the position.

*   The angle protection has to protect the axis against hitting the end stops. Furthermore, the angle protection has to prevent the angle between two connected axes from becoming too small. The protection method is a direct method, each

angle is measured and when its value exceeds a limit the interference action is started.

- The purpose of the position protection is to avoid obstacles. Here it is not sufficient to act on a single angle. A 3-D combination of angles leads to a certain position of the gripper or other parts of a robot to enter a forbidden area.
- A third protection mechanism is the fail-safe mechanism. It operates according to checks on:
  - the interface, to check if the control data arrives on time
  - the control path, by means of a model of the robot
  - the status path, using a model of the digital states of the robot signals.

During failures a large number of hazardous situations may occur depending on the type and place of the failure. Therefore these failures have to be monitored continuously and as soon as a failure is detected, the robot has to be switched off and no further action is allowed any more. The protection against these situations is called the fail-safe protection. The failures may be thought of as occurring in either the control path or the status path of the system. The control path consists of the path from the link control output of the computer, the D/A - servo-motor - drive to the actual link path. This path is closed via the angle measurement and an A/D to the control computer. The status path consists of the digital input and output signals generated by or input to the control computer. These hazardous situations can be checked with an interface check, a control check, the status check and the system check. In order to create a better overview of the protection measures they have been classified in hierarchical levels as follows. Also the relation with the previously defined layers has been indicated.

control system	*control layer*
interface check	
position protection	
angle protection	*protection layer*
control path check	
status path check	
system check	*communication layer*
status check	*system hardware layer*

At the first level the status check may be incorporated in hardware and is consequently considered part of the hardware layer. The system check may be incorporated by checking the computer activity at regular intervals. This leads to the proper application of a watchdog timer circuitry. An edge triggered watchdog timer is preferred so that this timer may be set in one place and reset somewhere else. This increases the safety. The time value should be related to the equidistant sampling time of the points of the complete controller. This way the watchdog timer may be set in the interrupt program and reset in the program of the main control loop. The absence of a trigger will cause the power to be switched off within one sampling interval.

The status path check may be implemented by checking all possible system error sources by means of digital input and output monitoring in hardware. Alternatively a software check may be implemented, by predicting the status of the system and comparing this with the measured status. The software method checks a larger range of errors than the hardware method because it is often not possible to detect every hardware failure with a hardware check. The disadvantage of the software method is that one does not know exactly which part of the control path fails. The software method also requires a model of the robot system. This has to be accurate enough so that the software does intervene whenever a failure occurs, but it should not cause intervention in the absence of errors. A complete model, taking into account parameter changes such as changing link angles, weight in the gripper etc., will in general be too complex to be realized in this part. A simpler model will have to be updated by means of a feedback loop, as indicated in Fig. 3.10, where the feedback factor L determines the feedback of the difference signal of the measured position and the predicted position. With a large L the model will be more accurate but less suited as a predictor, with a small L the model itself has to be more accurate but as a predictor it works very well.

A first order model may be used if non-linear phenomena such as friction and current limiting effects of servo amplifiers are taken care of if necessary. The model with feedback may be realized as in Fig. 3.11. The voltage check is a check on the control

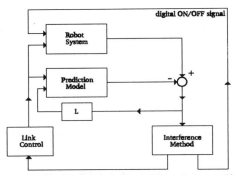

Fig. 3.10 Control path check using prediction

voltage between Umax and Umin in which case the control voltage is changed to zero. This is not a full model for the compensation of Coulomb friction but it is sufficient.

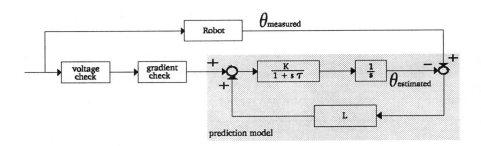

Fig. 3.11 Model with feedback

The current limiting effects of the servo amplifiers may in its simplest form be compensated for by limiting the gradient of the control voltage. The parameters K and τ of the first order model have to be measured using proper parameter estimation techniques. The feedback system has the following transfer function:

$$H(s) = \frac{1}{1 + \dfrac{1}{LK}s + \dfrac{\tau}{LK}s^2} \qquad (3.1)$$

this system has a damping factor of:

$$\delta = \frac{1}{2\sqrt{\tau LK}} \qquad (3.2)$$

Next the feedback factor L has to be determined by analysis of the step response of the system. When L is large the system follows the real system very well and it will be difficult to detect failures. Therefore the L has to be chosen as small as possible, however a large control voltage will also require a large L in order to better follow the model. This leads to a new model for the feedback factor as follows:

$$L = L_{min} + UL_{max} \qquad (3.3)$$

This model gives a good estimate of L between its limits of L_{min} and L_{max}. An important aspect of the safety system is that it should never be blocked in its execution. Due to the fact that occam communication in principle is synchronous a conversion to a synchronous parameter passing to the safety layer should be implemented. This can be done using an overwriting buffer process.

3.5.1 Angle Protection

The next component in the protection layer is the angle protection layer. The purpose of the protection measure is to avoid that the robot links hit end stops or each other. The method selected here uses a p-controller that steers the link to its end stop. The method only intervenes when the control voltage calculated by the user is larger than the control voltage calculated by this controller. This controller is implemented as follows. When the angle position is between a plus and a minus offset value the control signal is passed through, as in Fig. 3.12. When the angle position is outside the plus or minus offset values, the p-controller calculates the control voltage that controls the position of the link to the end stop. The required calculation in that case simply is:

$$U = K_p (\theta_{max} - \theta)$$ (3.4)

With this controller the trajectory depends on the selected K_p value. A large K_p value causes the link to overshoot. A small K_p value causes the protection measure to react too early resulting in a large deceleration trajectory. This method is easy to implement, it does not require a velocity measurement and the velocity can still be limited by choosing the proper K_p value. On the other hand for small K_p values the unrestricted workspace of the robot decreases.

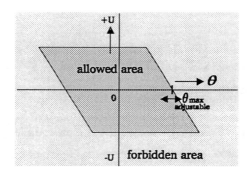

Fig. 3.12 Angle protection range limits

3.5.2   Position Protection

The purpose of this protection is to avoid the situation where the robot would hit an obstacle or another robot. This method requires the calculation of the Denavit-Hartenberg transformation to calculate the position of those parts of the robots that have to be protected. This method poses a heavy burden on the computing power of the protection layer. As soon as the robot is steered to a position that is not allowed, the position protection has to control the robot to a safe end position. In this case a P-controller may be used as with the angle position. However the required controller is not for just one link but instead has to react on all robot links. The realization of this P-controller is different from the one described before.

3.5.3 Conclusions

The protection measures discussed include the following:

- The required deceleration for *angle protection* is implemented by means of a P-controller. This method results in a very smooth deceleration trajectory. Besides the method is easy to implement.

- For the *position protection* the Denavit-Hartenberg transformation has to be calculated and the workspace of the robot has to be determined. The control voltage should be calculated by some form of a P-controller, or a PD-controller.

- A *fail-safe protection* implemented by means of a watchdog circuit to perform a system check. The status path is realized by predicting the states in order to minimize the required hardware. For the control path check, a model of the robot is implemented that predicts the real robot position rather accurately and still is sensitive enough to detect failures in the control path. Blocking of the protection circuitry caused by absence of data is prevented using overwriting data buffers.

3.6 THE COMMUNICATION LAYER

The primary purpose of the communication layer is to support the modular and flexible development and maintenance of complex control systems. Typical for such control systems is their hierarchical nature. The communication layer provides the communication between the different layers of the control system as illustrated in Fig. 3.1. These layers communicate setpoint and measurement data with each other. It is also necessary to provide some kind of supervisory system to monitor the behaviour of the control modules and to send commands. Preferably a user should be able to develop a new controller module without any detailed knowledge of the implementation of other parts of the system. This means that it is necessary to support dynamic loading, starting and stopping of controller modules, monitor the status of controller modules and change module parameters. Considering this, a set of design requirements was defined that have to be fulfilled by the communication layer.

The communication layer is specifically intended to support the development and implementation of control systems. Because control systems have a rather specific nature, special requirements must be supported. This results in the following two system requirements.

- The system must support communication between controller modules. Control data must be transported with a minimal delay, command messages may be treated differently.
- The system must support networks with an arbitrary configuration.

Furthermore, the communication layer is intended as a development environment. This poses the following requirements that must be met unless contradicted by the first two requirements.

- The system must be user friendly.
- A control engineer, programming a control module, should require only minimal knowledge of the system.
- The system must support projects with several people working on the same control system.

Finally, some practical considerations are important:

- The delay in communications and the overhead of the system must be kept to a minimum. The goal was to reduce the overhead caused by the system to below 30% at a 1 kHz sample frequency. The communication delay between modules on neighbouring transputers should not exceed 150 micro seconds.
- The system must support the loading of programs developed under the Transputer Development System. The principal language is occam.

• The memory requirements of the system must be kept to a minimum. The goal is to keep the size of the kernel below 8 kbyte.

3.6.1   The Architecture of the Communication Layer

The communication layer itself also has a layered architecture as illustrated in Fig. 3.13. The first layer in the system is the *application layer*. This layer contains the controller module specified by the user. The second layer in the system, called the *interface layer*, contains the protocol conversion, buffering and manager processes. The protocol conversion provides for the translation of the different protocols between the network layer and the application layer. The element manager takes care of basic functions like loading, starting and stopping controller modules. The third layer consists of a network-wide communication protocol called the *network layer*. This layer must be present on each transputer in the system.

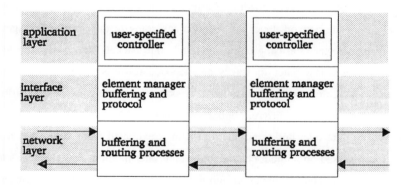

Fig. 3.13   Architecture of communication layer

3.6.2   The Application Layer

The application layer contains the user-specified controller module. This controller module consists of a single separately compiled (SC) code module, as defined by the

Inmos TDS. This code module can be loaded and started at run-time. To start such a controller module, a special starter process is a part of the operating environment. Each controller module can communicate transparently with the other controller modules. The routing and the actual location of the other controller modules need not be known by the controller modules; this information is hidden in source and destination translation tables in the protocol conversion layer, and in the routing tables in the network layer. A controller module just has four channels to communicate with. Two of these channels are intended for the transport of control data, the other two for the transport of command messages. The command messages consist of a tag, followed by the relevant data. Control data just consists of a block of data.

3.6.3   The Interface Layer

The interface layer contains the protocol conversion and manager layer and takes care of the conversion between the network protocol and the controller module protocol. Besides, it manages the code loading, starting and stopping of processes. Incoming messages from the network layer are decoded according to their type. Messages for the element manager (start/stop commands and code packets) are passed on to the manager process. The other messages are decoded towards a control data and a command message protocol. Because these messages are to be converted to different protocols, they are sent to different buffering processes. The buffering processes also check that no data overruns occur. Control data is extracted from the packet that is received and passed on without change to the controller module. The physical source number of the message is converted into a logical source number for the controller. Command messages are decoded to the different protocols that are used for the different types of command messages, thus relieving the controller module from this task.

3.6.4   The Network Layer

The network layer in the operating environment takes care of the distribution of the messages. In the network layer all messages have the same protocol. Important information for the network layer is the type of the message, the destination of the message and the size of the message. Several different implementations of the network layer have been investigated. These implementations differ in the nature of the messages at the network level, and in the type of buffering used. The results show that the performance of the system is mainly determined by the processing overhead of the network layer and the protocol conversion layer. The network layer has been designed in such a way that it will be relatively easy to port to new transputer types such as the T9000. On these types of transputers with automatic routing facilities, most of the functionality of the network layer will already be implemented in the hardware.

3.6.5   The Network Addressing Scheme

Important for the description of a communication layer is the type of addressing that is used. The addressing scheme used in the communication layer is an indirect addressing scheme. Within a controller module a logical destination address is used to refer to other controller modules. These logical destination addresses are translated to physical destinations in the interface layer. The translation is module dependent and is specified separately in a project file. From this project file, a source table and a destination table are generated automatically. At the network layer level, the source and destination of a message are identified by the element numbers of the sending and receiving transputers. The routing strategy used is the network is fixed. A routing table exists on each transputer that contains the link number that must be used for each other network element number. If a message enters via a given link, the destination transputer number is used as an index into the routing table. This yields the number of the outgoing link. The use of the different tables is shown in Fig. 3.14.

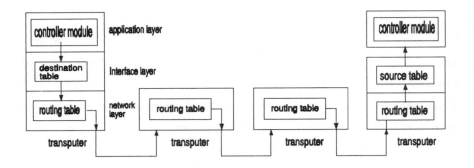

Fig. 3.14 Routing a message through the network

3.6.6   Implementation

The total operating environment has been implemented in occam. There are several
reasons for doing this:

*   Ease of programming

    Parallel programming is a rather difficult topic without sufficient language support.
    Though occam may be less suited for applications requiring dynamic memory
    allocation, it is very well suited for describing parallelism. Primitives for
    specifying parallel processes and communication are incorporated in the language,
    and can be applied in a safe way.

*   Correctness

    Due to the strict nature of occam it is a safe language. This is especially important
    when writing parallel programs, because the correctness is difficult to prove. When
    a programmer adheres to the characteristics of the language, it is easier to write
    correct programs. Furthermore, formal verification is possible.

*   Efficiency

    Occam is a very efficient language for the transputer. Compared to the standard
    C and Pascal compilers on the market it generates highly efficient code, without
    having to resort to tricks. Because the transputer has been designed specifically

for executing occam code, most of the language constructs are supported very well in the hardware.

Most of the code for the operating environment is rather straight-forward, and will therefore not be treated in detail here. Only a few more interesting topics will be addressed below. For better understanding an overview of the different processes in the operating environment is given in Fig. 3.15.

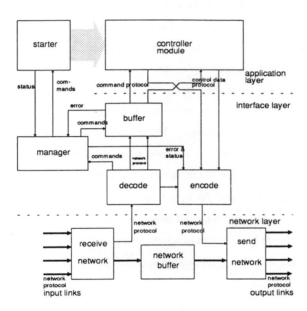

Fig. 3.15 Implementation of communication layer

3.6.7 The Network Layer Message Formats

During the development of the operating environment, it was discovered that the message formats in both the network layer and the decoding/encoding layer have a great impact on the performance of the system. In a first implementation of the operating environment, a variable length message format was used at the network layer level. This message format consists of a three byte header indicating the type of the message, the source and the destination, followed by a size and an array of bytes. The array of bytes contains the actual data. The advantage of this method seems to be that no more data is sent than is actually needed. However, to send a message, three communications have to be performed: one for the header, one for the size of the variable part of the message and one for the variable part of the message itself. A reduction of the number of communications can be obtained by changing to a format that incorporates the header into the data field. In this case, the message format is as shown in Fig. 3.16. Only two communications have to be performed per message. The speed-up is rather significant. This message format still has the memory advantages of a variable length message format. The only disadvantage is that more effort is needed to pack the data into the messages and to extract the data from the messages. Finally, a further reduction in the effort needed for communication can be obtained by changing to fixed size messages. These messages will always have the same maximum length. Because of this, the time taken for the actual communication will be equal to the maximum. For the relatively small message sizes used in the operating environment (between 6 and 76 bytes), this disadvantage does not outweigh the advantage of having only one communication performed. Furthermore, only the control data messages have to meet strict timing requirements, but these messages will always have the maximal size. Therefore, only fixed size packets are used.

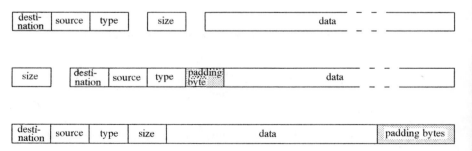

Fig. 3.16   Message format in the network layer

3.6.8   Buffering in the Network Layer

As can be seen from Fig. 3.15 the network layer contains some buffering. When measuring the performance of the system and determining the time taken by the different parts of the system, it was found that the buffering processes require a relatively large amount of time. Therefore, the buffering processes have been analyzed and other solutions have been looked at.

I   The first type of buffer process in the system used array retyping and parallel input and output processes. While the input process was inputting messages in the free parts of the array, the output process was outputting a single message. The buffer is accepted by the usage checker of the TDS occam compiler. Because of the time needed for starting and ending the two parallel processes and for all the array retyping, the performance of this buffer is relatively poor.

II   The second type of buffer is a more conventional cyclic buffering scheme, using fixed size buffer slots of the maximal message size. Due to this mechanism, retyping can be avoided, thus decreasing the overhead.

III The third type of buffering process is a so-called sleeping barber buffer. Because both processes run at high priority, mutual exclusion of the processes is guaranteed. It is therefore safe to use a common shared area for the buffering. Both processes read and write into this area. If the output process is idle, it will deschedule. If the input process receives a message while the output process is idle, it will restart the output process by communicating to it. This type of buffer gives the best performance. Because of the use of shared memory in this implementation, the usage checker of the TDS occam compiler had to be switched off.

3.6.9   Results

In this section, the results of measurements on the network are presented. Before the results are given, the performance indicators used for the measurements and the measurement method will be explained.

Performance indicators

The performance indicators are numbers indicating the performance of the network. In practice, several different types of performance indicators have been used, like the average throughput of the network, the average delay, and the number of messages generated by the different nodes. Furthermore, throughput can be measured in the number of messages per second or as the total number of bytes per second. However, one should be very careful when judging the performance of a network in terms of these indicators, because they often give a misleading indication.

For the measurements on the operating environment, the requirement was that they should deliver useful numbers for the practical system. This means that the performance indicators chosen must reflect the reality in a control system. A control system is a hard real-time system, meaning that no deadlines may be missed. This means the average throughput and the average delay are not interesting, because they only reflect the average situation. More important are the maximum throughput at which no deadlines are missed, and the maximum delay of a message. Furthermore, idle time on a processor as a function of the throughput is important, because this determines how much time is left for the actual controller computations. The following performance indicators were therefore chosen:

- The maximum throughput between neighbouring transputers. This maximum throughput determines the speed at which control loops can be executed. A fixed packet size was chosen
- The maximum delay between neighbouring transputers. This maximum delay determines the amount of time left in the sample interval of the control loop for computations. It has been measured as a function of different maximum throughput values.
- The maximum delay for each extra transputer between two communicating transputers. Often the data has to be distributed to a transputer further down the network. The delay for this communication determines the amount of computational time left for this controller module. This measurement was

performed by inserting "empty" transputers between the communicating transputers.

- The processor utilization as a function of the maximum throughput. The processor utilization determines the computational effort that a controller module in a heavily communicating transputer can perform.

Results of the measurements

The measurements have been carried out for five different configurations of the system. These configurations differ in the protocol and in the kind of buffering used. All four performance indicators mentioned in the previous section have been measured. The first three indicators are given in Table 3.3. It was not necessary to perform the delay measurements for a different throughput, because exploratory measurements confirmed that the delay is almost independent of the throughput.

For CIII the delay increased to 138 µsec worst-case at the maximum throughput of 10.4 kpacket/s. This small difference between CII and CIII is caused by the fact that intermediate buffering is not allowed. Therefore, the maximal throughput in our definition will be reached before the delay will start to rise significantly. The behaviour of the controller utilization as a function of the throughput using the control data protocol is shown in Fig. 3.17. In practice the command message throughput will be very low. Therefore, only the control data throughput is of interest for actual control applications.

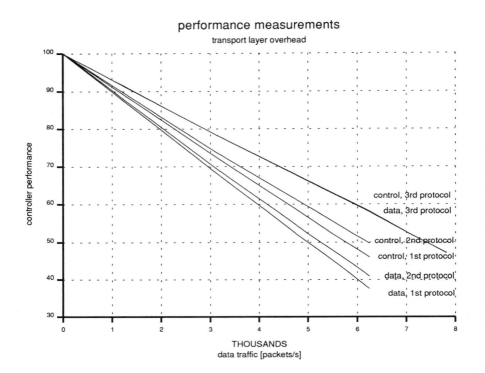

Fig. 3.17 Measured utilisation versus throughput

		buffer 1	buffer 2	buffer 3
protocol A		throughput=6.2kpackets/s delay = 274µs int.delay = 121µs		
protocol B		throughput=6.2kpackets/s delay = 252µs int.delay = 112µs	throughput=6.2kpackets/s delay = 178µs int.delay = 110µs	
protocol C			throughput=10.4kpackets/s delay = 143µs int.delay = 88µs	throughput=10.4kpackets/sd elay = 138µs int.delay = 81µs

Table 3.3 Measured results

It can be concluded from Fig. 3.17 and Table 3.3 that the buffering scheme has a great influence on the utilization, and that the message format mainly affects the throughput and the delay. The total memory use of the operating environment is approximately 7 kbyte in the current version. This includes the vector space requirements for the buffers and the workspace requirements for the operating environment processes.

3.6.10 Conclusions

The operating environment described here works well in practice. Due to the small delay, the added flexibility and the small code size it is very well suited for real-time control applications. Currently, the system is used for this purpose at the University of Twente in robot systems. The goals of combining a high maximal throughput with a low delay have been reached for implementation CIII. Due to this low delay, the system can be used for the operation of neighbouring controller modules at rates of 1 kHz. For an intermediate controller, which has to handle 2 kpacket/s in both directions, the utilization by the communications network is restricted by 10%, leaving a controller performance of 90%. Because the operating environment is intended specifically for control system applications, the performance indicators and measurement methods have been chosen to reflect this. These indicators are more strict than the generally used "average" indicators, but are more useful in practice. It can be concluded from the measurements for the three different implementations that the message format mainly affects the delay and thus the maximal throughput that can be obtained. The buffering scheme mainly affects the utilization on a heavily communicating transputer. Especially buffering scheme III performs very well in this respect. The goal of keeping the size of the kernel restricted to at most 8 kbyte has been fulfilled. The kernel size is approximately 7 kbyte in the current system. From the experiences with the operating environment implementation it can be concluded that it is important to keep the efficiency of communications protocols and buffering strategies in mind. It is shown that the delay can be reduced significantly by choosing a suitable communications protocol. A suitable protocol performs a minimal number of communications. For small packet sizes this is more important than the actual size of the communication due to the communication set-up times. The buffering strategy chosen can influence the utilization of the system very much. It is therefore important to use an efficient buffering strategy, that performs a minimal number of actions for each message received. The sleeping barber buffer meets this requirement.

REFERENCES

[3.1]   JSME: *The International Conference on Advanced Mechatronics*, May 21-24 Tokyo, Japan, The Japan Society of Mechanical Engineers, 1989.

[3.2]   Bakkers AWP, Verhoeven WLA: A robot control algorithm implementation in transputers, *Proc Intelligent Autonomous Systems Conference*, Amsterdam, pp118-122, Elsevier, 1986.

[3.3]   Stavenuiter ACJ, Ter Reehorst G, Bakkers AWP: Transputer control of a flexible robot link, *Microprocessors and Microsystems*, **13**, 3, pp227-232, 1989.

[3.4]   Hilhorst R: Parallelisation of computational algorithms for a transputer network, *Proc 7th Occam User Group Technical Meeting*, Grenoble, France, pp420-424, IOS Press, 1987.

[3.5]   Sunter JPE, Koenders EC, Bakkers AWP: Post-game analysis on transputers, development of a measurement kernel, *Proc Transputing '91 Conference*, Sunnyvale, CA, pp330-341, IOS Press Amsterdam, 1991.

Chapter 4
Parallel Processing for Real-Time Flight Control

GS Virk and JM Tahir

4.1 INTRODUCTION

An aircraft in flight is a complex, nonlinear and rapidly time-varying system (see for example [4.1], [4.2]), which can be demanding to control adequately over its entire flight regime. Although optimal control techniques can provide the ability to design suitable strategies, the on-line computing requirements are excessive. The normal procedure is to make various assumptions so that the processing demands are reduced for calculating the optimal controls. These include

(a) linearizing the aircraft about some operating point and considering a simpler optimisation problem;

(b) assuming that the aircraft is time-invariant over short time intervals; and

(c) making assumptions about the flight conditions so that the cross-coupling between the longitudinal and lateral motions can be ignored, and then the two motions can be considered independently of each other.

Using such assumptions, a sequence of linear quadratic performance (LQP) optimal control problems needs to be considered. These in turn give rise to standard two-point-boundary-value problems (TPBVP), see, for example, [4.3]. As is well known, the solution to such problems involves a "backward" integration phase where the Riccati equations are computed, and a "forward" phase, where the optimal controller gains for the feedback design are calculated and applied to the system under consideration.

For adequate control performance of flight control systems, it is necessary to use sample rates of $\approx$ 100-200 Hz. It is normal practice to select the fastest possible sampling rate so that the control performance is optimised; for this reason we propose to develop a strategy capable of cycling at the higher end of this range, that is, at 5 ms. Although this may appear straightforward to achieve, a critical point to realise is that in optimal flight control, it is usually not possible to linearize the aircraft every 5 ms (see [4,4], [4.5]), but after much longer time intervals dictated by the computing hardware. Since the aircraft is a time-varying system, the approximations may therefore yield poor descriptions. As demonstrated in Section 4.4.1, this has consequences which are detrimental to the performance of the flight controller. To improve the performance, the linearization update rate can be increased by using faster and more powerful (sequential) computer hardware, but usually with a significant price penalty.

An alternative to the traditional uni-processor approach is made possible by the use of parallel processing techniques. Here the overall computing task is partitioned into sub-tasks which are mapped onto a multi-processor system. If the individual processors can communicate effectively with each other (see Bertsekas [4.6]; Hockney and Jesshope [4.7]), good performances can be achieved. In this respect, a recent development in parallel computer systems has been the Inmos transputer whose attractions have been described in Chapter 1.

Because of the processing demands of real-time flight control systems, parallel processing methods may prove extremely useful and such an investigation is considered here. More specifically we shall be using transputer hardware to develop a parallel processing approach to obtain a real-time optimal autopilot for an aircraft whose engineering data was supplied by British Aerospace, Brough [4.8].

An optimal regulator control problem formulation is considered where the controller is designed to drive initial errors towards the origin. The problem can be reformulated in a straightforward way to yield the tracking problem case where the objective is to calculate the optimal control laws in response to pilot demands. Similar reasoning to the longitudinal autopilot, discussed in Tahir and Virk [4.4], is used to arrive at a suitable control strategy for the whole aircraft. The cross-coupling effects between the longitudinal and lateral motions of the aircraft are assumed to be constant over the linearization intervals. It is shown that when the processing is partitioned over several processors the linearization time intervals can be reduced significantly enabling accurate representations of the nonlinear time-varying aircraft, and thereby achieving good control performances as compared to the results when a single computing device is used.

In applications where there is strong inherent parallelism, it is relatively straightforward to achieve efficiencies of 0.8 or higher (see Virk et al [4.10]; Kourmoulis [4.11]); but in other cases the computations are highly sequential in nature and much effort is needed to obtain efficient parallel versions. In some cases it may be impossible to achieve dramatic improvements. Although automatic parallelising compilers are being developed, these are in their infancy and far from ready for general use. They essentially look at procedures such as nested loops or for matrix algebra where the parallelisation is straightforward.

What is required is the ability to automatically look at a particular application from a "high" abstract level and establish which sections can be best parallelised. Unfortunately such generic automation is not yet possible and it is up to the designer to perform the problem analysis and determine which parts can be parallelised and which must be executed sequentially. In addition the determination of the most appropriate hardware configuration for the final implementation needs to be determined. Again no firm rules are yet available, and it is clear therefore that many different parallelisations are possible, with some solutions being more efficient than others. The autopilot design considered here is parallelised in a number of ways to demonstrate this, and the efficiencies of the different parallel implementations are studied and compared with a uni-processor solution. Timings of the multi-processor designs are also analysed.

The use of multiple processor devices offer several advantages other than mere speed-up. These include

(a) easier reprogramming since the distributed nature of the computing hardware normally dictates that the computing tasks have been partitioned into discrete modules which also allows for better understanding;
(b) a certain level of redundancy, and hence improved system reliability;
(c) mutual supervision and checking of the units within the processor network is possible so that the operations of each device are correct; and
(d) reconfiguration under failure conditions.

The last three points are related to fault tolerance and reliability issues. For example, if an individual processor fails it is possible to distribute its task onto the remaining functional processors (see Ayuk [4.10]). Such reconfiguration can be repeated if further failures occur, leading to the concept of "graceful degradation". The use of fault-tolerant design using parallel processing techniques is receiving significant attention and some reliability features for aircraft flight control are discussed in Virk and Tahir [4.13]. We start our discussions by giving a brief statement of the mathematical model of the aircraft, and an introduction to general optimal control problems; these are included essentially for completeness.

4.2   AIRCRAFT EQUATIONS

When considered as a rigid body (see Fig. 4.1) the motion of the aircraft is defined by a set of nonlinear equations, see [4.1], [4.2]:

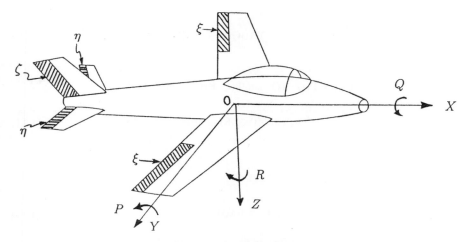

Fig. 4.1 Aircraft in flight

$$\dot{U}(t) = \frac{X_f(t)}{M} - Q(t)W(t) + R(t)V(t) \tag{4.1}$$

$$\dot{W}(t) = \frac{Z_f(t)}{M} + Q(t)U(t) - P(t)V(t) \tag{4.2}$$

$$\dot{Q}(t) = \{ P_m(t) + (I_z - I_x)P(t)R(t) + I_{xz}(R^2(t) - P^2(t)) \} / I_y \tag{4.3}$$

$$\dot{\Theta}(t) = Q(t) \cos\Phi(t) - R(t) \sin\Phi(t) \tag{4.4}$$

$$\dot{H}(t) = U(t) \sin\Theta(t) - W(t) \cos\Theta(t) \cos\Phi(t) - V(t) \sin\Phi(t) \cos\Theta(t) \tag{4.5}$$

$$\dot{N}(t) = \bar{f}(N(t),V_r(t),H(t),\gamma(t)) \tag{4.6}$$

$$\dot{V}(t) = \frac{Y_f(t)}{M} + P(t)W(t) - R(t)U(t) \tag{4.7}$$

$$\dot{P}(t) = \{R_m(t) + (I_y - I_z)Q(t)R(t) + I_{xz}(\dot{R}(t) + P(t)Q(t))\} / I_x \tag{4.8}$$

$$\dot{R}(t) = \{Y_m(t) + (I_x - I_y)P(t)Q(t) + I_{xz}(\dot{P}(t) - Q(t)R(t))\} / I_z \qquad (4.9)$$

$$\Phi(t) = P(t) + (Q(t)\sin\Phi(t) + R(t)\cos\Phi(t)) \tan\Theta(t) \qquad (4.10)$$

$$\Psi(t) = \{Q(t)\sin\Phi(t) + R(t)\cos\Phi(t)\} / \cos\Theta(t) \qquad (4.11)$$

or in compact form as

$$\dot{x}(t) = f(x(t), u_{in}(t)) \qquad (4.12)$$

where the state vector $x = [x_1 \ x_2]^T$ is made up of variables related to the longitudinal motion ($x_1 = [U,W,Q,\Theta,H,N]^T$) and those connected with the lateral motion ($x_2 = [V,P,R,\Phi,\Psi]^T$) and the control input vector ($u_{in}(t) = [\eta,\gamma,\xi,\zeta]^T$). The notation used in this Chapter is defined in the Appendix.

These equations can be written in a linearized form to highlight the cross-coupling terms between the longitudinal and lateral motions as

$$
\begin{bmatrix} \dot{u} \\ \dot{w} \\ \dot{q} \\ \dot{\theta} \\ \dot{h} \\ \dot{n} \\ \hline \dot{v} \\ \dot{p} \\ \dot{r} \\ \dot{\phi} \\ \dot{\psi} \end{bmatrix}
=
\left[\begin{array}{cccccc|ccccc}
f_{1u} & f_{1w} & f_{1q} & f_{1\theta} & 0 & f_{1n} & R & 0 & V & 0 & 0 \\
f_{2u} & f_{2w} & f_{2q} & f_{2\theta} & 0 & f_{2n} & -P & -V & 0 & f_{2\phi} & 0 \\
f_{3u} & f_{3w} & f_{3q} & f_{3\theta} & 0 & f_{3n} & 0 & f_{3p} & f_{3r} & f_{3\phi} & 0 \\
0 & 0 & f_{4q} & 0 & 0 & 0 & 0 & 0 & f_{4r} & f_{4\phi} & 0 \\
f_{5u} & f_{5w} & 0 & f_{5\theta} & 0 & 0 & f_{5v} & 0 & 0 & f_{5\phi} & 0 \\
f_{6u} & 0 & 0 & 0 & f_{6h} & f_{6n} & 0 & 0 & 0 & 0 & 0 \\
\hline
f_{7u} & f_{7w} & 0 & f_{7\theta} & 0 & 0 & f_{7v} & f_{7p} & f_{7r} & f_{7\phi} & 0 \\
f_{8u} & f_{8w} & f_{8q} & 0 & 0 & 0 & f_{8v} & f_{8p} & f_{8r} & 0 & 0 \\
f_{9u} & f_{9w} & f_{9q} & 0 & 0 & f_{9n} & f_{9v} & f_{9p} & f_{9r} & 0 & 0 \\
0 & 0 & f_{10q} & f_{10\theta} & 0 & 0 & 0 & f_{10p} & f_{10r} & f_{10\phi} & 0 \\
0 & 0 & f_{11q} & f_{11\theta} & 0 & 0 & 0 & 0 & f_{11r} & f_{11\phi} & 0
\end{array}\right]
\begin{bmatrix} u \\ w \\ q \\ \theta \\ h \\ n \\ \hline v \\ p \\ r \\ \phi \\ \psi \end{bmatrix}
+
\left[\begin{array}{cc|cc}
f_{1\eta} & 0 & 0 & 0 \\
f_{2\eta} & 0 & 0 & 0 \\
f_{3\eta} & 0 & 0 & 0 \\
0 & 0 & 0 & 0 \\
0 & 0 & 0 & 0 \\
0 & f_{6\gamma} & 0 & 0 \\
\hline
0 & 0 & 0 & f_{7\zeta} \\
0 & 0 & f_{8\xi} & f_{8\zeta} \\
0 & 0 & f_{9\xi} & f_{9\zeta} \\
0 & 0 & 0 & 0 \\
0 & 0 & 0 & 0
\end{array}\right]
\begin{bmatrix} \eta \\ \gamma \\ \xi \\ \zeta \end{bmatrix}
$$

$$(4.13)$$

where $f_{1a} = \partial f_1/\partial a$ is the partial derivative of the first element of function **f**, that is, f_1, with respect to state a, etc., and u,w,q,....,ψ are the state perturbations about the linearized point. In compact form this reduces to

$$\begin{bmatrix} \dot{x}_1(t) \\ \dot{x}_2(t) \end{bmatrix} = \begin{bmatrix} A_{11} & A_{12} \\ A_{21} & A_{22} \end{bmatrix} \begin{bmatrix} x_1(t) \\ x_2(t) \end{bmatrix} + \begin{bmatrix} B_1 & 0 \\ 0 & B_2 \end{bmatrix} u_{in}(t) \qquad (4.14)$$

where A_{11}, A_{12}, A_{21} and A_{22} are the partial derivations of the nonlinear function f in equation (4.12) with respect to the states and B_1 and B_2 are the derivatives with respect to the controls. Hence A_{12} and A_{21} represent the cross-coupling terms, and if these are absent the longitudinal and lateral motions are decoupled and can be handled independently of each other. It is well known that the cross-coupling terms can be removed by assuming:

(a) the aircraft is in straight and unaccelerated flight and then disturbed by deflections of the control surfaces;

(b) the elevator deflection causes only a pitching moment about the OY axis and causes no rolling or yawing moments; and

(c) the aileron and rudder deflections cause rotations only about the OX and OZ axes respectively.

These assumptions are not strictly valid in many modern aircraft. Furthermore, the designs are evolving towards aircraft having more weight concentrated in the fuselage and their wings are becoming thinner, shorter and hence lighter. This weight shift is causing the cross-coupling effects to increase because the magnitudes of the moments of inertia in equations (4.1)-(4.11) are changing significantly. As more weight is concentrated along the longitudinal axis, the moment of inertia about the OX axis, I_x, decreases while the moments of inertia about the OY and OZ axes increase. This phenomenon increases the interaction between the longitudinal and lateral motions, and can best be seen by examining the basic moment equations (4.3), (4.8) and (4.9). As I_x becomes much smaller than I_y and I_z the moment of inertia difference terms (I_z - I_x) and (I_x - I_y) become large. Hence if a rolling moment is introduced, it results in some yawing moment and the $P(t)R(t)(I_z - I_x)$ term may become large enough to cause considerable pitching. Other factors which must be considered are the aerodynamic cross-coupling effects. For example, the lateral aerodynamic derivatives are proportional to the angle of attack (α) which is dependent upon the longitudinal states (i.e. $\alpha = \tan^{-1} W/U$). Also, in the design of standard flight controllers, pointwise linearizations of the aircraft are commonly used - this means the aircraft may not be in straight and level unaccelerated flight at the linearization instants as normally assumed above leading to errors in the models used in the controller design.

It is clear that the standard assumptions are not always valid and so a more general approach is necessary for obtaining improved system performance. In this respect we propose to consider the longitudinal and lateral motions separately because this leads to a more efficient parallel solution. However, the cross-coupling effects are taken into account but are assumed to be constant over the linearization intervals. Equation (4.13) shows that the longitudinal motion can be separated if we assume that the lateral state perturbations, that is $[v,p,r,\phi,\psi]^T$ have small values and can be neglected. In the same way we can separate the lateral motion equations by neglecting the longitudinal perturbations. Therefore, if X is a vector of the state variables, then

$$X(t) = X_0(t) + x(t)$$

$$(4.15)$$

where X_0 is the value of the state vector at the linearization instant and $x(t)$ is the state perturbations vector. This forms the basis for the decoupling of the aircraft motions; the equations for the two motions are presented next.

4.2.1   "Decoupled" Aircraft Motions

4.2.1.1   Longitudinal Motion

When considering the longitudinal motion, the lateral state perturbations are assumed to be small, and so their rates of change can be neglected during an interval T_1

between two successive linearizations. Hence $\dot{V}=\dot{P}=\dot{R}=\dot{\Phi}=\dot{\Psi}=0$, and this leads to the following longitudinal equations (not showing the time dependence for convenience):

$$\dot{U} = \frac{X_f}{M} - QW + (R_0V_0)^{\bullet} \qquad (4.16)$$

$$\dot{W} = \frac{Z_f}{M} + QU - (P_0V_0)^{\bullet} \qquad (4.17)$$

$$\dot{Q} = \{P_m + (I_z - I_x)P_0R_0 + I_{xz}(R_0^2 - P_0^2)\}/I_y \qquad (4.18)$$

$$\dot{\Theta} = Q\cos\Phi_0 - (R_0\sin\Phi_0)^{\bullet\bullet} \qquad (4.19)$$

$$\dot{H} = U\sin\Theta - W\cos\Theta\cos\Phi_0 - V_0\sin\Phi_0\cos\Theta \qquad (4.20)$$

$$\dot{N} = \overline{f}(N,V_r,H,\gamma) \qquad (4.21)$$

4.2.1.2   Lateral Motion

In the same way, the effects of the longitudinal perturbations can be ignored by assuming $\dot{U}=\dot{W}=\dot{Q}=\dot{\Theta}=\dot{H}=\dot{N}=0$, which gives rise to the following lateral equations:

$$\dot{V} = \frac{Y_f}{M} + PW_0 - RU_0 \qquad (4.22)$$

$$\dot{P} = \{R_m + (I_y - I_z)RQ_0 + I_{xz}(\dot{R}+PQ_0)\}/I_x \qquad (4.23)$$

$$\dot{R} = \{Y_m + (I_x - I_y)PQ_0 + I_{xz}(\dot{P}-RQ_0)\}/I_z \qquad (4.24)$$

$$\Phi = P + (Q_0 \sin\Phi + R\cos\Phi) \tan\Theta_0 \qquad (4.25)$$

$$\Psi = \{Q_0 \sin\Phi + R\cos\Phi\} / \cos\Theta_0 \qquad (4.26)$$

These sets of equations will be used for short time intervals, of length T_1, over which the aircraft is linearized and suitable optimal control laws designed. It is clear that in this way the cross-coupling effects between the two motions are allowed for, but are assumed to be constant over the linearizing intervals. For example when considering the longitudinal motion, the lateral variables (V,P,R,Φ,Ψ) are assumed to be constant at their values $(V_0,P_0,_0,\Phi_0,\Psi_0)$ when the linearization is performed, and vice versa.
In the longitudinal motion equations (4.16)-(4.21), some of the cross-coupling terms (assumed constant) appear as constants, and hence will vanish in the linearization process.

Other terms however, for example $Q \cos\Phi_0$, in equation (4.19) are combined with the longitudinal terms and will not vanish. In the lateral motion equations (4.22-4.26), all the (assumed constant) longitudinal terms are combined with the (assumed time-varying) lateral terms. Therefore (U_0,W_0,H_0,N_0) will not vanish from the linearized lateral equations, and hence they will be included in the calculation of the optimal feedback gains.

A procedure for handling the cross-coupling terms which vanish in the linearization in the longitudinal motion equations (4.16)-(4.21) is possible along the lines indicated below.

(a) The terms marked * in equations (4.16) and (4.17) normally have a small effect on the longitudinal motion and can therefore be removed from the equations without affecting the performance significantly.

(b) The inertial cross-coupling terms in equation (4.18) are normally the most important terms. They can be neutralised by applying an equal and opposite amount of pitching moment using the elevator. Such a result can be achieved by setting

$$\Delta \eta = \{PR(I_x - I_z) + I_{xz}(P^2 - R^2)\} / \frac{\partial P_m}{\partial \eta} \qquad (4.27)$$

(c) The term marked ** in equation (4.19) can be eliminated by changing the pitch rate, Q, by an amount, ΔQ, where

$$\Delta Q = R \tan \Phi \qquad (4.28)$$

This ΔQ can be added to the demanded pitch rate, Q_d, causing an error which generates (when multiplied by the corresponding feedback gain) an elevator control action dependent upon yaw rate and roll angle to keep the pitch angle and aircraft height at their desired values.

In this way it is not necessary to wait until significant errors accumulate in the longitudinal states before remedial action is taken since such an action can be computed and applied as soon as the errors arise in the lateral attitude angles and rates using equation (4.27) and (4.28). In this way these cross-coupling effects can be kept to a minimum.

4.3 OPTIMAL CONTROL PROBLEM

The approach taken here is to formulate two optimal control problems for the linearized aircraft (one for the longitudinal and one for the lateral motion dynamics), taking into account some of the cross-coupling effects explicitly and others implicitly in the control algorithm, and solve the two "decoupled" sub-problems using a multi-transputer network in real-time.

The nonlinear aircraft system represented by equation (4.12) can be linearized about an operating point $(\mathbf{X_0}, \mathbf{U_0})$ and the equations written as

$$\dot{e}(t) = A(t)e(t) + B(t)\Delta u(t) \tag{4.29}$$

where the A and B matrices are of the form shown in eqn. (4.14), $\mathbf{e}$ is the error in the system states and $\Delta\mathbf{u}$ is the control deviation from the operating point $\mathbf{U_0}$. The elements of the A and B matrices are obtained using the aircraft engineering data supplied by British Aerospace, Brough, [4.9]. Equation (4.29) is assumed to be time invariant for a short interval, T_1, over which the optimisation is performed. The cross-coupling effects over the interval T_1 for the longitudinal and lateral problems are assumed to be constant and handled as discussed above. The resulting control actions are applied to a simulation of the nonlinear time-varying aircraft for performance assessment. The shorter the interval T_1, the more accurate the approximation, but also the more demanding the processing requirements for real-time execution.

Several optimal control problems can be formulated for real-time control; possibilities include

(a) considering a fixed optimisation time horizon, T, over which the optimal control inputs are calculated. Once the end point of the optimising horizon is reached a further optimising window of length T can be considered, etc.;
(b) calculating the steady-state Riccati solution for each linearization; and
(c) considering an optimising horizon which moves forward as time progresses, that is, the horizon recedes and is never reached.

The receding horizon technique has various advantages in terms of computational and memory requirements and so is used here to compute the optimal control inputs in real-time. Starting at time t_0 two linear quadratic performance indices having the form

$$J(\mathbf{u}, t_0) = \frac{1}{2}\int_{t_0}^{t_0+T} [e^T(t)Qe(t) + \Delta u^T(t)R\Delta u(t)]\ dt \tag{4.30}$$

are considered and minimised, where Q is a 6 x 6 positive semi-definite matrix for the longitudinal motion and a 5 x 5 positive semi-definite matrix for the lateral motion, R is a 2 x 2 positive definite matrix for each motion and T is the length of the optimising horizon interval.

It is well known that the receding horizon optimal control law, see Kwon and Bruckstein [4.14], is given by

$$\Delta \mathbf{u}^*(t) = -R^{-1}B^TP(t_0)e(t) \tag{4.31}$$

$$\mathbf{u}^*(t) = U_0 + \Delta \mathbf{u}^*(t) \tag{4.32}$$

where P(.) is computed by solving the following Riccati equation backwards

$$\dot{P}(t) = -P(t)A - A^TP(t) - Q + P(t)BR^{-1}B^TP(t) \tag{4.33}$$

$$P(t_0 + T) = 0 \tag{4.34}$$

Once the time t has reached $t_0 + T_1$, a new linearizing interval of length, T_1, can be started by setting $t0 = t_0 + T_1$ and repeating the cycle indefinitely. The receding horizon, T, is made approximately equal to the settling time of the aircraft so that stability is ensured. T is made larger than the linearizing interval, T_1, so that several linearizations are done within a single horizon and hence good control performance is achieved. The actual size of T_1 is dependent on the processing hardware used, but for real-time, the control signals must be updated every 5 ms.

4.4   REAL-TIME IMPLEMENTATION

The above optimisation and control procedure can be stated in the following algorithmic form:

Step 0   Initialise control, U_c, initial time, t_0, receding horizon length, T, linearization interval, T_l, sampling interval, T_s integration stepsize, Δt, demanded state, x_d.

Step 1   Linearize the aircraft equations ((4.16)-(4.21) or (4.22)-(4.26)) about the current state, X_0, and the midpoint control, U_c.

Step 2   Integrate the Riccati equation from $t_0 + T$ to t_0, and store the gains $P_T = P(t_0)$.

Step 3   Set $t = t_0$ and compute the control, $u_{in}(t)$, $t \in [t_0, t_0 + T_l]$, using Step 4.

Step 4   Calculate

$$\Delta u(t) = -R^{-1}B^TP^Te(t) \tag{4.35}$$

where

$$e(t) = x(t) - x_d \tag{4.36}$$

Set

$$u_{in}(t) = U_c + \Delta u(t) + u_{cc} \tag{4.37}$$

$$\tag{4.38}$$

$$t = t + T_s$$

Step 5   Calculate $x(t)$ by integrating the nonlinear aircraft eqns. (4.1)-(4.11) from initial condition, $x(t - T_s)$ and using the new control, $u_{in}(t)$.

Step 6   If $t \geq t_0 + T_l$, set $X_0 = x(t)$, $t_0 = t$ and go to Step 1; else go to Step 4.

Note that the aircraft linearizations are performed about the control U_c, where the control surfaces are at the centre (zero) position, and the throttle control is at the centre (0.5) position. The use of U_c instead of the current control, $u_{in}(t)$, at the instant of linearization is to prevent integral action difficulties in the calculated control from equation (4.37), caused by the high repetition rate of the linearizations. Also, in the above algorithm, it should be noted that the extra controlling terms needed to account for the cross-coupling terms are added and shown as u_{cc} in equation (4.37). Clearly for real-time performance all these computations have to be performed iteratively within the time scales of the aircraft and as already mentioned, a sampling rate of ≈ 200 Hz is required to achieve satisfactory control; hence the above algorithm should be processed to provide control updates every 5 ms.

4.4.1   Single Transputer Implementation

The aircraft data supplied by British Aerospace was coded in Parallel C to run on a single T800 transputer, using the ATMOS Routine [4.15] based on the International Standard Atmosphere model [4.16]. As a benchmark to assess the parallel implementations, the above optimal control algorithm was executed on another single T800 transputer interacting with the aircraft simulator processor as shown in Fig. 4.2, where the ellipses represent processes mapped onto the diferent processors (represented by the rectangles).

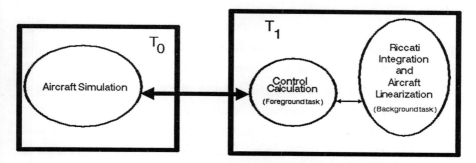

Fig. 4.2 Single transputer autopilot implementation

Since the transputer devices currently available have only two levels of priority, the linearization and Riccati integrations for the lateral and longitudinal motions were executed as background tasks (non-urgent tasks) and the control updates as foreground tasks (urgent tasks) so that the control signals could be be provided every 5 ms. (see, for example, Bennett [4.17]). It was found that real-time performance was achieved using an optimising horizon, $T = 5s$, integration step size $\Delta t = 20ms$. and linearizing updates every $T_l = 600ms$. This time is quite satisfactory for the aircraft system considered in this paper, but for advanced military aircraft with faster dynamics, and which are required to perform complex manoeuvres, much faster linearizing rates are required to maintain good system representations at all times. To illustrate this aspect for the aircraft under consideration the linearization update rate was deliberately slowed to illustrate the difference in the control performance from that obtained using the faster update rate. Fig. 4.3 shows the longitudinal responses for $T_1 = 600$ms and $T_1 = 4$s, when an initial state,

x_{ic} [180, 0, 0, 0, 4900, 6615, 0, 0, 0, 0, 0]^T, and a desired state,

x_d = [150, 5, 0, 0.033, 5000, 6615, 0, 0, 0, 0, 0]^T, are assumed. The lateral states are not shown because there is no significant change in them.

Fig. 4.3 clearly shows that the control action is slower for the $T_1 = 4$ s   case because the aircraft linearization is carried out at a high velocity, but as time passes the aircraft velocity reduces, thus changing the aircraft dynamics, but these are not followed adequately with the slow linearizing rate and it leads to the poorer response. The faster update implementation is able to follow the aircraft changes more closely and leads to a better control performance. It is conceivable that slow linearization update rates, and hence poor dynamic modelling, in this way can lead to situations where the controlled performance of the aircraft is unsatisfactory, and even to instances where the aircraft is driven into instability. In addition, fast linearization updates are useful in instances where aspects such as fault tolerance are considered (see Virk and Tahir [4.13]), and which use analytical redundancy to detect and isolate failures; such applications require fast updates in the reference models so that quick and reliable fault detection can occur, enabling remedial action to be initiated rapidly.

To improve the uni-processor situation the linearization update time can be reduced by using a multi-processor system, as discussed next.

4.4.2 Multi-Transputer Implementations

It has been shown in Tahir and Virk [4.4], that the longitudinal motion of aircraft can be optimally controlled using a parallel processing approach where the linearizing intervals, T_1, can be made equal to the execution time for Steps 1 and 2 of the control algorithm. Therefore if extra processors are used to execute the algorithm, the time interval, T_1, can be reduced as required.   A number of different   parallel

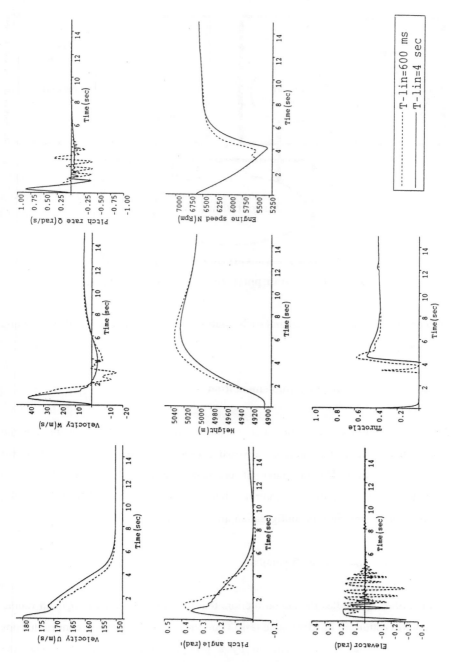

Fig. 4.3 Control performances of fast and slow linearization updates

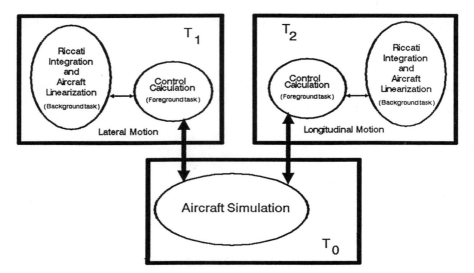

Fig. 4.4 Two transputer autopilot implementation

implementations are presented and each solution is analysed in terms of its timing and efficiency.

4.4.2.1   Two transputer implementation

The first multi-processor solution to be presented is obtained by partitioning the longitudinal and lateral motions into two sub-tasks which are mapped onto two separate processors. The transputer network system shown in Fig. 4.4 can be used to provide the real-time optimal control solution for this approach. The tasks of the separate processors in this configuration are as follows:

Transputer T_0 is the aircraft simulator.

Transputer T_1 handles the lateral motion, that is, it provides aileron (ξ) and rudder (ζ) control actions in its foreground task. Transputer T_1 performs these control updates by using the gains, P_T, calculated by a background task which computes the linearizations and performs the Riccati integration, that is, Steps 1 and 2 of the control algorithm for the lateral motion.

Transputer T₂ controls the longitudinal motion of the aircraft, that is, it provides the elevator (ζ) and engine throttle (γ) controls. Essentially T_2 performs the same operations as T_1 but for the longitudinal motion.

Both the lateral and longitudinal transputers (T_1 and T_2) read the complete state vector from the simulator transputer T_0 so that the cross-coupling effects can be allowed for as discussed earlier. For a receding horizon interval, T, of 5 s, and if the integration step used in Step 2 is 20 ms, then it was found that the lateral Riccati equations can be updated every 215 ms ($= T_{l,lat}$) and the longitudinal ones every 345 ms ($= T_{l,long}$). These figures can be further reduced if the control calculations, aircraft linearizations and Riccati integration sub-tasks are separated and distributed onto extra processors as discussed next.

4.4.2.2   Tree network autopilot implementation

Since the Riccati integration sub-task is performed after the aircraft linearization sub-task has been completed, it is not worthwhile to map these two tasks onto separate processors as they are essentially sequential in nature. It may however be useful to distribute the individual sub-tasks onto more processors so that the cycle time is reduced. This is not done here but we speed up the cycle rate of the linearization by separating the control calculation sub-tasks and mapping them onto a separate transputer as shown in Fig. 4.5. The control calculation sub-tasks are relatively lightweight and so this transputer (T_1) has significant spare processing capacity which can be used in a variety of ways to speed up the overall cycle time. For example, T_1 can be used to share some of the processing for the aircraft linearization and/or assisting in the Riccati integration calculations. Another possibility, as discussed in Virk and Tahir [4,13] is to use the spare capacity to monitor and maintain other aircraft functions such as fault tolerance by being able to reconfigure the control forces under failure conditions.

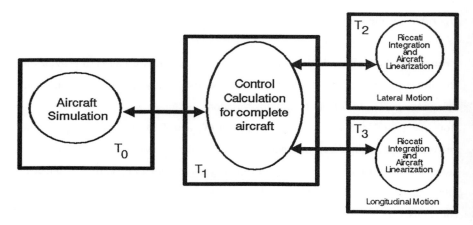

Fig.4.5 Tree network implementation

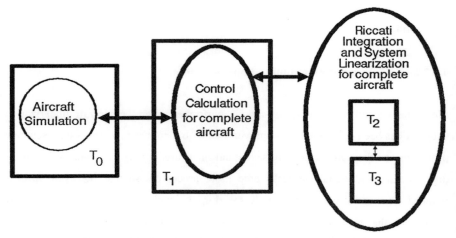

Fig. 4.6 "Collective Mode" network implementation

Using the network shown in Fig. 4.5 it was found that the lateral motion transputer T_2 could update the gains every 190 ms and the longitudinal transputer T_3 every 295 ms. The control calculation transputer T_1 required 993 µs to perform the controlling and communication tasks leaving the remainder of the 5 ms sample time to perform "other operations".

It should be noted that if the transputer T_2 and T_3 are used together collectively to perform the aircraft linearization and Riccati integration for the whole aircraft as shown in Fig. 4.6, that is, not splitting the processing into the longitudinal and lateral parts, then the results are not as effective as the tree network implementation of Fig. 4.5. In the collective mode, transputers T_2 and T_3 first solve the linearization task of the two motions together and then perform the Riccati equation integrations by sharing the processing for each motion between them. Extra communications are necessary for this implementation and so the efficiency is reduced. When this case was implemented, it was found that the linearization and feedback gains could be updated every 342 ms.

The processing and communication times are significantly increased if the whole aircraft is considered as one optimisation problem due to the larger dimensionality of the problem.

Network		Cycle time	Processing time	Communication time
Two transputers	T_1	215 ms	208.9 ms	6.2 ms
	T_2	345 ms	335.1 ms	9.9 ms
Tree Network	T_1	5 ms	728 µs	275 µs
	T_2	190 ms	189.89 ms	110 µs
	T_3	295 ms	294.86 ms	132 µs
"Collective Mode" network	T_1	5 ms	728 µs	385 µs
	T_2	342 ms	242.8 ms	99.2 ms
	T_3	342 ms	242.8 ms	99.2 ms

Table 4.1 Timings for different transputer implementations

The timings for the various parallel implementations discussed can be broken down into actual processing times, and communication times as shown in Table 4.1, and Table 4.2 shows the performances of the various transputer autopilot implementations.

Network	Cycle times /ms	Efficiency	Spare capacity
Uni-processor	$T_l = 600$	1.0	No
Two processors	$T_{l,lat} = 215$ $T_{l,long} = 345$	0.87	No
Tree network	$T_{l,lat} = 190$ $T_{l,long} = 295$	0.68	Yes
"Collective Mode"	$T_l = 342$	0.59	Yes

Table 4.2 Performances for different transputer autopilot implementations

The efficiency of the multi-transputer implementations are calculated as defined by eqn. (1.1) in Chapter 1.

4.5   RESULTS AND CONCLUSIONS

The real-time algorithm was run on the various T800 transputer networks considered in Section 4.4. For the state vector $x = [U, W, Q, \Theta, H, N, V, P, R, \Phi, \Psi]^T$, an initial value of $x_{ic} = [150, 5, 0, 0.033, 5000, 6615, 0, 0, 0, 0, 0.2]^T$ and a desired value of $x_d = [150, 5, 0, 0.033, 5000, 6615, 0, 0, 0, 0, 0]^T$ was assumed, and so the aircraft was required to change its direction by 11.5°. The weighting matrices shown in Table 4.3 were used. Note that for good control performance over the entire working range of the aircraft, some of the weights are chosen to be dependent upon the aircraft velocity; for further discussion on this, see Virk and Tahir [4.18].

Longitudinal motion	Lateral motion
$Q_{long} = \mathrm{diag}[1.3, 0.6, 200, 40, 0.004, 2 \times 10^{-5}]$ $R_{long} = \mathrm{diag}[r11(V_r), 2]$	$Q_{lat} = \mathrm{diag}[q_{11}(V_r), 1, 20, 30, 200]$ $R_{lat} = \mathrm{diag}[20, 20]$

Table 4.3 Weights used in the autopilot

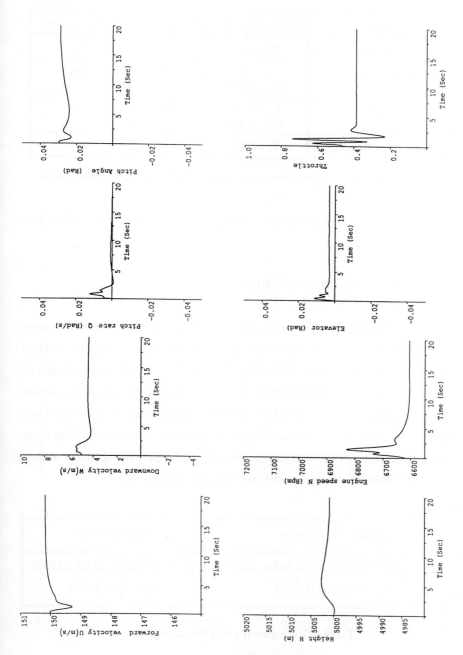

Fig. 4.7 Longitudinal aircraft motion

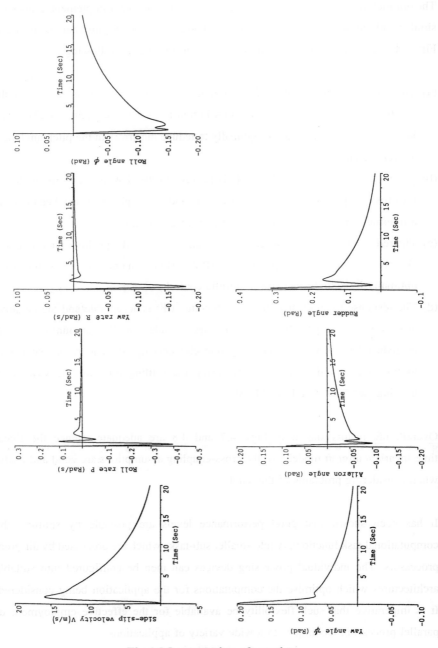

Fig.4.8 Lateral aircraft motion

The optimal trajectories and controls for the different transputer implementations were similar and sample responses are shown in Fig. 4.7 (the longitudinal motion) and Fig. 4.8 (the lateral motion). From these we can observe the following:

(a) The large elevator positive deflection in the first few seconds is due to the additional cross-coupling control contribution from $\Delta\eta$ in equation (4.27), while later on the elevator responds optimally to reduce the errors in the pitch angle and aircraft height.

(b) The reduction in Θ, even though Q is positive in the first few seconds, is due to the cross-coupling effect from the yaw rate and roll angle but it has been kept to a minimum due to the additional ΔQ term of equation (4.28).

(c) The reduction in forward speed U is caused mainly by the positive pitch rate and slightly by the cross-coupling term (RV). This reduction in U is remedied optimally by a slight increase in throttle control.

(d) The response to an error in the yaw direction (Ψ) is acceptable and the negative error in the roll angle (Φ) reduces the angle of side-slip. The amount of roll can be reduced by increasing the weighting elements q_{11}, q_{33} and r_{11} in the lateral motion, but at the expense of increasing the settling time for the yaw angle heading, see Virk and Tahir [4.18].

Overall, the results shown in Figs. 4.7 and 4.8 are adequate. Hence the linear time-invariant aircraft model, and the cross-coupling assumptions are valid and useful when considering problems of this kind.

It has been shown that good performance levels are possible by splitting the computational task functionally into smaller sub-tasks which are processed by different processors. The individual processing devices can then be configured into suitable architectures which optimise the computations for the application being considered. It is imperative that such flexibility be available for the effective employment of parallel processing techniques to a wide variety of applications.

ACKNOWLEDGEMENT

The authors would like to express their gratitude to British Aerospace (Military Aircraft), Brough for providing the aircraft engineering data.

APPENDIX

Table of notation

U	m/s	forward component of aircraft velocity
W	m/s	downward component of aircraft velocity
V	m/s	velocity of side-slip
V_r	m/s	aircraft relative velocity
Q	rad/s	pitch rate
P	rad/s	roll rate
R	rad/s	yaw rate
Θ	rad	pitch attitude angle
Φ	rad	roll attitude angle
Ψ	rad	yaw attitude angle
H	metres	aircraft height
N	rev/min	engine speed
η	rad	elevator deflection
ξ	rad	aileron deflection
ζ	rad	rudder deflection
γ	dimensionless	engine power setting
X_f	N	total force acting along OX axis
Y_f	N	total force acting along OY axis
Z_f	N	total force acting along OZ axis
P_m	Nm	total pitching moment
Y_m	Nm	total yawing moment
R_m	Nm	total rolling moment
M	kg	total aircraft mass
I_x	kgm^2	moment of inertia about OX axis
I_y	kgm^2	moment of inertia about OY axis
I_z	kgm^2	moment of inertia about OZ axis
I_{xz}	kgm^2	cross product of inertia about OZX axes
T_s	ms	sampling period
T_l	ms	time between successive linearizations
T	s	horizon depth
x, X		vector of state variables
$\mathbf{x}_d$		vector of desired states
$\mathbf{u}_{in}$		vector of control variables
α	rad	angle of attack

REFERENCES

[4.1]   Babister AW: *Aircraft dynamic stability and response*, Pergamon Press, 1980.

[4.2]   Blakelock JH: *Automatic control of aircraft and missiles*, John Wiley, 1965.

[4.3]   Banks SP: *Control systems engineering*, Prentice-Hall, 1986.

[4.4]   Tahir JM and Virk GS, A real-time distributed algorithm for an aircraft longitudinal optimal autopilot, *Concurrency: Practice and Experience*, Vol 2(2), pp 109-121, 1990.

[4.5]   Virk GS and Tahir JM: Parallel optimal control algorithms for aircraft, *IEE Colloquium on Navigation, guidance and control in aerospace*, Digest No 1989/142, pp3/1-3/5, 1989.

[4.6]   Bertsekas DP and Tsitsiklis JN: *Parallel and distributed computation: numerical methods*, Prentice-Hall, 1989.

[4.7]   Hockney RW and Jesshope CR, *Parallel computers 2: Architecture programming and algorithms*, Adams Hilger, 1988.

[4.8]   Inmos Ltd: *IMS T800 Transputer architecture*, Technical note 6, 1987.

[4.9]   British Aerospace PLC: *Aircraft engineering data*, (Private correspondence).

[4.10] Ayuk JT: *Fault tolerant reconfigurable architectures for flight control*, MSc Thesis, University of Sheffield, 1989.

[4.11] Virk GS, Tahir JM, and Kourmoulis PK: Parallel processing in aerospace control systems, *Proc Int Conference on Applications of Transputers 2*, DJ Pritchard and CJ Scott (eds), IOS Press, pp 124-134, 1990.

[4.12] Kourmoulis PK: *Parallel processing in the simulation and control of flexible structure systems*, PhD Thesis, University of Sheffield, 1990.

[4.13] Virk GS and Tahir JM: A fault tolerant optimal flight control system, *Proc IEE Int Conf Control 91*, Vol 2, pp 1049-1055, 1991.

[4.14] Kwon WH, Bruckstein AM and Kailath T: Stabilising state feedback design via the moving horizon method, *Int J Control*, Vol 37, No 3, pp 631-643, 1983.

[4.15] *The ATMOS Routine*, British Aerospace Report BAe-KSE-R-GEN-51478/9006/SDD, Issue 1, 1986.

[4.16] International Standard Atmosphere, B.S.2G 199: *British Standard Aerospace Series*, 1984.

[4.17] Bennett S: *Real-time computer control*, Prentice-Hall, 1988.

[4.18] Virk GS and Tahir JM: Selection of weights in time-varying optimal flight control, submitted to *Optimal Control Applications and Methods*, 1991.

Chapter 5

Parallel Adaptive Control of a Synchronous Generator

LP Maguire and GW Irwin

5.1   INTRODUCTION

Recent developments in power systems, arising from advances in technology, changes in generation and load patterns and economic considerations have exposed various problems and requirements. For example, large power stations have been constructed in locations remote from load centres leading to the possibility of dynamic instability under certain circumstances. Furthermore, a modern turbogenerator is a non-linear system which encounters frequent changes in operating conditions and may be subject to very large disturbances. To achieve the most effective and efficient control of such a system it is desirable that the controllers are capable of adapting to the non-linearities of the plant and the consequent changes in the values of the parameters.

There has been considerable research interest directed towards the possible application of modern control theory to generator excitation control. In particular, self-tuning regulators (STRs) have been proposed for such control and shown to provide improvements in system stability [5.1-5.4]. However practical issues such as parameter tracking, violation of the preconditions for the estimation procedure and rejection of unmodelled disturbances [5.5-5.7] all impede the practical implementation of self-tuning controllers and necessitate the introduction of a comprehensive and fully automatic supervision scheme in the form of jacketing software. These problems have been addressed and the resulting STR has been successfully applied to the control of a simulated generator model [5.8].

The STR algorithm, outlined in the Appendix, uses a generalised minimum variance control strategy [5.9, 5.10], together with an auxiliary predictor, to minimise the variance between the output of the system and a desired track of the output. This restrains excessive control signals and supplies better damping to the system. The supervision scheme is realised by introducing moving boundaries for the estimated parameters, modifying the covariance matrix by monitoring the gain vector and turning the estimator on or off, according to the results of a statistical T-test. However the introduction of all these features results in a complex controller which is difficult to implement in real-time.

With conventional sequential processors, the STR can operate at 50 Hz to produce an updated control signal every 20 msecs. The objective of this work was to achieve a 100 Hz realisation with control intervals of at most 10 msecs through the introduction of low cost, parallel transputer hardware. Furthermore, this improvement in computational power facilitated an increase in the complexity of the control algorithm, to include estimation of the noise parameters, which removed biases in the parameter estimates with coloured noise. This Chapter reports on two approaches to parallel adaptive control, one involving heuristic partitioning of the regular sequential algorithm, the other using systolic array descriptions. Real-time implementation results on transputer networks are included and the performance is evaluated in terms of implementation times, relative speed-up, computational capability of the processor and numerical inaccuracy for a range of problem sizes.

More generally the work was motivated by the realisation that if parallel processing hardware, specifically transputers, are to find widespread use in control it is essential that systematic mapping procedures emerge from the largely ad-hoc methods currently employed [5.11]. In particular, we were interested in looking at the potential of systolic array descriptions in this context. The Chapter therefore contains results on both the performance of transputer based adaptive control for a particular application and also partly addresses the more general issues involved in mapping adaptive control algorithms onto hardware architectures.

5.2   APPLICATION OF THE STR TO THE TURBOGENERATOR SYSTEM

A laboratory-scale model of the turbogenerator, the micromachine [5.12], is available for practical implementation studies. The existing control hardware employs a PDP 11 MINC computer to calculate the root-mean-square (rms) terminal quantities from phase measurements and optical transducers to provide digital measurements of rotor angle and speed. The control algorithm is implemented in C on an IBM PC with an Intel 80286 processor and 80287 co-processor. This hardware allowed a reduced form of the STR algorithm (in terms of the supervisory calculations) to be implemented within a 20 msecs sampling interval.

The computational limitations of this configuration has prompted an investigation [5.13] into a new architecture based on Inmos transputers combined with an advanced VME bus-based measurement system, as shown in Fig. 5.1. The proposed modular structure employs Motorola 68020 microprocessors to calculate the terminal quantities from phase measurements. The Fourier analysis algorithm used can provide accurate measurements under all conditions, rather than relying on a balanced 3-phase supply as at present. The control algorithm is resident on a transputer which facilitates the application of parallel processing. At the time of writing the new hardware system is being commissioned and hence the performance of the STR and its supervision scheme were evaluated by simulation.

The STR was tested on an occam simulation of a turbogenerator, connected to a power system through a transformer and two transmission lines as shown in Fig. 5.2. The total system was described by a 14th order, nonlinear state model which is well established in power system studies [5.12]. The generator was represented as a

7th-order system based on Park's equations, the exciter by a first-order system with a small time constant and limits on both the positive and negative ceilings of the field voltage. Furthermore, it was assumed that the mechanical power input from the turbine remains constant during brief transient disturbances thereby reducing the system to single-input, single-output.

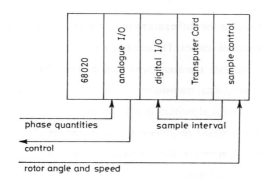

Fig. 5.1 Proposed hardware architecture

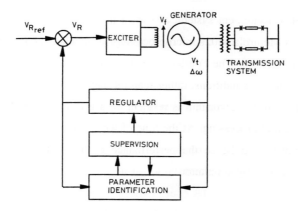

Fig. 5.2 STR implemented on the turbogenerator

Three versions of the STR algorithm were investigated, differing in the number of parameters in the estimated ARMA model. The first implementation involved a five parameter ARMA model, with measurement and parameter vectors :

$$\phi(t) = [\ y(t),y(t-1),y(t-2),u(t-1),u(t-2)\ ]^T$$
$$\theta(t) = [\ f_0\ ,\ f_1\ ,\ f_2\ ,\ g_1\ ,\ g_2\ ]^T$$

(5.1)

This self-tuning regulator has been tested in previous studies [5.8] and, when realised on conventional processors, produces an updated control signal every 20 msecs. Regulators based on nine and fifteen parameter ARMA plant models, with noise parameters included, were also studied.

Transient performance was assessed by simulating a three-phase short circuit, cleared after 120 msecs, at the sending end of the transmission lines. The simulation was allowed to run for 10 seconds with a white noise disturbance on the input signal. This allowed the estimator to determine the ARMA model before the fault was initiated. The total run time for the simulation was 15 seconds. The initial operating point was chosen as $P_t = 0.8$ p.u. and $Q_t = 0.2$ p.u., which constitutes quite a stringent test of the controller. Furthermore, a disturbance was applied to the output using prbs (pseudo-random binary sequence) and a second-order filter to simulate coloured noise.

Fig. 5.3 compares the transient responses of the rotor angle, real power, terminal voltage and field voltage produced with no control and with adaptive control. The graphs contain the responses from time $t = 8$ secs to the end of the run, since the initial part of the simulation involves the start-up of the estimator. Three traces are presented for each variable corresponding to no control, STR control with a five-parameter model, and finally STR control with a nine-parameter model. The benefit of adaptive control is clearly shown as the uncontrolled responses are more oscillatory and take longer to return to their initial values. Severe oscillations in the uncontrolled rotor angle response, for example, may force the generator to lose synchronism. The graphs also illustrate the advantage of the nine-parameter ARMA model; the responses are more damped than those of the five parameter case.

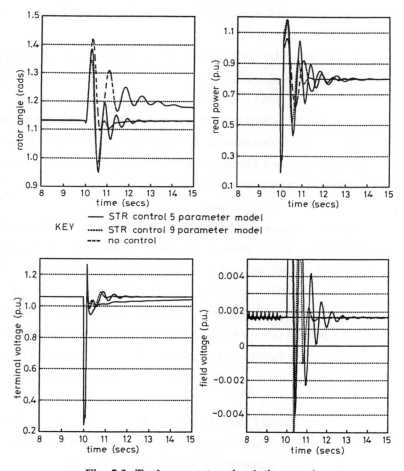

Fig. 5.3 **Turbogenerator simulation results**

It was found that there was no further improvement in performance with the controller based on the fifteen parameter ARMA model, however the higher order dynamics of this model may prove beneficial on the real plant. Previously this controller was not practically realisable on the turbogenerator system, because of its computational demands, but is included here to illustrate the potential benefits of parallel processing as discussed in the following Sections.

5.3   A HEURISTIC APPROACH TO ADAPTIVE PARALLEL CONTROL

The flow chart in Fig. 5.4 shows that the STR requires a strict sequential data flow, which limits the scope for parallelism. However, further investigation revealed that, although the supervision scheme and control law calculations are inherently sequential, the matrix-based parameter estimator is suitable for parallel implementation. Furthermore, during any sample interval the parameter estimator accounted for more than 60% of the computational requirements of the algorithm. This percentage increases with n, the dimension of parameter vector θ, because the estimator requires $O(n^2)$ computations while the remainder of the algorithm requires $O(n)$ computations.

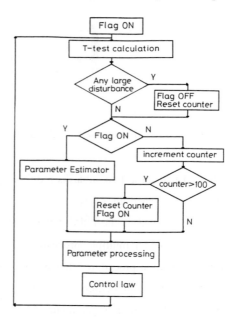

Fig. 5.4 Flow chart for STR implementation

Recursive least squares, with exponential data weighting via a forgetting factor, eqns. (A.17-A.20), was employed for parameter estimation. The heuristic approach to partitioning this algorithm involved using a Gantt chart [5.14], a project management tool for matching available resources to tasks in an efficient manner. The Gantt chart describing the partitioning strategy, as applied to the STR algorithm, is contained in Fig. 5.5. This chart has been drawn to scale, using timing information for a T414-G20 transputer and 20 Mbit/sec link speeds. It was derived for the five-parameter ARMA model and suggested that the estimation procedure could be partitioned coarsely into two subtasks, one involving the gain vector calculation and parameter vector update, the other the update of the covariance matrix.

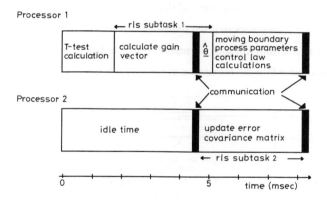

Fig. 5.5   Gantt chart for heuristic STR partitioning

The Gantt chart also indicated that these two subtasks required approximately equal computation times and hence a speed-up of two could be obtained using two transputers (where speed-up is defined as the ratio of the computation time on one processor to the computation time on multiple processors [5.15]). However, this speed-up relates only to the estimation procedure whereas the actual speed-up of the control algorithm also depends on the computation time of the supervision and control calculations and the idle time. For the five-parameter ARMA model, the actual speed-up of the control algorithm on two processors would be approximately 1.5.

This figure would increase with the ARMA model size, since the estimation algorithm dominates the computational requirements thereby reducing the relative effect of the idle time.

The actual performances, when the self-tuning regulator was implemented on T414-G20 transputers, are given in terms of the average iteration time versus the number of estimated parameters in the ARMA model (Fig. 5.6). Average iteration times, calculated by taking measurements over 750 intervals, measure the total time required for the estimation, supervision and control calculations during one sample interval. As expected, this iteration time increases by $O(n^2)$. The results also show that the time required to implement the STR algorithm on two transputers decreases relative to the single transputer implementation as the number of estimated parameters increases, i.e. the speed-ups range from 1.44 to 1.86. This is because parallel processing is directed only towards parameter estimation which dominates the computational requirements of the algorithm when using the larger ARMA models. A disappointing feature of the results was that only the implementation of the five parameter ARMA based STR was performed within the required 10 msecs sampling interval, all the other implementations being too complex to meet this target. This prompted an investigation into the use of T800-G20 transputers.

The T800 transputer provides, on average, a factor of 10 increase in performance over the T414 processor. As we have seen in Chapter 1, it contains an on-chip 64-bit floating-point unit and twice the on-chip RAM capacity of the T414 transputer. The T414 implements floating-point arithmetic in software which sustains about 10^5 floating-point operations per second (flops) whereas the hardware floating-point unit in the T800 sustains 1.5Mflops. One disadvantage of the T800 is that it provides only a slight improvement in actual link speed over the T414 transputer.

Fig. 5.7 contains the corresponding iteration times for T800-G20 transputers. These exhibit approximately a factor of fifteen improvement over the T414 results as the implementations were all carried out using double precision (64-bit floating-point) arithmetic to maintain a high degree of accuracy. This hardware facilitated the implementation of all the adaptive controllers within 5 msecs, which readily meets the 10 msecs target.

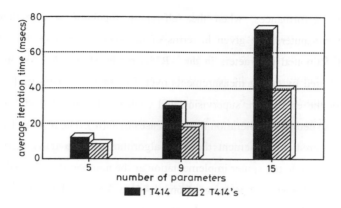

Fig. 5.6 STR with heuristic partitioning (T414's)

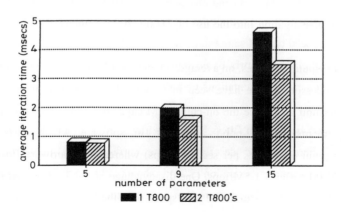

Fig. 5.7 STR with heuristic partitioning (T800's)

The results also contain the same trends with increasing number of parameters as before. However, the two transputer implementations do not provide a comparable performance improvement, with speed-ups ranging from 1.04 to 1.33. This is because the T800 simulations provide a finer-grained implementation than the T414 ones. Here granularity is defined as the ratio of computational to communication requirements [5.16]. This is a major limitation of the T800 processor; its superior computational performance together with a relatively slow communication speed supports only a coarse-grained partitioning strategy. Relatively large computational tasks which interact infrequently have to be mapped onto each processor in order to utilise the hardware efficiently. Thus, the considerable communication overheads of the heuristic partitioning approach reduce its effectiveness when using high performance parallel processors. (The granularity issue is further discussed in Chapter 10.)

5.4   A SYSTOLIC ARRAY APPROACH TO ADAPTIVE PARALLEL CONTROL

The shortcomings of the heuristic approach, discussed in the previous Section prompted an investigation into the use of systolic arrays in the mapping procedure. This approach was studied earlier in relation to transputer based Kalman filtering [5.17], and, with certain assumptions, least-squares parameter estimation may be regarded as a special case of state estimation [5.18]. Systolic array descriptions extract the natural parallelism of matrix-based algorithms and thus offer a more useful starting point for transputer implementations than the conventional description.

Analysis of systolic Kalman filters [5.19] has identified a square-root filter [5.20] as the most efficient systolic description. The corresponding square-root systolic architecture for parameter estimation [5.21] is shown in Fig. 5.8. This architecture has been customised for a scalar measurement problem, thereby reducing the dimensions of the array to two rows. The array implements the RLS algorithm by using Given's rotations to perform the required orthogonal decomposition, followed by a matrix multiplication procedure to provide the results required for the next iteration.

Comparisons with other systolic parameter estimation architectures have shown that this array provides a higher processor utilisation and a relatively lower latency [5.21].

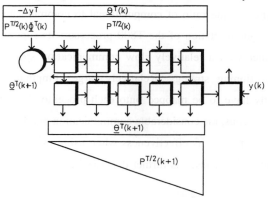

Fig. 5.8 Systolic array for RLS algorithm

The initial transputer implementations of this systolic algorithm used T414-G20 transputers to produce the results shown in Fig. 5.9. The single transputer implementation involved coding the systolic array description as a sequential task to maximise performance by removing the overheads associated with parallel occam processes. The average iteration times increase with the number of parameters, as before.

The application of parallel processing required an efficient mapping strategy to assign partitioned tasks onto transputers. To maintain a fairly coarse-grained realisation it was decided to target the parallel implementations at two processors. The mapping strategy utilised the inherent linear schedule of the systolic architecture, which is based on a set of uniformly spaced equitemporal hyperplanes [5.22], as shown in Fig. 5.10. The schedule vector **S,** which specifies the sequence of operation of the processes, points in a direction normal to these hyperplanes since processes along a hyperplane can be performed simultaneously. If the array is treated as a wavefront array, the data-driven structure allows the schedule vector to be resolved into orthogonal components in the horizontal and vertical directions respectively S_h, S_v. This permits the description of the array in terms of pipelines in these directions. The processes can then be mapped

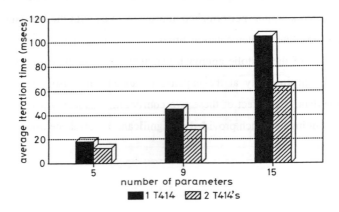

Fig. 5.9 STR using systolic approach (T414's)

efficiently onto a linear array of processors by projecting parallel to one of these
schedule vectors and using the parallelism in the resulting pipeline. The imbalance
between the computational requirements of the rows of this particular array restricts
the projection to the vertical direction. The projected cells are then coalesced into two
sequential subtasks and implemented on the two processors.

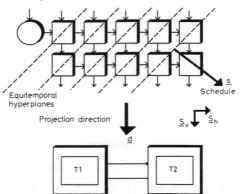

Fig. 5.10 Systolic array mapping strategy

The results when this strategy was implemented on two T414-G20 transputers are also
included in Fig. 5.9. The performance of the estimation algorithm was improved by

a factor of two but the actual speed-up of the control algorithm ranged from 1.45 to 1.7. This provided a similar performance improvement as with the heuristic approach but again the absolute implementation times did not meet the 10 msec target. The major advantage of the systolic approach was that the communication requirements were reduced, unfortunately at the expense of added supervisory requirements in setting up the data. The effect of these two conflicting characteristics explained why the systolic mapping approach provided no significant performance improvement over the heuristic one.

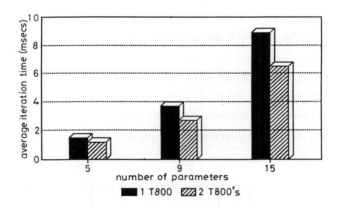

Fig. 5.11 STR using systolic approach (T800's)

The T414 iteration times did not meet the 10 msec target but T800-G20 realisations produced the results given in Fig. 5.11. On these transputers the reduced communication requirements of the systolic approach provided a coarser grained partitioned system resulting in more efficient implementations, with the speed-ups ranging from 1.26 to 1.4. However, the additional supervisory requirements, discussed above, restricted the resulting speed-up of the STR even though the parallel estimator was implemented more efficiently than before.

These results highlight the fact that the systolic array approach constitutes a systematic mapping procedure which allows task granularity to be matched to the target hardware. However, the systolic approach involved a square-root form of the parameter estimation algorithm whereas the regular form was employed with the heuristic approach. Comparisons of these two indicated that the square-root form is a factor of 1.5 more computationally intensive than the regular form, as is evident from the results presented in Figs. 5.7 and 5.11. The major advantage of the square-root algorithm is that the propagation of the Choleski factors of the covariance matrix force it to remain symmetric, increasing robustness to numerical inaccuracies [5.20]. Similar investigations applied to a target tracking problem suggest that the same robustness to numerical errors can be obtained using either a single-precision square-root filter or a double-precision regular filter [5.23]. This assumption can be justified by considering the dynamic range of the covariance matrix since, in square root form, half the number of bits are required to represent this range as compared to the regular form.

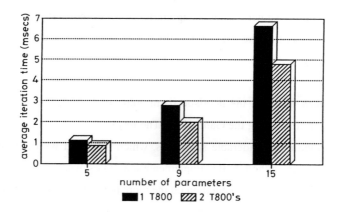

Fig. 5.12 STR using systolic approach (T800's and single precision arithmetic)

Implementation of the STR algorithm using single-precision arithmetic on T800-G20 transputers produced the results in Fig. 5.12. This provided a factor of 1.35

performance improvement over the comparable double-precision results because the on-chip, 64 bit floating point unit on the T800 transputer implements double-precision arithmetic relatively more effectively. Nevertheless, this facilitated the implementation of both the square-root and regular forms in comparable times. One further point is that the square-root form may reduce the supervision requirements, thereby improving the performance, by removing the need to reset the covariance matrix as the propagation of the Choleski factors ensures that it remains positive definite. This point refers to the stability of the algorithm and can only be verified by initiating a long-term operation test.

5.5 DISCUSSION AND CONCLUSIONS

The initial Sections of this Chapter introduced a robust self-tuning regulator which has been successfully applied to the control of a turbogenerator system. The objective of this research was to develop systematic approaches to the realisation of a parallel implementation on transputers, using sampling times of, at most, 10 msecs. Analysis of the algorithm identified the parameter estimator as the most suitable candidate for parallel processing.

The first approach involved the heuristic partitioning of the conventional recursive least squares algorithm using the Gantt chart. The results on T414 transputers proved encouraging providing considerable speed-ups, which increased with the number of estimated parameters, although the implementation times were outside the target sampling time. However, implementation on the more powerful T800 transputers were well within the 10 msec sampling time target for estimated ARMA model sizes ranging from 5 to 15 parameters. The disadvantage of this approach was that the relatively fined-grained partitioned system did not match the coarser granularity required by the hardware.

The second approach introduced the systolic array description and a novel mapping strategy for partitioning the algorithm. The T414 and T800 implementations showed similar trends as before. The systolic method, however, provided a coarser-grained parallel estimation algorithm which utilised the T800s more effectively. Nevertheless the added supervisory requirements of the systolic algorithm reduced the effect of this parallelism within the whole control scheme. Furthermore, the systolic architecture described a square-root form of the RLS algorithm, whereas the heuristic approach used the regular form. The different computational requirements resulted in a factor of 1.5 difference in performance. However, the former algorithm is more robust to numerical errors and it was shown that with equivalent numerical robustness properties the two forms can be implemented in comparable times.

One disappointing feature of the results is that the actual realisable parallelism extracted from the algorithm permitted the use of a maximum of two transputers. This can be attributed to the relatively small size of the problem needing only a coarse-grained partitioning of the algorithm onto the powerful transputer. However, the performance improvements provided by parallel processing have facilitated the introduction of more complex algorithms which improve the control performance.

This suggests that a more complex algorithm may be worth considering. For example, a multi-input, multi-output (MIMO) controller may be considered, with the turbine mechanical power as another input and the real electrical power as another output. Using the same number of estimated parameters in the ARMA models, would only increase the computational requirements of the regular estimation slightly as $\phi(t)$ becomes a matrix rather than a vector. A mathematical analysis of this algorithm, in terms of the number of floating point operations, suggests that the heuristic approach provides the same performance improvements as with the SISO case. This is again due to the inherent communication requirements reducing the effectiveness of the implementations on a coarse-grained target hardware. However, the MIMO problem increases the dimensions of the systolic array twofold. This allows the extraction of a coarser grained parallelism which can then be readily implemented on T800's to give predicted speed-ups in the range 1.3 to 1.8. In addition, this larger systolic array allows the introduction of more transputers into the target network. The major drawback of the MIMO algorithm is that the considerable increase in the computational requirements of the systolic array suggest that the implementation time of the nine parameter algorithm, on two transputers, would just meet the 10 msecs objective.

ACKNOWLEDGEMENTS

Liam Maguire would like to acknowledge the financial support of the Institute of Advanced Microelectronics and the Department of Education for Northern Ireland. The assistance and advice of Dr Q.H. Wu and M. Brown of the Control Engineering Research group is gratefully acknowledged.

REFERENCES

[5.1]   Sheirah MAH, Hope GS and Malik OP: Self-tuning voltage and speed regulators for a generating unit, *Proc IEEE/ASME/ASCE Joint Power Conf*, Dallas, **A78**, pp810-4, 1978.

[5.2]   Xia DZ and Heydt GT: Self-tuning controller for generator excitation control, *IEEE Trans. Power Apparatus Systems*, **102**, 6, pp1877-1885, 1983.

[5.3]   Kanniah J, Malik OP and Hope GS: Excitation control of synchronous generators using adaptive regulators, *IEEE Trans Power Apparatus Systems*, **103**, pp897-910, 1984.

[5.4]   Ibrahim AS, Hogg BW and Sharaf MM: Application of self-tuning control techniques to a turbogenerator system, *AMST 87*, Plymouth, UK, pp193-198, 1987.

[5.5]   Wittenmark B and Astrom KJ: Practical issues in the implementation of self-tuning control, *Automatica*, **20**, 5, pp595-605, 1984.

[5.6]   Kresselmeier G and Anderson BDO: Robust model reference adaptive control, *IEEE Trans Automatic Control*, **31**, 2, pp127-133, 1986.

[5.7]   Isermann R and Lachmann KH: Parameter adaptive control with configuration aids and supervision functions, *Automatica*, **21**, pp625-638, 1985.

[5.8]   Wu QH and Hogg BW: Robust self-tuning regulator for a synchronous generator, *IEE Proc, Pt D*, **135**, 6, pp463-473, 1988.

[5.9]   Harris CJ and Billings SA (Eds): *Self-tuning adaptive control : Theory and applications*, IEE Control Engineering Series 15, Peter Peregrinus Ltd, 2nd Edition, 1985.

[5.10] Clarke DW and Gawthrop PJ: Self-tuning controllers, *Proc IEE*, **122**, 9, pp625-638, 1975.

[5.11] Irwin GW and Fleming PJ (Eds): *Special Issue IEE Proc Pt D*, **137**, 4, 1990.

[5.12] Hogg, BW: Representation and control of modern turbogenerators, in Nicholson H (Ed): *Modelling of dynamical systems - Vol 2*, Peter Peregrinus, Ch 5, pp112-149, 1980.

[5.13] Brown MD and Swidenbank E: Supervisory control of a self-tuning automatic voltage regulator, *Proc IEE Int Conf Control '91*, **1**, pp449-454, 1991.

[5.14] Kruatrachue B: Static task scheduling and grain packing in parallel processing systems, *PhD dissertation*, Oregon State Univ, Corvallis, 1987.

[5.15] Eager DL et al: Speed-up versus efficiency in parallel systems, *IEE Computers*, **38**, 3, pp408-422, 1989.

[5.16] Stone HS: *High-performance computer architecture*, Addison-Wesley, 1987.

[5.17] Maguire LP and Irwin GW: Transputer implementation of Kalman filters *Proc ACC*, San Diego, pp2945-2946, 1990.

[5.18] Sorenson HW: Least-squares estimation : from Gauss to Kalman, *IEEE Spectrum*, **7**, pp63-68, 1970.

[5.19] Gaston FMF: Systolic algorithms and architectures for Kalman filtering *PhD dissertation*, Queen's University Belfast, 1989.

[5.20] Morf M and Kailath T: Square root algorithms for least squares estimation, *IEEE Trans Autom Contr*, **20**, 4, pp487-497, 1975.

[5.21] Gaston FMF and Irwin GW: A systolic parameter for real-time adaptive control, *Proc UK Information Technology Conf*, pp111-116, 1990.

[5.22] Kung SY: *VLSI array processors*, Prentice Hall, 1988.

[5.23] O'Hallaron DR and Baheti RS: Parallel implementation of the Kalman filter on the WARP computer, *Proc Int Conf on Parallel Processing*, **3**, pp108-111, 1988.

[5.24] Goodwin GC and Sin KS: *Adaptive filtering prediction and control*, Prentice-Hall Inc, 1984.

[5.25] Wu QH, Hogg BW: Laboratory implementation of self-tuning automatic regulator for turbogenerator, in Whalley R (Ed) *Applications of multivariable system techniques*, Elsevier Science Publishing Co, pp94-101, 1990.

Appendix THE SELF-TUNING REGULATOR AND SUPERVISION SCHEME

A.1   List of principal symbols

V_t machine terminal voltage

P_t power delivered at machine terminals

Q_t reactive power delivered at machine terminals

V_R exciter input voltage

ω rotor speed

θ parameter vector

ϕ data vector

A.2   The control algorithm

The implementation of the self-tuning controller as applied to a turbogenerator system is illustrated in Fig. 5.2. The turbogenerator system [5.12] can be represented as a SISO system by the following equation :

$$A(z^{-1})y(t) = z^{-k}B(z^{-1})u(t) + C(z^{-1})\xi(t) \qquad (A.1)$$

Here u(t) and y(t), the input and output of the system at the sample instant t, are defined as :

$$y(t) = \Delta V_t(t) + \gamma\Delta\omega(t) \quad -1 < \gamma < 0$$
$$u(t) = \Delta V_R(t) \qquad (A.2)$$

Also $\xi(t)$ is a zero mean, white noise sequence disturbing the system and k represents the system time delay in an integer number of sample intervals. $A(z^{-1})$, $B(z^{-1})$ and $C(z^{-1})$ are polynomials in the backward shift operator z^{-1} of order N,M and S respectively, as follows :

$$A(z^{-1}) = 1 + a_1 z^{-1} + \dots + a_N z^{-N}$$

$$B(z^{-1}) = b_0 + b_1 z^{-1} + \dots + b_M z^{-M} \tag{A.3}$$

$$C(z^{-1}) = 1 + c_1 z^{-1} + \dots + c_S z^{-S}$$

A predictive model of the system can be derived from eqn. A.1 and is described in the following form :

$$y(t+k) = EC^{-1} y(t) + DBC^{-1} u(t) + D\xi(t+k) \tag{A.4}$$

where the monic polynomial D is the quotient of C/A and is of degree k-1. The polynomial E is the remainder of C/A and is of degree N-1. C/A is resolved by replenishing the degree of C to be N with zero coefficients. A, C, D and E satisfy the following identity :

$$1 = ADC^{-1} + z^{-k} EC^{-1} \tag{A.5}$$

The cost function to be considered for choosing the control takes the form :

$$J = E\{ Q[y(t+k) - w(t+k)]^2 + Ru^2(t) \} \tag{A.6}$$

where $E\{.\}$ is the expectation operator and Q and R are weighting factors. The sequence $w(t+k)$ defines the desired track which the system should follow and can be obtained by designing an auxiliary predictor according to the following equation:

$$w(t+k) = z^{-k} P(z^{-1}) y(t+k)$$

$$P(z^{-1}) = p_0 + p_1 z^{-1} + \dots + p_{N-1} z^{N-1} \tag{A.7}$$

The coefficients of the P polynomial are selected by the designer.

The use of the auxiliary predictor in the cost function restrains excessive control signals, but it does not overcome the problems of nonminimum-phase systems. Thus, it is necessary to include a weighting factor R, into the cost equation, chosen so as to move the unstable zeros of B into the unit circle. The control law is then given by:

$$u(t) = \frac{(EC^{-1} - P)\ y(t)}{DBC^{-1} + (R/b_0)} \qquad (A.8)$$

The analysis above assumes known model parameters. If the system model parameters are unknown then their estimates are assumed to be the true values by the Certainty Equivalence Principle. The function $\Psi(t+k)$ and its estimated quantity are defined :

$$\Psi(t+k) = [\ y(t+k) - w(t+k)\ ]$$
$$\hat{\Psi}(t+k) = [\ \hat{y}(t+k) - w(t+k)\ ] \qquad (A.9)$$

Thus,

$$\Psi(t+k) = \hat{\Psi}(t+k) + e(t+k) \qquad (A.10)$$

where $e(t+k)$ is the prediction error between y and $\hat{y}$:

$$y(t+k) = \hat{y}(t+k) + e(t+k) \qquad (A.11)$$

For simplicity, it is assumed that

$$F = EC^{-1} - P$$
$$G = DBC^{-1} \qquad (A.12)$$

where,

$$F(z^{-1}) = f_0 + f_1 z^{-1} + \ldots + f_N /z^{-N'}$$

$$G(z^{-1}) = g_0 + g_1 z^{-1} + \ldots + g_M /z^{-M'} \tag{A.13}$$

Here F is of degree N'=N-1, G is of degree M'=k-1+M and g_0 is equivalent to b_0 because D and C are monic. The following equation is then used to predict Ψ (t+k)

$$\Psi(t+k) = Fy(t) + Gu(t) + Qe(t+k) \tag{A.14}$$

where the coefficients of F and G need to be estimated. Substituting eqn. (A.9) into eqn. (A.6) gives :

$$J = E\{ Q \Psi^2(t+k) + R u^2(t) \}$$

$$\therefore J = E\{ Q[\hat{y}(t+k) - w(t+k) + e(t+k)]^2 + Ru^2(t) \} \tag{A.15}$$

This function is minimised by selecting u(t) such that

$$Q [\hat{y}(t+k) - w(t+k)] + (R/b_0)u(t) = 0 \tag{A.16}$$

Assuming b_0 can be fixed, the method of recursive least squares (RLS) can be used to estimate the parameters in eqn. (A.14). Thus

$$\hat{\theta}(t) = \hat{\theta}(t-1) - K(t-1)[\Psi(t) - b_0 u(t-1) - \hat{\theta}(t-1)\phi^T(t-k)] \tag{A.17}$$

$$K(t-1) = (P(t-1)\phi(t-k)) / D \tag{A.18}$$

$$D = \lambda(t-1) + \phi^T(t-k)P(t-2)\phi(t-k) \tag{A.19}$$

$$P(t-1) = [I - K(t-1)\phi^T(t-k)]P(t-2)/\lambda(t-1) \tag{A.20}$$

where λ is a forgetting factor and where the vectors $\theta(t)$ and $\phi(t)$ are defined by

$$\phi(t) = [\ y(t),...,y(t-N'),\ u(t-1),..,u(t-N')\ ]^T \tag{A.21}$$

$$\hat{\theta} = [\ f_0,..,f_N \ \text{\textit{/}}\ g_0,...,g_M \ \text{\textit{/}}\ ]^T \tag{A.22}$$

The control law is then :

$$u(t) = \frac{-b_0}{b_0^2 + R}\ \theta^T(t)\phi(t) \tag{A.23}$$

If the noise parameters are included in the estimation procedure, and if b_0 is not assumed to be fixed, a more computationally intensive algorithm results. Eqns. (A.18-A.20) are unchanged but eqn. (A.17) becomes :

$$\hat{\theta}(t) = \hat{\theta}(t-1) - K(t-1)\ [\ \Psi(t) - \hat{\theta}(t-1)\phi(t-k)\ ]^T \tag{A.24}$$

The quantities $\theta(t)$ and $\phi(t)$ are now defined as :

$$\phi(t) = [y(t),..,y(t-N'),u(t),..,u(t-M'),e(t),..,e(t-S)]^T \tag{A.25}$$

$$\hat{\theta}(t) = [f_0,..,f_N \text{\textit{/}} g_0,..,g_M \text{\textit{/}},c_1,..,c_S]^T \tag{A.26}$$

and the control law can be obtained from

$$u(t) = \frac{-b_0\ [\ F(z^{-1})y(t) + G(z^{-1})u(t)\ ]}{R\ C(z^{-1})} \tag{A.27}$$

A.2   The supervision scheme

The STR must be able to handle any nonlinearities, unmodelled dynamics and unmodelled disturbances which may arise during the operation of the turbogenerator.

These problems are overcome by the implementation of a supervision scheme to monitor the operation of the parameter estimator and to take appropriate actions to guarantee the successful control behaviour of the STR. Three components of this supervision scheme are discussed below.

a) Moving boundaries are introduced for every estimated parameter to protect them from large modelling errors caused by the unmodelled disturbances. This is particularly important in power systems where a variety of sudden disturbances can occur. The moving boundaries are realised by utilising the mean values of the estimated parameters at each time instant. Thus

$$\beta_i(t) = (1/T'') \sum_{k=1}^{T''} \theta_i(t-k) \tag{A.28}$$

where $\theta_i(t)$ is the ith unknown parameter and $T'' = 10$ to ensure the stability of the parameters and the adaptability of the boundaries. The high and low boundaries for each parameter are given by

$$\beta_{iH}(t) = \beta_i(t) + \eta \mid \beta_i(t) \mid$$
$$\beta_{iL}(t) = \beta_i(t) - \eta \mid \beta_i(t) \mid \tag{A.29}$$

Here $0 < \eta < 1$, with a larger value of η the more likely it is for the parameters to vary. At each sampling instant the estimated parameters are bounded as follows

$$\beta_{iH}(t) \; ; \; \theta_i(t) \geq \beta_{iH}(t)$$
$$\theta_i(t) = \theta_i(t) \; ; \; \beta_{iL}(t) < \theta_i(t) < \beta_{iH}(t) \tag{A.30}$$
$$\beta_{iL}(t) \; ; \; \theta_i(t) \leq \beta_{iL}(t)$$

b) Modification of the covariance matrix is required because linearly dependent rows can arise after excessive variations in the output variables and control signals. The parameter vector will then not be updated correctly. The normal method of overcoming this problem is to modify the covariance matrix either by resetting [5.24], or by using a random walk procedure [5.9]. The method used here was to monitor the gain vector K(t) as follows

$$\upsilon(t) = \Sigma_{j=1}^{T'} \Sigma_{i=1}^{m} \mid k_i(t-j) \mid \qquad (A.31)$$

where m is the number of estimated parameters, and $k_i(t)$ is the ith element of K(t). The function $\upsilon(t)$ is similar to the power spectrum of K(t) over the interval t-1 to t-T'. The RLS algorithm is then modified by the introduction of a forgetting factor, eqns. (A.19) and (A.20), which specifies an asymptotic sample length in which useful measurements are included. This modification ensures that the covariance matrix does not "wind-up" [5.5] because the forgetting factor will be reset to 1 when $\upsilon(t)$ is greater than some specified value σ.

c) The parameter estimator is the critical part of the STR and should only be turned on when the measurement vector is providing information that could improve the model. In practice sudden disturbances, such as faults at transmission lines, will lead to a sudden change in the estimated parameters which does not result from changes in the process behaviour. Although moving boundaries are used to protect the system parameters, it is also necessary that the measured values of the system model and the control signals are evaluated before they are used for parameter estimation to prevent an unrealistic model of the system being found. The method used to turn the parameter estimator on and off was based on a statistical T-testing of the prediction error of the estimator [5.25]. This recursive error detector generates a value at each sample interval, and, if this is greater than that specified by the designer, the estimator is switched off for a set number of samples until the fault is cleared.

The flow chart of Fig. 5.4 illustrates the implementation of the STR control strategy: the supervision scheme, the estimation algorithm and the control law calculation.

Chapter 6

Control of High-Performance AC Induction Motor Drives

M Sumner and GM Asher

6.1   INTRODUCTION

For variable speed drive applications such as machine tool drives, traction, paper and steel mill rollers, the dc drive was the automatic choice until the mid 80's. The drive permits operation in all four quadrants of the torque-speed plane, gives good efficiency and excellent dynamic response. The dc machine itself suffers from several economic disadvantages when compared to the ac induction motor: the induction motor is cheaper, more reliable, and requires less periodic maintenance. Moreover, the induction motor has a lower rotor inertia for a given power rating than the dc machine. The induction motor thus has the capability of higher dynamic performance for a given power rating. The advantages of the dc drive result from the simplicity of the power converter and control circuitry required to complete the variable speed drive.

The power converter employed by power dc drives is based on the line commutated thyristor bridge rectifier. The induction motor needs a converter capable of transforming fixed frequency ac into a variable frequency, variable voltage source at low losses. This originally necessitated the use of thyristors using forced commutation. The extra components required for forced commutation increased the cost of the converter substantially.

The simplicity of the dc drive control circuitry derives from the fact that the dc motor has a simple control structure wherein the torque and air-gap fluxes of the machine are able, by the action on the commutator, to be controlled independently. By contrast the induction motor has a complex control structure as the voltage, current, torque and speed are all interdependent, resulting in a highly coupled, non-linear, multivariable control problem. The development of ac drives, over the last 15 years, as variable speed drives has derived from the power switching devices developed over the same period as an alternative to thyristors [6.1],[6.2]. The introduction of such devices as the Gate Turn Off Thyristor and high power Bipolar Junction and Field Effect Transistors, for low to medium power applications, has removed the need for auxiliary commutating circuits. The resulting reduction in cost of the power converter means that the ac drive has become more commonplace in low performance, variable speed drive applications.

The problem of obtaining a fast torque response from the induction motor has received considerable attention for many years [6.1],[6.3]. In the early seventies the "Vector" or "Field Orientated" control strategy was derived by Blaschke [6.4]. This technique involves the transformation of the machine dynamics into those of a "pseudo-dc machine equivalent" in which a torque and field component of the machine currents can be obtained. It derives its transformations from the instantaneous rotor flux vector and allows the torque and flux to be controlled independently in a similar manner to the dc machine. However, due to the complexity of this control algorithm, it was not until the early 1980's and the advent of powerful digital controllers, that experimental work to verify this strategy could be performed [6.5],[6.6].

The recent development of microprocessor technology (outlined in Chapter 1) has been such that the control engineer now has a large selection of processor hardware from which to choose. The advent of Very Large Scale Integration (VLSI) means that processor design is no longer a restriction and dedicated processors for drive control can now be manufactured.

For real-time control problems of low to medium complexity, microcontrollers and ASICS are principally exploited for direct commercial application. For the modern state-variable based control problems, with matrix manipulation based strategies, DSP chips may be thought to be very attractive with their pipe-lined architecture. Parallel architectures based around the transputer have proved effective for processing complex, real-time control strategies. Superficially they offer an increase in speed and hence an increase in the degree of processing within the control system sample time. Furthermore, system expansion and modification are relatively straightforward as both hardware and software are designed in a modular manner. Thus for a drive development rig, they are the ideal choice for control processor.

6.2   CONTROL OF INDUCTION MOTORS

A typical induction motor drive using a voltage source inverter is illustrated in Fig. 6.1. The base drive signals for the switching elements are derived from a Pulse Width Modulation (PWM) strategy used by the controller and provide a three-phase voltage source of variable amplitude, phase and frequency for the induction motor. Rotor position, and thus speed, are derived from an absolute encoder mounted on the shaft of the induction motor, and line currents are measured using current sensors. A dc generator is directly coupled to the induction motor to provide a means for varying the load torque. A Regenerative Braking Unit is connected across the dc link of the inverter to provide a means for dissipating regenerative energy from the induction motor during braking. This consists of a switching transistor and resistance bank. The transistor is turned on when the link voltage exceeds a preset limit and the regenerative energy is dissipated as resistor heating.

In order to derive the vector control strategy for the induction motor, it is necessary to define two orthogonal components of the stator current such that one acts as a torque producing component and one acts as an air-gap flux producing component.

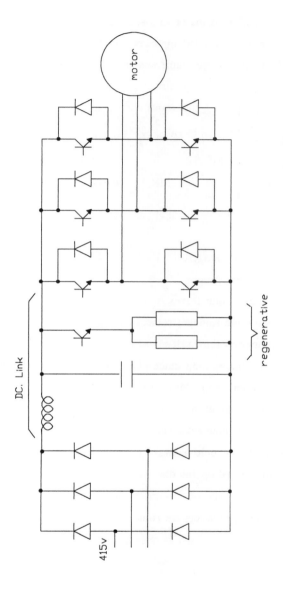

**Fig. 6.1 Typical voltage source inverter driven
induction motor.**

The typical starting point is the generalised d-q axis dynamic model of the induction motor in a synchronously rotating frame of reference, [6.2]. Slot effects, spatial harmonics and end effects are ignored as are the harmonics of the voltage source.

$$
\begin{bmatrix} v_{sd} \\ v_{sq} \\ 0 \\ 0 \end{bmatrix} = \begin{bmatrix} R_s + s\sigma L_s & -w_e\sigma L_s & sM/L_r & -w_e M/L_r \\ w_e\sigma L_s & R_s + s\sigma L_s & w_e M/L_r & sM/L_r \\ -MR_r/L_r & 0 & (R_r/L_r)+s & -(w_e-pw_r) \\ 0 & -MR_r/L_r & w_e-pw_r & (R_r/L_r)+s \end{bmatrix} \begin{bmatrix} i_{sd} \\ i_{sq} \\ \phi_{rd} \\ \phi_{rq} \end{bmatrix}
$$

(6.1)

The symbols represent :-

v_{sd}, v_{sq}	d-q axis voltages,
i_{sd}, i_{sq}	d-q axis currents,
ϕ_{rd}, ϕ_{rq}	d-q axis rotor fluxes,
R_s, R_r	stator and rotor resistance,
L_s, L_r	stator and rotor self-inductance,
M	magnetising inductance,
σ	total leakage factor,
w_e	stator angular velocity,
w_r	rotor angular velocity,
p	number of pole pairs,
s	differential operator.

The torque equation for this system is :-

$$
T_e = (3pM/L_r)(i_{sq}\phi_{rd} - i_{sd}\phi_{rq})
$$

(6.2)

It can be seen that if the d axis of the rotating frame of reference is aligned to the rotor flux axis, then the d - q model simplifies significantly, particularly :-

$$\phi_{rq} = 0 \tag{6.3}$$

$$|\phi_r| = \phi_{rd} \tag{6.4}$$

$$T_e = (3pM/L_r)(i_{sq} \phi_{rd}) \tag{6.5}$$

Putting $\phi_{rq} = 0$ as demanded by the orientation described above, then row 4 of eqn. (6.1) becomes :-

$$w_e = pw_r + (MR_r/L_r)(i_{sq}/\phi_{rd}) \tag{6.6}$$

The second term on the right-hand side is seen to represent the slip angular velocity. Considering row 3 of eqn. (6.1) gives :-

$$i_{sd} = \{(1/M) + s(L_r/(MR_r))\} \phi_{rd} \tag{6.7}$$

If a new term is introduced, the magnetising current vector i_{mr} where :-

$$i_{mr} = \phi_r/M \tag{6.8}$$

then eqn. (6.7) can be rewritten as :

$$i_{sd} = (L_r/R_r) \frac{d(i_{mr})}{dt} + i_{mr} \tag{6.9}$$

For an induction motor operating with a constant rotor flux,

$$\phi_{rd} = Mi_{mr} = Mi_{sd} \tag{6.10}$$

and the torque equation becomes :-

$$T_e = (3pM^2/L_r)i_{mr}i_{sq} \qquad (6.11)$$

Eqns (6.6), (6.9) and (6.11) are the fundamental equations for vector control. Eqn. (6.9) is directly analogous to the field equation of a dc machine where i_{sd} is the steady-state field current and is directly proportional to the rotor flux. It is qualitatively analogous to the applied field voltage in the dc machine and i_{mr} is analogous to I_f. Eqn (6.11) corresponds to the torque equation of a dc machine and thus i_{sq} is the torque producing component of the stator current. Under field weakening control eqn. (6.9) becomes important as the rotor flux, being proportional to i_{mr} through eqn. (6.8), responds to changes in i_{sd} with a significant time constant L_r/R_r.

For implementation of vector control for induction motor drives some means for identifying the instantaneous position of the rotor flux vector is essential. Early experimentation with this technique employed flux sensing coils mounted in the stator slots [6.7] and provided a good flux measurement down to about 0.5Hz. This method, however, requires the use of modified or specially constructed machines, not considered generally practicable. A second method, used in the early history of Vector Control employed the stator voltages (either measured again using sensing coils again or by using the reference values controlling a PWM generator) and by means of integration provided an estimate of the rotor flux vector [6.7]. This method, however, proved unreliable at low speed due to the cut-off frequency of the integrators employed. Variations in the stator parameters due to temperature and saturation had a marked effect on the control scheme. Techniques employing direct sensing of the rotor flux signal are known as "Direct Vector Control".

An alternative, and simpler, approach to this control strategy is to employ a technique known as "Indirect Vector Control" where the rotor flux is not directly measured or derived and no modifications to the induction motor are required. This strategy imposes vector control in a feedforward manner [6.6]. It implicitly aligns the d axis to the rotor flux vector, by controlling the slip angular velocity, according to eqn. (6.6), using the controller reference values of i_{sq} and ϕ_{rd} rather than the actual machine values. It thus relies upon the precise control of the d and q axis currents using fast stator current controllers. A general scheme for such an indirect vector controller employs two quadrature current controllers for i_{sd} and i_{sq} and controls the inverter frequency according to eqn. (6.6). The controller imposes a rotor flux vector angle Θ_e which is implicitly aligned to the d axis such that

$$\theta_e = \theta_r + \theta_{slip} \qquad\qquad (6.12)$$

$$w_{slip} = (1/T_r)(i_{sq}^{ref}/i_{mr}^{ref}) \qquad\qquad (6.13)$$

where Θ_r is the absolute position of the rotor. Its magnitude is controlled directly by i_{sd}. The torque current reference is derived from the speed controller, whereas the flux current reference under base speed is maintained constant at just under saturation level. For operation above base speed field, weakening is introduced whereby the flux current reference is reduced gradually with speed in a similar manner to field weakening operation of a dc machine.

6.3   IMPLEMENTATION OF INDIRECT VECTOR CONTROL

The general schematic for the "indirect" vector control algorithm employed is illustrated in Fig. 6.2. It can be seen that the structure is similar to that of a dc motor drive, whereby the inner feedback loops control the field and torque currents, and the reference values for these controllers are derived from the outer speed feedback loop.

The instantaneous rotor flux position Θ_e is defined at any instant by eqn. (6.12), where Θ_r is the measured rotor position and Θ_{slip} is the slip angle demand. The rotor flux angle is then used to transform the instantaneous measured line currents to the field

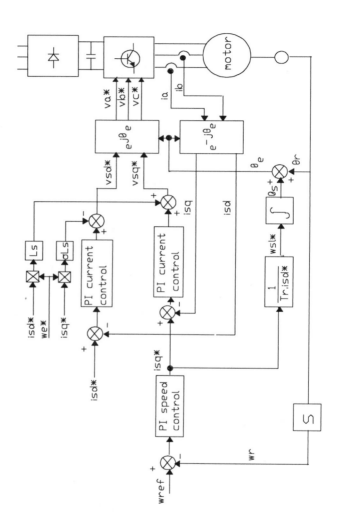

Fig. 6.2 Indirect vector control using impressed stator voltages

orientated frame of reference, using a 3-2 phase transformation (demodulation) as
follows:-

$$i_{s\alpha} = i_a/2 \tag{6.14}$$

$$i_{s\beta} = (1/6)(i_b - i_c) \tag{6.15}$$

$$i_{sd} = i_{s\alpha}\cos\theta_e + i_{s\beta}\sin\theta_e \tag{6.16}$$

$$i_{sq} = i_{s\beta}\cos\theta_e - i_{s\alpha}\sin\theta_e \tag{6.17}$$

The absolute values of these transformed currents reflect the phase rms quantities in
the motor and are consistent with the torque equation used. This transformation is
abbreviated for the schematic diagrams by use of the equivalent complex operator $e^{j\Theta e}$.
The corresponding modulation routines (i.e. transformation of d and q axis values to
instantaneous stator reference frame values) are represented by the complex operator
$e^{-j\Theta e}$.

The precise control of the stator currents is achieved using current feedback to provide
closed-loop control of the d and q axis currents, and is based on the stator dynamic
equations derived from eqn. (6.1).

The current controllers themselves were designed using Laplace techniques and
employed proportional-plus-integral (PID) control. The controllers were designed on
the basis of the following equations :-

$$v_{sd} = (R_s + s\sigma L_s)i_{sd} - w_e\sigma L_s i_{sq} \tag{6.18}$$

$$v_{sq} = (R_s + s\sigma L_s)i_{sq} + w_e L_s i_{sd} \tag{6.19}$$

It can be seen that the terms on the right hand side of eqns. (6.18) and (6.19)
constitute additional coupling terms which must be compensated for at the output of
each current controller.

The three-phase voltage demands are derived from v_{sd} and v_{sq} using the inverse of eqns. (6.14) - (6.17). These are then compared with a high frequency triangular wave carrier in a technique known as sine weighted PWM [6.8] in order to calculate the desired switching pulses for the inverter.

The major disadvantages of indirect control over direct control result from the need for precision control of the d and q axis currents, and accurate knowledge of the rotor time constant. This is because the flux vector angle, imposed by the controller, is derived directly from i_{sd}^{ref}, i_{mr}^{ref} and T_r on the assumption that these match the corresponding parameters in the machine itself. If this is not the case, then the torque and flux will not be controlled independently by i_{sq} and i_{sd} respectively.

In order that the controller may truly follow the position of the flux vector in the machine, the controller parameters L_r and R_r must accurately reflect those parameters in the machine itself, such that eqn. (6.6) is validly imposed on the motor by the controller. If the rotor resistance or rotor self inductance varies during operation of the drive, due to temperature, frequency or saturation effects, then the values of the control parameters L_r and R_r become "detuned" and the flux axis set by the controller becomes misaligned from the real flux axis in the motor, as illustrated by Fig. 6.3.

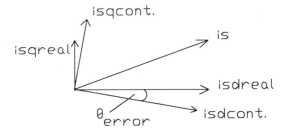

Fig. 6.3 Angular relationship of the current vectors when "detuning" occurs.

Changes in the rotor resistance during operation may be compounded by saturation or underfluxing effects caused by the resultant misalignment of the real and controller flux vectors. If a change in i_{sq} is imposed by the controller, then there will be an undesired significant change in the d axis current of the motor i.e. coupling effects. A reduction of the d axis current will result in underfluxing of the motor, and can result in a significant change in L_r itself (the motor will now be operating on a different part of its magnetisation curve). The effect of detuning on the torque and flux response in the induction motor has been described by Garces [6.9], Matsuo and Lipo [6.10], Sugimoto and Tamai [6.11] and Krishnan and Doran [6.12].

The net conclusion from these papers is that an on-line method for T_r identification is essential for correct implementation of an indirect vector controller, particularly for T_r deviation due to temperature and frequency effects, but preferably also to estimate changes in L_r during changes in flux levels such as field weakening.

An algorithm for T_r identification has been proposed by Garces [6.9] and is here termed "Reactive Power Measurement". The basis of this method is the comparison of demanded and measured reactive powers. He relates the discrepancy to a δT_r function and provides analogue computer simulations to justify the method. Krishnan [6.13] and Koyama [6.14] describe experimental implementations of this algorithm with some success, both in steady-state and transient T_r identification. The basis of this technique is the derivation of a function which gives the necessary information on the position and magnitude of the flux vector. The function (F_o) itself is derived from the reactive power expression [6.9] and can be calculated in two ways. The first method uses the demanded values for vsd and v_{sq} (assuming that these are correctly imposed on the motor) and measured values for i_{sd} and i_{sq} to calculate F_o as :-

$$F_o = v_{sd}i_{sq} - v_{sq}i_{sd} + \sigma L_s w_e(i_{sd}^2 + i_{sq}^2) \tag{6.20}$$

A corresponding function (F_o*) can be calculated from the controller reference values:-

$$F_o^* = -w_e(M^2/L_r)i_{sdref}^2$$

(6.21)

The calculation of the correction term for the controller value of rotor time constant, δT_r, is based on the error between F_o and F_o^* and provides a correction term for the value of T_r used by the slip frequency controller. The block diagram for this control scheme is illustrated in Fig. 6.4. This scheme operates in parallel with the speed control and will only work if the slip frequency and the stator frequency are not zero. It will identify changes in rotor resistance, but does not consider changes due to under-fluxing or over-fluxing.

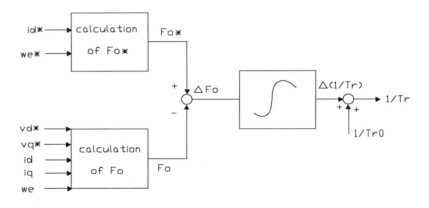

Fig. 6.4 Rotor time constant identification using reactive power measurements

This method requires background computational ability from the controller to carry out the T_r update. The main advantage of this strategy, however, is that no extra sensory devices are required. Assuming that the motor voltage and current references are correctly imposed on the machines, then the controller reference signal can be used for identification. It is assumed that a fast PI current controller can overcome the effects of changes in the stator parameters due to temperature.

6.4　THE PARALLEL STRUCTURE OF MOTOR CONTROL

A general motor drive tasking schemat is shown in Fig. 6.5. The low level consists of signal input, conditioning, control processing and actuator output for the power converter. This level corresponds to the conventional "interrupt" processing that must be serviced for the drive function. For example, in dc drives this equates to speed, armature current and field current measurement, speed and current control, and then the production of the firing pulses for use with a three-phase bridge converter. A switched reluctance drive requires speed and current measurement, control calculation and then suitable energisation of the required phases. In a basic slip controlled induction motor drive, speed measurement is again required, calculation of the slip frequency and voltage amplitude is then performed, and finally production of the transistor base drives for a PWM inverter.

The next level covers the drive's intelligence, supervision and memory. Intelligence is used to describe on-going background calculations, the principal examples being parameter estimation procedures for a partly or wholly undefined drive system. The supervision function covers the assessment of drive performance, and arbitration with respect to faults and perhaps various drive control modes such as self commissioning and piecewise control. System memory is the drive's data logger, providing the information as to performance and system status upon a drive fault. User input/output is shown at the highest level. For a development rig, this is normally of the form of a local keyboard/terminal for on-line commands, parameter modification, data display and software development. For commercial drives, it is more likely to take the form of a user control panel or a remote communication link either to a modem or programmable controller.

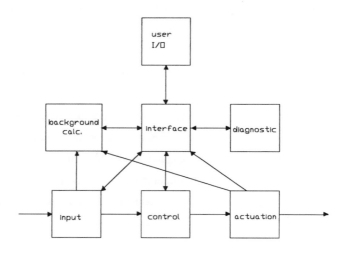

Fig. 6.5 Tasking schemat for motor control

The development of vector control for induction motors has utilised parallel processing techniques which use networks comprised of conventional sequential processors. Gabriel [6.7] describes a multiprocessor "direct" vector controller for a current controlled, voltage source inverter which uses two Intel 8085 microprocessors. One performs the speed, torque and flux control algorithms and input/output routines. The second performs the flux detection (using sensing coils mounted within the machine) and current control with coordinate transformations. Harashima [6.15] describes the implementation of two "indirect" control structures based on three microprocessors :- two i-8031 chips are assigned to the 3-2 and 2-3 phase transformations and an i-8086 performs vector and speed control. For both of these structures, the signal actuation for the power converter are not derived from the microprocessors. Kubo [6.8] describes "indirect" vector control using four 16 bit 8086 microprocessors for speed control and slip frequency calculation, current control and vector calculation, current component and speed detection, and PWM waveform generation.

These implementations have proved the effectiveness of applying parallel processing architectures to vector control of induction motors. It is obvious that the major consideration when applying parallel processing techniques to a control algorithm is the breakdown of that algorithm into subroutines which can run concurrently. It is also apparent that the actual processor time for each of these processes will differ, resulting in some redundancy of the individual processors. It is therefore necessary to strike a balance between the reduction of this process redundancy, and obtaining a low process time per sample of information. A further consideration in this respect arises from the amount of inter-process communication required by the algorithm, as experience has shown that this is the principal factor in determining processor performance (see Chapter 10).

The parallel implementation of the vector control scheme is derived from the tasking philosophy of Fig. 6.5. The philosophy rests on the assumption that, since transputer inter-process communication time can be significantly longer than arithmetic operation times, mathematical operations such as background calculations, control processing and coordinate transforms should not be parallelised. The parallel operation acts on the strategic functions within the overall controller, all of which operate on data pertaining to each sample instant. It can be seen that, to some extent, this results in a "pipelining" of sample data through successive strategic processes, the most obvious of which is the delay between measurement and control calculation on T2, and the calculation and output of the pulsewidths on T3. These delays, however, can be accounted for by the z-transform delay operator.

It is apparent that, within the low level of the tasking schematic, the processes employed (ie. on T2 and T3) are sequential: there are no parallel constructs within these processes. All procedures within a process are timed to execute within the system sample time, (in this instance derived from T3 and communicated to other processors via the communication protocol) otherwise loss of synchronization would occur. The only communication which is not synchronized is that between the host and the interface transputer.

6.5   TRANSPUTER IMPLEMENTATION OF VECTOR CONTROL

The three processors employed for this project were Inmos T800 transputers [6.16], mounted upon a B008 motherboard. This was resident in an expansion slot of an IBM PC clone. Rotor angle was measured using a custom-built interface board, which placed the absolute encoder value onto an Inmos C011 Link Adaptor [6.16] when required. Line currents were measured using another interface design which multiplexed the signals through an A/D converter, and then placed the measured value onto another link adaptor. The details of the cage induction motor used are contained in the Appendix.

The breakdown of the vector control algorithm into parallel processes running on the individual transputers (T1 - T3) is illustrated in Fig. 6.6. The overriding consideration is that the communication time, t_s, must be equal to the sample time corresponding to the fastest, closed-loop dynamics of the drive itself. The fastest drive dynamics invariably relate to the motor drive's current or torque feedback loops, which for power drives is generally not less than 2ms. It was found that the calculation routine for the PWM signal generation required a significant process time. This was thus solely assigned to a T800 processor (T3) and dictated the system sample time t_s (ie. acted as synchronisation master). For this project t_s was chosen to be 500μs, primarily as 2kHz was the maximum switching frequency of the power converter used. The minimum on- and off-times of the switching transistors was 50μs, resulting in a significant distortion of the resultant PWM waveform if a switching period of greater than 500μs is used. It was then found that the signal acquisition, speed control, vector control calculations and current control could be implemented on a single T800 transputer (T2) running in parallel. The control calculations would be initiated by communication with T3 and would be completed before the next communication with T3 to ensure synchronisation of the processes.

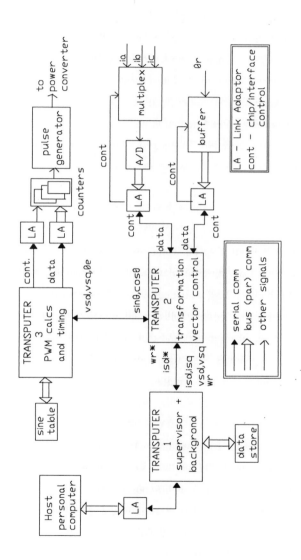

Fig. 6.6 Transputer implementation of the vector control strategy

The supervisory routine for the drive was implemented on the master T800 (T1) of the B008 board so that the 2Mbyte memory array could be used for data capture. During operation, T1 oversees diagnostic storage and user interface, the parallelism allowing transient performance data to be passed to the host for display whilst reference and control parameters can be input by the user and passed to the control transputer during drive operation. T1 also provides the capability for the background calculations demanded by T_r identification. Connected directly to T1 is the host machine which provides user interaction and access to the hard disk for permanent data storage, graphics and plot utilities. The concurrent software strategy for the controller is illustrated by Fig. 6.7 where the process times (in μs) are indicated by the figures in brackets.

The transputer T2 handles speed, rotor angle and line current acquisition, speed control, i_{sd}, i_{sq} control, flux angle calculation, and stator dynamic voltage compensation. Speed is calculated every 2ms, whilst currents and rotor position are sampled at 500μs intervals. Sine and cosine lookup tables are employed to transform the currents to the field orientated frame of reference, and then two independent PI controllers calculate the reference v_{sd}, v_{sq} values. The rotor flux reference is also calculated and these values are communicated to the actuation transputer T3.

T3 employs the transputer's high priority (1μs) timer using the PRI PAR statement, to create a sample time of 500μs. This sample time effectively simulates a 2kHz carrier wave which is used for asynchronous, asymmetrically sampled, PWM [6.17]. Pulsewidths are computed in real-time using sine and cosine lookup tables. The pulse times for the three phases are then downloaded via link adaptors to three 16-bit counters for PWM wave synthesis.

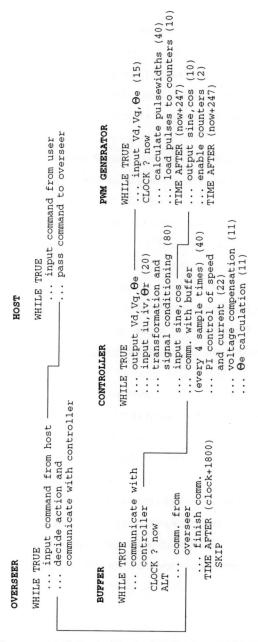

Fig. 6.7. Occam pseudo-code for the vector controlled drive

It can be seen that no independent timer is required for T2. Synchronisation is achieved by communication of v_{sd}, v_{sq}, and θ_e to T3. Only when this communication has been accepted can the process proceed. The creation of a 2ms sample time for speed calculation, and passing of data to the supervisor, is simply achieved by making these procedures skip seven out of eight samples.

The supervisory transputer T1 makes use of the ability of a single transputer to execute parallel processes on a time slicing basis. Two procedures are defined, one high and one low priority process. The high priority process (Buffer) provides synchronised communication with T2 whereas the low priority process (Overseer) interfaces between the buffer and the host, and provides background computational facilities. Buffer makes use of the occam ALT statement in conjunction with a "timeout" of 1.8ms in order to prevent the long interface and calculation process times from extending the sample time of the control system. If Overseer demands a communication from Buffer at a time when communication is expected from T2, Overseer is ignored until the communication from T2 has been received.

Overseer, in conjunction with a Turbo Pascal routine running on the host, provides the user interaction. Speed demands and changes to controller parameters are read by the host and passed to Overseer. These are passed via Buffer to the controller and then the subsequent measured data read from the controller is stored over a 2s period, and passed to the host for display and hard disk storage. The user can also initiate the T_r identification routine. This is performed by Overseer and dynamically changes the controller value of T_r over a 2s period. Again measured data is passed to the host on completion of this procedure. Two further procedures provided by the host and Overseer allow instantaneous measurements to be read, and a steady-state data capture facility.

6.6   EXPERIMENTAL RESULTS

The performance of the induction motor drive is illustrated by the speed transients shown in Figs. 6.8 - 6.10. Also shown are the measured field and torque components of the stator current through the transient. For these tests the field current demand was set at 1.8A (this corresponds to the no-load or magnetising current of the machine), and field weakening was not employed. The torque current limit was set to 5A, 10A and 15A respectively for Figs. 6.8 - 6.10, corresponding to one, two and three times the rated current of the machine. Torque and flux currents are controlled accurately, and the rate of acceleration for the system increases proportionally with the torque current limit. This is good evidence that the vector control strategy is working well.

The performance degradation due to "detuning" of the rotor time constant is illustrated in Fig. 6.11. In this instance the controller value of rotor time constant has been set to 75% of the actual motor time constant. The degradation in performance can be seen by the lower rate of acceleration, as compared to Fig. 6.9, and the increased curvature of the speed slope.

Fig. 6.12 illustrates the performance of the rotor time constant identification procedure. The controller value is initially 75% of the actual motor value, and it can be seen that the procedure hones in on the correct value within 1s.

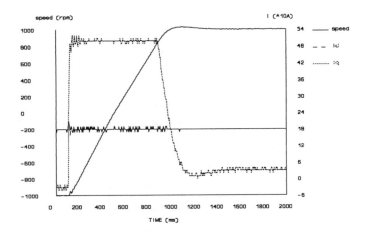

Fig. 6.8 Speed transient (torque current limit - 5A)

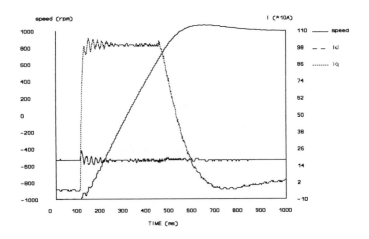

Fig. 6.9 Speed transient (torque current limit - 10A)

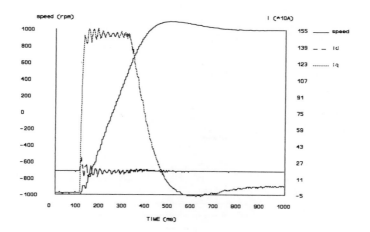

Fig. 6.10 Speed transient (torque speed limit - 15A)

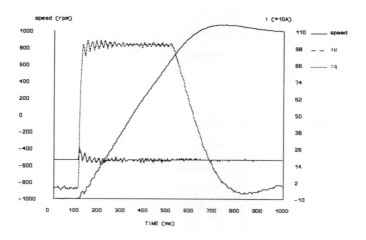

Fig. 6.11 Speed transient subject to "detuning" of rotor time constant

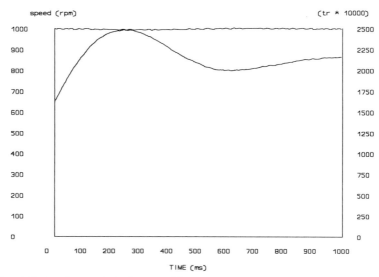

Fig. 6.12 Performance of rotor time constant identification procedure

6.7   DISCUSSION

Many forms of digital controller have been employed for vector control purposes, most of which appear to have correctly met their design specification. In order to assess this project it is worth considering the primary requirements of a research rig, as well as the project objectives.

The aim of the project was to develop an effective, vector controlled, induction motor drive using parallel processing techniques, and to evaluate/justify the need for a multiprocessor network. The drive performance was demonstrated by the speed transients shown. Furthermore, if a higher switching frequency had been used, it can be seen from the process times of Fig. 6.7 that the sample time could be easily reduced to 200μs. This would be sufficiently fast to control most servo-drives. The background computational ability for parameter estimation was demonstrated, and it is felt that the processor power of this system would be sufficient to implement dynamic estimation techniques, such as the Extended Kalman Filter [6.18], for parameter identification.

It can thus be seen that a parallel processing network will be superior to a single processor controller, as it reduces the sample period, allows a greater degree of processor power for the same sample period, and is thus capable of providing the user with more information for control and diagnostic purposes. The fact that most reported digital implementations of vector control have employed parallel processing to some degree reinforces this belief.

The true benefits of the parallel processing network and the transputer in particular are apparent when the nature of the drive is considered. For a research and development drive, the main requirements are for a system that is easily modified (both hardware and software) to meet multifarious specifications. The transputer network provides such a system by its very nature: both hardware and software construction is done on a modular basis, with each component part easily connected into the network.

On the hardware side, the serial link interconnection and the link adaptors provide a straightforward means of connecting processors and peripherals directly. The hardware structure itself is implicitly non-hierarchical, and a true grid modular structure results. Communication priorities and the parallel and hierarchical planning are designated by user-defined software and system configuration, using the transputer development system. It is worth emphasising that the occam high level programming language and the TDS are as instrumental in producing a flexible parallel-processing system as the transputer hardware itself. The processes for each transputer are edited and compiled separately, and a higher level editor is then invoked to assign a particular process and communication links to each transputer or peripheral in the network.

In comparison, the parallel bussed architectures used for multiprocessor systems using conventional sequential microprocessors provide quite a challenge to the circuit designer. For example, arbitration logic for establishing priority between sending and receiving processes must be implemented in hardware. This reduces the system flexibility with regard to system expansion. Any alleviation of hardware complexities results in a hierarchical system involving master/slave architectures. This reduces the options for task assignment. Software development for such systems is cumbersome, with the user generally being responsible for code to download the programs to the appropriate processors.

The flexibility of the transputer network has been demonstrated by the research work performed so far. The drive described is a typical, high performance, vector control drive but other forms of induction motor control have been implemented [6.19]. The first employs a scheme known as scalar control where slip frequency is controlled proportional to load, and voltage magnitude is controlled proportional to stator frequency. The second is a variation of the vector control scheme described, whereby no current feedback is used. The reference voltages for the PWM generator are derived simply from the steady-state voltage equations. It can be seen that both of these control algorithms require only minor modifications to the process running on T2, with the processes running on T1 and T3 remaining the same. A further form of indirect vector control termed "current controlled vector control" [6.6] was implemented by modifying the programs on T2 and T3. With this scheme, the actuation signals are derived from a comparison of the instantaneous measurements of line current with the reference values of line current at that instant. It is thus necessary to use T3 to measure directly the line currents, and use T2 to perform speed control, calculate reference currents and demodulate these to the stationary frame of reference.

The present subjects of research are the areas of self-commissioning, and on-line parameter identification. Both of these techniques are being performed on the vector control described and require modifications only to the host and overseer routines. These modifications are simply an increase of user options available. The software modifications have been trivial, allowing development time to be concentrated purely on algorithm development and testing.

6.8   CONCLUSIONS

It has been demonstrated that the functions of a generalised drive controller exhibit a natural parallelism, which must be exploited for high performance drive applications. It is certain that this aspect of drive control will become increasingly important as a single drive package becomes more capable of optimised performance over a wide range of user applications. The particular parallelism between supervisor and controller provides enhanced facilities for self commissioning, on-line parameter estimation and fault monitoring, with user interaction performed from a remote rather than local monitor.

The choice of microprocessor for such a network will undoubtedly be dependent on the drive application. At present the cost of transputers prohibits their use in low to medium power commercial drives. It is envisaged that a hardware specific parallelism involving conventional processors with a defined, restrictive specification is likely to remain the most economic option for some time. However they are the ideal basis for a research or development rig, whereby modularity and ease of modification are the main criteria. In this application they are particularly useful for evaluating algorithms over the whole spectrum of drive controller functions.

The authors also have experience in interfacing the transputer with a number of TMS320c25 DSP processors for real-time signal processing applications. This illustrates that parallel networks may be constructed on the basis of each processor being chosen specifically for its task, with parallelism and intercommunication simplified by a transputer overseer. Such a network, where say at the low level a DSP performs computationally intensive, modern control algorithms and an ASIC provides PWM generation, and at the higher level a transputer provides host interaction, supervision, low-level coordination, and possibly communication to another DSP providing background parameter estimation capability, may provide the future for commercial vector control drives for high performance applications.

APPENDIX

The parameters of the three phase, 50Hz, 415V, 5.5Hp, 1420rpm, squirrel-cage induction motor are :-

R_s 5.27 Ω R_r 3.1 Ω
L_s 0.64 H L_r 0.65 H
M   0.61 H
Moment of Inertia $0.121 kgm^2$ (coupled to dc generator)

REFERENCES

[6.1]   Lipo TA: Recent progress in the development of solid-state ac motor drives, *IEEE Trans Power Electronics*, **3**, April 1988, pp105-117.

[6.2]   Bose BK: *Power electronics and ac drives*, Prentice Hall, New Jersey, 1986.

[6.3]   Kume T and Iwakane T: High-performance vector-controlled ac motor drives: applications and new technologies, *IEEE Trans Ind Appl*, **IA-23**, September/October 1987, pp872-880.

[6.4]   Blaschke F: The principle of field orientation as applied to the new Transvektor closed-loop control system for rotating field machines, *Siemens Review*, 1972, pp217.

[6.5]   Leonhard W: *Control of electrical drives*, Springer Verlag, 1985.

[6.6]   Leonhard W: Field-orientation for controlling ac machines - principle and application, *IEE PEVD Conference*, London, July 1988, pp277-285.

[6.7]   Gabriel R, Leonhard W and Nordby CJ: Field-oriented control of a standard ac motor using microprocessors, *IEEE Trans Ind Appl*, **IA-16**, March/April 1980, pp186-192.

[6.8]   Kubo K, Watanabe M, Ohmae T and Kamiyama K: A fully digitalized speed regulator using multimicroprocessor system for induction motor drives, *IEEE Trans Ind Appl*, **IA-21**, July/August 1985, pp1001-1007.

[6.9]   Garces LJ: Parameter adaption for the speed-controlled static ac drive with a squirrel-cage induction motor, *IEEE Trans Ind Appl*, **IA-16**, March/April 1980, pp173-178.

[6.10] Matsuo T and Lipo TA: A rotor parameter identification scheme for vector-controlled induction motor drives, *IEEE Trans Ind Appl*, **IA-21**, May/June 1985, pp624-632.

[6.11] Sugimoto H and Tamai S: Secondary resistance identification of an induction-motor applied model reference adaptive system and its characteristics, *IEEE Trans Ind Appl*, **IA-23**, March/April 1987, pp296-303.

[6.12] Krishnan R and Doran FC: Study of parameter sensitivity in high performance inverter-fed induction motor drive systems, *IEEE Trans Ind Appl*, **IA-23**, July/August 1987, pp623-635.

[6.13] Krishnan R and Doran FC: A method of sensing line voltages for parameter adaption of inverter-fed induction motor servo drives, *IEEE Trans Ind Appl*, **IA-23**, July/August 1987, pp617-622.

[6.14] Koyama M, Yano M, Kamiyama I and Yano S: Microprocessor-based vector control system for induction motor drives with rotor time constant identification function, *IEEE Trans Ind Appl*, **IA-22**, May/June 1986, pp453-459.

[6.15] Harashima F, Kondo S, Ohnishi K, Kajita M and Susono M: Multimicro-processor-based control system for quick response induction motor drive, *IEEE Trans Ind Appl*, **IA-21**, May/June 1985, pp603-609.

[6.16] *The transputer reference manual*, INMOS Publication, INMOS Ltd, UK, 1989.

[6.17] Sumner M and Asher GM: PWM induction motor drive using the Inmos transputer parallel processor", *IEEE APEC 88 Conference,* New Orleans, pp121-129.

[6.18] Zai LV and Lipo TA: An extended Kalman filter approach to rotor time constant identification in PWM induction motor drives, *IEEE IAS,* 1987, pp177-183.

[6.19] Asher GM and Sumner M: Parallelism and the transputer for real-time control of ac induction motors, *IEE Proc* Pt D, **137,** 4, 1990.

Chapter 7

The Application of Parallel Processing Techniques to Eddy-Current NDT

S Hill and JO Gray

7.1   INTRODUCTION

In the present competitive engineering climate it is important that flawless materials can be produced with a high degree of quality assurance, particularly in an area such as the nuclear power industry where quality assurance is essential. To achieve this a number of techniques have been developed that allow flaws in the materials to be detected without testing the material to destruction. These non-destructive techniques (NDT) include the use of x-rays, ultrasound and electromagnetism to detect inhomogeneities within the sample. In this Chapter electromagnetic eddy-current NDT is used to detect inner and outer wall defects in tubular metal samples.

Extensive work on eddy current non-destructive testing of metal samples was first conducted by Forster [7.1]. The impedance of a test coil in the vicinity of a metallic object changes if inhomogeneities are present within the sample and Forster carried out a series of experiments to relate the response of eddy current NDT instruments to the shape, size and location of defects in the sample under test. This technique, known as phase analysis, uses a single frequency sinusoidal excitation signal and was later incorporated into a range of commercial instrumentation [7.2-7.4], where the output is presented as a polar oscilloscope display which an operator will attempt to interpret.

Experimental work has been carried out that will aid operators in the interpretation of these displays by the simulation of defects in samples [7.1,7.5-7.8].

More recently, increasing use is being made of different excitation methods, such as multi-frequency excitation [7.9,7.10] and pulse excitation [7.11,7.12], which provide the operator with more information due to the multi-frequency nature of the signals. However it is difficult for the operator to interpret this additional information at production line speeds using current instrumentation.

Ideally, what is required is a fully automated inspection system that indicates not only the presence of a surface flaw or inner wall defect in a metal sample but also the position, depth and type of flaw that exists. Such information should be immediately available to the operator so that he can use his judgement to accept or reject the sample under test. This Chapter is concerned with the development of such an automated procedure which employs digital signal processing techniques. It is based on an algorithm which is amenable to parallel decomposition and the use of concurrent computing procedures.

A lumped parameter system model of the eddy current test phenomena is first derived. This results in a state space discretised representation of electromagnetic behaviour of the test coil and sample system. Such a representation has system elements, consisting of resistors and inductances, which relate to the current distribution at discrete levels within the wall of the metal sample. It is hypothesised that surface and inner wall defects can be represented by changes in the resistance values of the individual resistor elements and that the resulting changing state relates directly to the position of such defects within the sample. Given that the defect detection and identification problem can be reduced to a state estimation procedure, a Multiple Model Estimation Algorithm (MMEA), based on Kalman filters, appears to be a natural choice for the identification of such faults. The algorithm is outlined here and its implementation, utilising a set of transputers, is described. The performance of the system is evaluated and experimental results presented which are obtained from a practical instrument using a set of tubular metal samples with no physical defects.

7.2   SYSTEM MODELLING

In this Section the lumped parameter model [7.13,7.14] is used to describe the circular test coil and sample arrangement generally found in commercial eddy current NDT test instrumentation. This is also the coil arrangement that has been employed in this particular implementation. From this model the hypothesis models required to classify faults in the layers of the sample will be derived, each model being implemented on a separate transputer as part of the MMEA.

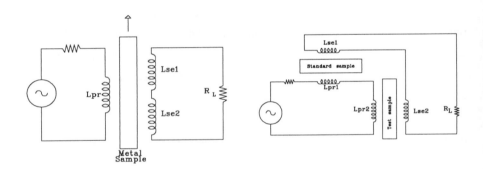

Fig. 7.1a Physical arrangement of coil systems   **Fig. 7.1b Equivalent coil circuit for test procedure**

The inspection coil consists of an inner primary coil and two similar, differentially wound, outer secondary coils all in close proximity to give an overall length of the order of a few millimetres around the tubular metal sample. The physical circuit for this arrangement is shown in Fig. 7.1a, with its Felici bridge representation in Fig. 7.1b. The energisation of the primary coil by a pulse waveform generates eddy currents in the metal sample which influences the coupling between the primary and the secondary coils. Suppose the metal sample has no defect in the vicinity of the coils. As it is passed through the coil system then this coupling will be the same for both secondary coils resulting in a net current flow of zero in the secondary coil circuit. However any defect present in the metal sample which affects the eddy current distribution, and hence the coupling between the primary and secondary coils, will cause a transient voltage in the secondary circuit when it passes under each secondary coil.

7.2.1   Coil and Sample Modelling

In the modelling process the metal sample is assumed to be decomposed into a set of concentric tubular elements, with an equivalent circuit representation as shown in Fig. 7.2. The complete equivalent circuit, Fig. 7.1(b), including the primary energising coil, the two areas of the metal sample being compared and the two secondary coils takes the form shown in Fig. 7.3. The following vectors and matrices may be assembled to represent the properties of the metal sample and primary coil system [7.13,7.14]:-

$$\mathbf{Q}_p = [\ m_{pr_1},\ \ldots\ ,\ m_{pr_n}\ ]^T, \tag{7.1}$$

$$\mathbf{x}_p = [\ i_1,\ \ldots\ ,\ i_n\ ]^T, \tag{7.2}$$

$$\mathbf{R}_p = \begin{bmatrix} R_1 & . & 0 \\ . & . & . \\ 0 & . & R_n \end{bmatrix}, \text{ and} \tag{7.3}$$

$$\mathbf{M}_p = \begin{bmatrix} L_1 & .\ . & M_{1n} \\ . & .\ . & . \\ . & .\ . & . \\ M_{n1} & .\ . & L_n \end{bmatrix}. \tag{7.4}$$

Here $\mathbf{Q}_p$ is an n-vector of mutual inductances of the coil and sample elements, $\mathbf{x}_p$ is an n-vector of currents induced in the sample elements, $\mathbf{R}_p$ is an nxn diagonal matrix of equivalent resistances and $\mathbf{M}_p$ is an nxn matrix of self and mutual

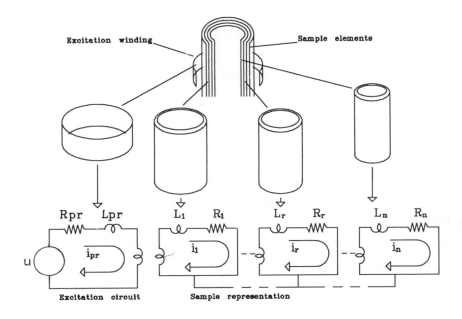

Fig. 7.2 Lumped parameter circuit of impedance loading effect due to distributed eddy currents in a cylindrical metal sample

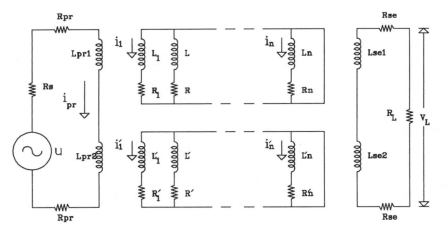

Fig. 7.3 Lumped parameter circuit of the eddy current test instrument

inductances of the sample elements. If Kirchhoff's laws are applied to the circuit of Fig. 7.2 the following equations are obtained.

$$(R_{pr} + sL_{pr})i_{pr}(s) + sQ_{p}^{T}x_{p}(s) = u(s)$$

(7.5)

$$(R_{p} + sM_{p})x_{p}(s) + sQ_{p}i_{pr}(s) = 0$$

For the purposes of modelling the complete coil and sample system, illustrated in Fig. 7.3, two sets of n-vectors x_a, x_b, Q_a, Q_b and nxn matrices R_a, R_b, M_a, M_b are defined representing the two areas of the tubular metal sample under each of the secondary coils with the elements of these vectors and matrices being the same as eqs. (7.1-7.4) above. Further n-vectors d_a and d_b are defined to represent the inductive coupling between the sample areas and the secondary windings:

$$\mathbf{d}_a = [M_{sa_1} , \ ..... \ , M_{sa_n}]^{T}$$

(7.6)

$$\mathbf{d}_b = [M_{sb_1} , \ ..... \ , M_{sb_n}]^{T}$$

where subscript n of m_{sa} is the mutual inductance of the nth element of one part of the metal sample and subscript n of m_{sa} is the mutual inductance of the nth element of the other part of the metal sample under test. Note that the secondary windings are arranged to cancel out the direct inductive coupling between the primary and secondary windings.

The following (2n+2)x(2n+2) matrices may now be assembled to represent the equivalent loop circuit shown in Fig. 7.3 :

$$R = \begin{bmatrix} r_p & 0 & | & 0 & | & 0 \\ 0 & r_s & | & 0 & | & 0 \\ - & - & & - & & - \\ 0 & 0 & | & R_a & | & 0 \\ - & - & & - & & - \\ 0 & 0 & | & 0 & | & R_b \end{bmatrix} \tag{7.7}$$

$$M = \begin{bmatrix} l_p & 0 & | & Q_a^T & | & Q_b^T \\ 0 & l_s & | & d_a^T & | & d_b^T \\ - & - & & - & & - \\ Q_a & d_a & | & M_a & | & 0 \\ - & - & & - & & - \\ Q_b & -d_b & | & 0 & | & M_b \end{bmatrix} \tag{7.8}$$

where R is a diagonal matrix of resistances and M is a symmetric matrix of self and mutual inductances. Also r_p, r_s, l_p and l_s are the total resistances and inductances in the primary and secondary circuits. As before, Kirchhoff's laws may be applied to give:

$$(R + sM)x(s) = bu(s) \tag{7.9}$$

where $x(s)$ is a $(2n+2)$ vector of currents given by:

$$x = [i_p , i_s , x_a^T , x_b^T]^T \tag{7.10}$$

and where b is a $(2n+2)$ vector given by:

$$b = [1 , 0 , ... , 0]^T \tag{7.11}$$

Eq. (7.9) may be expressed in space-state form:

$$\dot{x} = -(M^{-1}R)x + (M^{-1}b)u \tag{7.12}$$

where **u** is the input signal and **ẋ** denotes the time derivative of the vector **x**. The associated measurement equation is as follows:

$$z = c^T x \qquad (7.13)$$

where

$$c^T = [\ 0 \ , \ R_L \ , \ 0 \ , \ 0 \ , \ ..... \ ,0 \ ] \qquad (7.14)$$

The matrix differential, eq. (7.12), can be converted to discretised form and represented by a matrix difference equation of standard form :

$$x_{k+1} = F x_k + G u_k \qquad (7.15)$$

and the measurement equation can be written as :

$$z_k = c^T x_k \qquad (7.16)$$

Eqs. (7.15 and 7.16) form the mathematical model for the system shown in Fig. 7.3. Using this model, a metal sample which may contain, say, q different types of defect will have q+1 models set up a priori, each with different matrix and vector parameters **F** and **G**. Thus (q+1) models are always required, as the defect free model has to be present in addition to the q models representing defects.

7.3   ESTIMATION ALGORITHM

In the above lumped parameter model, any deviation in the nominal resistance of one of the circuits represented in Fig. 7.3 will correspond to a defect in one of the tubular elements of the metal sample. The state space representation of the configuration detailed above allows a state estimation procedure to be used to examine the values of the system states.

The MMEA is an algorithm which uses a set of predefined systems and can identify which of these systems matches the input data stream to the algorithm. Hence, the algorithm will have one predefined system for each element of the metal sample in the above model, plus one additional system which corresponds to a defect free sample. Each of these predefined systems basically consists of a Kalman filter and forms one unit of the MMEA. These units are combined with a probability update mechanism which will update the probability of a given system being the correct one by using the prediction error obtained in the Kalman filter.

7.3.1   Kalman Filtering Algorithm

A Kalman filter [7.15] may be applied to noisy measurements to estimate the state or unknown parameters of a dynamical system. A discrete time process that is corrupted by noise can be represented by :

$$\mathbf{x}_k = \mathbf{F}\mathbf{x}_{k-1} + \mathbf{G}\mathbf{u}_{k-1} + \mathbf{\Gamma}\mathbf{w}_{k-1} \tag{7.17}$$

where $\mathbf{w}_k$ is a Gaussian white noise sequence. The measurement model can also be expressed in a similar form :

$$z_k = \mathbf{c}^T\mathbf{x}_k + v_k \tag{7.18}$$

where v_k is an independent Gaussian white noise sequence. The disturbances in the system have the following statistics:

$$E\{w_i\} = 0 , \quad E\{v_i\} = 0$$
$$E\{w_i w_j\} = \mathbf{Q}\delta_{ij} , \quad E\{v_{ij}\} = \mathbf{R}\delta_{ij} , \quad E\{w_i v_j\} = 0 \tag{7.19}$$

The following equations are used in the Kalman filter algorithm to estimate the state of the system at each iteration:

$$\hat{x}_{k/k-1} = F\hat{x}_{k-1/k-1} + Gu_{k-1} \tag{7.20}$$

$$P_{k/k-1} = FP_{k-1/k-1}F^T + GQG^T \tag{7.21}$$

$$K_k = P_{k/k-1}c(c^TP_{k/k-1}c + R)^{-1} \tag{7.22}$$

$$\bar{z}_k = z_k - c^T\hat{x}_{k/k-1} \tag{7.23}$$

$$\hat{x}_{k/k} = \hat{x}_{k/k-1} + K_k\bar{z}_k \tag{7.24}$$

$$P_{k/k} = P_{k/k-1} - K_kc^TP_{k/k-1} \tag{7.25}$$

where K_k is the Kalman filter gain at the time instant k and $\hat{x}_{k/k}$ is the estimate of the state at the same time instant, utilising the measurements up to that time instant. Similarly, $\hat{x}_{k/k-1}$ gives a prediction for the state at time instant k based on measurements up to time instant k-1. $P_{k/k}$ and $P_{k/k-1}$ are the corresponding error covariance matrices. In order to initialise the algorithm, $\hat{x}_{0/0}$ and $P_{0/0}$ must be preset with relevant information.

Now to estimate the state of a system using the Kalman filter, K_k and $\hat{x}_{k/k-1}$ are required at each time instant. Obviously $\hat{x}_{k/k-1}$ can be obtained from eq. (7.20) quite easily with little computation, but the calculation of K_k involves a much greater computational overhead; $P_{k/k-1}$ must be formed, which can be a lengthy procedure, and $P_{k/k}$ must be updated for each iteration of the filter. Hence, in the computational realisation of the Kalman filter, K_k will be the time limiting factor. In the current implementation of the filter, the time invariant process is assumed to be Gauss-Markov with stationary noises, and the steady-state values of Kalman gains are used for all iterations [7.16]. Hence, for the practical application of this filter, the steady-state Kalman gains and the sequence of prediction error variances are determined for all the possible systems in the predefined set, prior to real-time operation. These are subsequently used in the real-time eddy current testing.

7.3.2   Probability updates

The following equation describes the mechanism by which the Kalman filter algorithm updates the hypothesis probabilities in the system [7.17] :

$$Pr_{hi/Z_k} = \frac{C}{\sqrt{\Omega_{k/hi}}} \exp\{\frac{-\overline{z}^2_{k/hi}}{2\Omega_{k/hi}}\}Pr_{hi/Z_{k-1}} \qquad (7.26)$$

where Z_k and Z_{k-1} are the set of measurements up to the time instants k and k-1, C is a factor which normalises the probabilities to unity, Pr_{hi/Z_k} is the probability of the ith hypothesis given Z_k and $\Omega_{k/hi}$ is the variance of the innovation sequence associated with the ith Kalman filter at the kth sampling instant which is given by the following equation:

$$\Omega_k = c^T P_{k/k-1} c + R \qquad (7.27)$$

Simulation has shown that the square root term in eq. (7.26) has an insignificant effect on the convergence of the MMEA. It has therefore been removed from all the calculations used in this system in order to reduce time overheads.

7.4   THE HARDWARE IMPLEMENTATION

The basic parallel nature of processing on the Inmos transputer makes it ideal for the implementation of an algorithm such as the MMEA. Fig. 7.4 shows the structure of the MMEA. Clearly, to obtain maximum computational speed, each of the Kalman filters would be implemented on its own processor. In the current implementation of the eddy-current tester there are three possible models, an inner surface defect in the tubing, an outer surface defect or the defect free model. The current instrument therefore uses three transputers to implement these models.

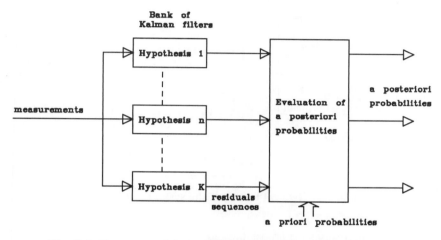

Fig. 7.4 Structure of the multiple model estimation algorithm

An overall diagram of the complete eddy current fault detection system is shown in Fig. 7.5 and a photograph of the original T414 implementation connected to a commercial eddy current test unit is shown in Plate 7.1. The instrument's hardware may be decomposed into three broad sections: the coil system and pulse generation and amplification circuits, the data acquisition unit, and the transputer network. In order to energise the metal sample, a pulse of 72μs duration is generated (P) and amplified (A_1) to approximately 15V in amplitude. This pulse is then applied to the primary of the coil system, producing the magnetic field which induces eddy currents in the metal sample. The resulting pulse generated in the pair of secondary coils is fed through a balancing unit (R_{se1}, R_{se2}) that will allow the operator to compensate for any matching imperfections in the secondary windings. The compensated output pulse then goes through multiple stages of amplification (A_2) to bring the pulse amplitude up to a level which effectively covers the dynamic range of the analogue-to-digital converter in the data acquisition unit.

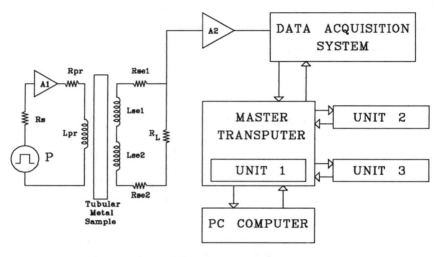

Fig. 7.5 General layout of the system hardware

The data acquisition unit consists of a 12-bit analogue-to-digital converter which has an 8µs sampling interval. This unit has an independent Z80 processor which can be instructed, from a transputer via a link adaptor device, to acquire a number of samples when it is triggered by the pulse input. This process does not require continuous monitoring by the transputer and hence does not consume precious computational time in data acquisition. This system also allows for overlapping data capture to be implemented so that the MMEA is never waiting for data input.When the acquisition of data samples is complete, they are sent in a burst via the link adaptor to the transputer network where the data is subsequently processed.

In its latest form, the transputer network now consists of three T800 transputer TRAM modules (Plate 7.2) on a motherboard (Plate 7.3) hosted on an IBM PC. The original implementation of this instrument was performed using four T414 transputers on a dedicated board system. For completeness, comparisons between the performances of these two transputer types will be made later in this Chapter. In the T800 system, each hypothesis of the MMEA is compiled into a separate unit and one unit is run on each transputer. The root transputer acts as the master transputer and, hence, also has the additional tasks of collecting the input data, screen handling and updating the probability of each hypothesis for 10 iterations of the MMEA, by which time the MMEA has usually converged and will send an appropriate message to the host PC which may be displayed to the operator.

7.5   COMPUTATIONAL REQUIREMENTS

Since the Kalman gain sequence $\{K_k\}$ and the variance sequence $\{\Omega_k\}$ are calculated prior to the real-time operation of the instrument the computation involved in each unit of the MMEA reduces to the following equations:

$$\hat{x}_{k/k-1} = F\hat{x}_{k-1/k-1} + Gu_{k-1} \tag{7.28}$$

$$\bar{z} = z_k - c^T\hat{x}_{k/k-1} \tag{7.29}$$

$$\hat{x}_{k/k} = \hat{x}_{k/k-1} + K_k\bar{z}_k \tag{7.30}$$

$$Pr_{hi/Z_k} = \exp\{\frac{-\bar{z}^2_{k/hi}}{2\Omega_{k/hi}}\}Pr_{hi/Z_{k-1}} \tag{7.31}$$

Here F is an $m \times m$ transition matrix and G, K_k and c^T are vectors with m components (where m = 2n+2, which is the order of the system). Computing the above equations will perform one iteration of one unit of the MMEA. It is possible to gain an additional saving in computation time by storing the variance sequence $\{\Omega_k\}$ in the form $1/2\Omega_k$, thus saving one division operation. For the current application m=6 since the tubular metallic sample is divided into only 2 elements (n=2) allowing the instrument to detect inner surface and outer surface defects only.

Operation	ADD/SUB	MUL	DIV	EXP
$F\hat{x}_{k-1/k-1}$	$m^2 - m$	m^2	0	0
Gu_{k-1}	0	m	0	0
$F\hat{x} + Gu$	m	0	0	0
Eq. (7.28)	m^2	$m^2 + m$	0	0
$c^T\hat{x}_{k/k-1}$	0	1	0	0
$z_k - c^T\hat{x}$	1	0	0	0
Eq. (7.29)	1	1	0	0
$K_k\bar{z}_k$	0	m	0	0
$\hat{x} + K_k\bar{z}$	m	0	0	0
Eq. (7.30)	m	m	0	0
$\bar{z}^2 / 2\Omega_k$	0	1	1	0
exp()	0	0	0	1
exp() x_{pr}	0	1	0	0
Eq. (7.31)	0	2	1	1
Total	$m^2 + m + 1$	$m^2 + 2m + 3$	1	1

Table 7.1 : Number of different operations for each equation
(n : number of element segments, m=2n+2 : order of the system)

The above equations are decomposed into their computational operations in Table 7.1. From Table 7.1 it can be seen that m^2+m+1 additions/subtractions, m^2+2m+3 multiplications, 1 division and 1 exponential function are required to complete the calculations for one iteration of the MMEA. In order to calculate the processing time required by the transputer to perform these calculations, it is necessary to know both the processor's clock speed and the number of processor cycles required to perform each of the required operations. In the case of the T414 and the T800 the clock speed was 20MHz. The number of clock cycles required for each arithmetic operation for each processor is given in Table 7.2. Using the figures from Tables 7.1 and 7.2 and the fact that a 20MHz T800 processor (clock period of 50ns) is being used, it is possible to calculate the computation time that will be required for each iteration of one MMEA unit. These calculations are shown in Table 7.3.

| operation | Number of clock cycles   (single length) | |
	T414	T800
ADD	230	7
SUB	230	7
MUL	200	11
DIV	246	17
EXP	6000 (typical)	900 (worst)

Table 7.2 : Performance table for T414 and T800

In addition to the processing time required on the arithmetic functions, there will also be a communications overhead. During one iteration of an MMEA unit, three 4 byte numbers are passed between the MMEA unit and the probability update mechanism. The transmission of a single 4 byte number requires 2.3μs of processor time on a 20MHz T800. Hence the total communication overhead for one iteration of an MMEA unit is 6.9μs. There will also be additional processor time required to execute occam instructions and perform some input processing, which is not taken into account in the straight arithmetic time period calculations. A factor of 10% of the total time taken for the calculations has been included in the final value obtained in Table 7.3. in order to take account of this additional time.

Operation	Time
ADD/SUB time	$(m^2+m+1)\times7\times50\times10^{-9} = 15.05\ \mu s$
MUL time	$(m^2+2m+3)\times11\times50\times10^{-9} = 28.05\ \mu s$
DIV time	$1\times17\times50\times10^{-9} = 0.85\ \mu s$
EXP time	$45\mu s$
COMM. time	$6.9\mu s$
Total	$95.85\mu s$
1.1 m Total	$105\mu s$

Table 7.3 : Total period of time for each unit and each iteration (T800)

A similar calculation for the execution of the MMEA on a T414 transputer running at the same clock speed gave a calculation time period of 1.47ms. Hence a factor of approximately 15 is gained in computation speed using the T800 processor.

7.6   RESULTS

The system was tested by passing a number of tubular metal samples through the coil system with known defects placed on the inner and outer surfaces. These defects consisted of circumferential grooves machined into the inner and outer surfaces of the metal samples that were approximately 5% of the wall thickness. Figs. 7.6-7.8 show the convergence histories of a selection of these defects.

It can be seen that, although the program allows 10 iterations of the MMEA for convergence, the system actually converges much quicker with the samples under test. However, it is probably desirable to maintain 10 iterations of the MMEA as a standard working number for defects that may present a less clear cut distinction between the available models.

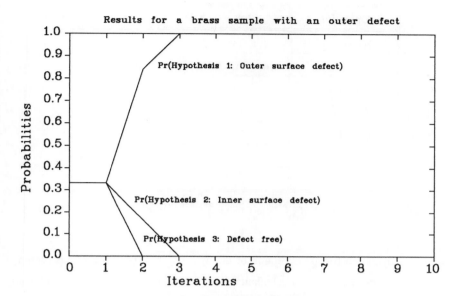

Fig. 7.6 Practical classification of defects in brass tubing

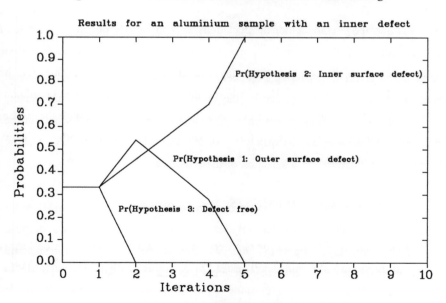

Fig. 7.7 Practical classification of defects in aluminium

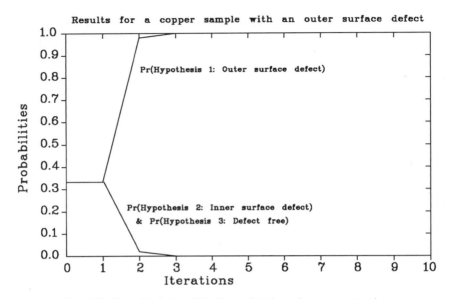

Fig. 7.8 Practical classification of defects in copper tubing

Based on the above computational calculations, it is possible to obtain an estimate of the performance of the system in a production line situation. Assuming that only one defect appears in the coil system at any one time, and allowing 1.05ms for the convergence of the MMEA (10 iterations), the maximum speed of a continuous sample through the coil system for fault detection would be 1.9m/s with the current secondary coil separations of 2mm. Such a performance is quite acceptable for many industrial test installations.

7.7   POSSIBLE IMPROVEMENTS

The computation time required for one iteration of an MMEA unit could be further improved by the use of 6 transputers instead of 3. In this configuration each MMEA unit would be processed on two transputers. The computational load would be divided such that one transputer processed eq. (7.31) (taking 50μs) whilst the other transputer performed the remaining calculations. Allowing for communication overheads, it should be possible to reduce the computational time required for one iteration of an MMEA unit to 60μs using this configuration. Innovative implementations of the Kalman filter algorithms, such as the implementation of Kalman filters on systolic arrays, [7.18] are now being explored in order to further reduce the computation time.

7.8   CONCLUSION

This Chapter has described the work performed in developing a practical instrument for eddy current non-destructive testing that would be suitable for real-time implementation. A model of the eddy current test phenomenon, based on an equivalent circuit representation, has been developed from earlier work. Extensive simulation studies had demonstrated the possibility of applying state-estimation procedures to a discretised form of this equivalent circuit model.

This model has been refined and implemented on a set of transputers to realise the estimation algorithm resulting in an instrument which demonstrates the essential features of on-line fault diagnostics at realistic throughput rates.

The present system only tests for two hypotheses, that of an outer surface defect and an inner surface defect on the tubular metal sample. With the addition of more processors it would be possible to also detect inner wall defects, although the system order would be increased which would affect the convergence time and hence the overall diagnostic speed of the instrument.

It should be noted that this system, like all similar systems using circular inspection coil arrangements, will have difficulty in detecting axial defects which do not present a significant change in their radial components over the length of the inspection coil.

The commercial development of this work will depend on the availability of inexpensive powerful processors which will support concurrent operations. The Inmos transputer is rapidly meeting these criteria as its price drops and processing speeds increase.

ACKNOWLEDGEMENTS

The authors wish to acknowledge the support provided by the SERC contract N2A 2K 0773 which allowed significant improvements to be implemented in the original experimental apparatus and the design parameter of a practical instrument to be defined.

REFERENCES

[7.1]   Forster F: Theoretische und Experimentelle Grundragin der Zerstorungsfreien Werkstoffprufung mit Wirbelstromverfahren, *Z Metallkunde*, **43**, pp 163-171, 1952.

[7.2]   Forster F: Nondestructive Inspection of Tubings for Discontinuities using Electromagnet Test Equipment, *Materials Evaluation*, **28**, 19A-23A, 26A-28A1, 1970.

[7.3]   Forster F: Sensitive Eddy Current Testing of Tubes for Defects on the Inner and Outer Surfaces, *Non Destructive Testing*, **10**, pp28-35, 1974.

[7.4]   Stumm W: Progress in Electromagnetic Tube Testing as an Economisation in Tube Production, *Ninth World Conference on Non Destructive Testing*, Melbourne, Australia, Session 4B, 1979.

[7.5]   McMaster RC: *Non-Destructive Testing Handbook*, New York: The Ronald Press Company Inc, 1963.

[7.6]   Hochschild R: Electromagnetic Methods of Testing Metals, *Progress in Non-Destructive Testing*, **1**, Standford EG and Fearen JH (Eds), pp59-109, 1961.

[7.7]   Aldeen A and Blitz J: Assessment of Oblique Cracks in Metal Tubes with Eddy Currents, *World Conference on Non-Destructive Testing*, Melbourne, Australia, Session 4B-1, 1979.

[7.8]   Blitz J and Rowse AA: The Investigation of Defects in Non-ferromagnetic Metal Tubes using Eddy Currents, *Applied Materials Research*, **3**, pp82-87, 1964.

[7.9]   Davis TJ: A Multifrequency Eddy Current System for the Inspection of Steam Generator Tubing, Non-Destructive Evaluation in the Nuclear Industry, *Proc International Conference*, Salt Lake City, Utah, 13-15 Feb 1978, Natesh R (Ed), American Society for Metals, Metal Parks, Ohio, pp421-436, 1978.

[7.10]   Larsson H: Multifrequency Eddy Current Testing of Case Hardened Cylinders - a Theoretical and Experimental Analysis, *Proc 1st European Conference on Non-Destructive Testing*, Mainz, Germany, pp24-26, 1978.

[7.11]   Morris RA: Quantitative Pulsed Eddy Current Analysis, *Proc 10th Symposium of Non-Destructive Evaluation*, San Antonio, Texas, 1975.

[7.12]   Wittig G: Application of Pulsed Eddy Current Methods in Non-Destructive Testing, *British Steel Corporation Tubes Division*, Translation no. TD1102. British Iron and Steel Industry Translation Service BISI 16234, (Translated from: *Materialprufung*, **19**, 9, pp365-370, 1977), 1977.

[7.13] Gorton P and Gray JO: The Classification of Defects in Electromagnetic Non Destructive Testing, *Proc 7th IFAC Symposium on Identification and System Parameter Estimations*, University of York, Pergamon Press, 1985.

[7.14] Bahramparvar MR and Gray JO: Application of Parallel Processing Techniques to Eddy Current Non Destructive Testing Instrumentation, *Proc IEE Pt D*, **137**, 4, 1990.

[7.15] Kalman RE: New Approach to Linear Filtering and Prediction Problems, *Trans ASME J Basic Eng*, **82**, pp34-45, 1960

[7.16] Candy JV: *Signal Processing the Model Based Approach*, McGraw-Hill, International Edition, 1986.

[7.17] Anderson BDO and Moore JB: *Optimal Filtering*, Prentice-Hall Inc, Englewood Cliffs, New Jersey, 1979.

[7.18] Gaston FMF and Irwin GW: Systolic Approach to Square Root Information Kalman Filtering, *Int J Control*, **50**, pp225, 1989.

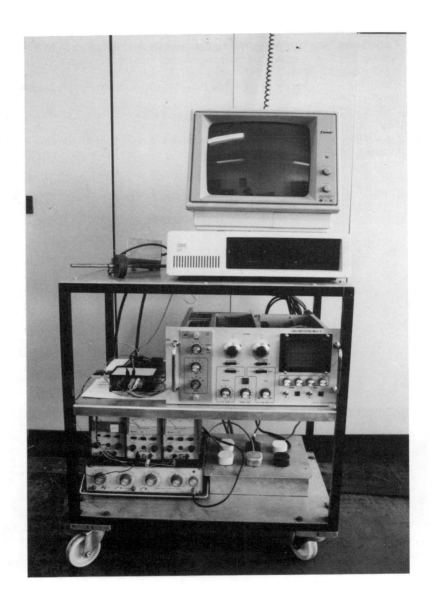

PLATE 1

PLATE 2

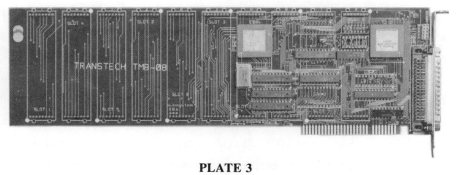

PLATE 3

Chapter 8

Hardware Fault-Tolerance: Possibilities and Limitations offered by Transputers

R Cuyvers and R Lauwereins

8.1   INTRODUCTION

Fault-tolerance techniques are applied in process control to guarantee human and environmental safety and/or to minimize production losses and equipment damage. In the past, fault-tolerant computers have only been used in a limited number of applications due to their high cost. Examples include the Space Shuttle, aircraft flight control systems and power system control. At present the areas of application are widening due to the increasing safety and production requirements, the constantly growing capabilities of integrated circuits, falling hardware prices and increasing digitisation.

Most fault-tolerant control systems are based on the redundancy provided by a second or third processor making a normal uniprocessor application fault-tolerant. However, due to the growing computation demands imposed by modern adaptive control algorithms, more and more interest is being shown in multiprocessor applications. On the one hand the increased number of components makes fault-tolerance even more stringent, while on the other it is possible to obtain an even more reliable system than with a conventional uniprocessor by efficiently utilizing the inherently available redundancy.

This Chapter studies the possibilities and limitations offered by transputers with respect to fault-tolerance. In particular, it will be shown that the availability of multiple communication links and a hardware scheduler makes the transputer an attractive processor for this kind of application. An introduction to fault-tolerance and a fault-study are given first. Subsequently, the possibilities and limitations of transputers are studied in making a single processor controller fault-tolerant, where different configurations are possible depending on the application. Finally, multiprocessor fault-tolerance will be considered with the emphasis put on a general purpose kernel which can be used for a wide range of applications.

8.2   FAULT-TOLERANCE : DEFINITIONS, PRINCIPLES AND FAULT-STUDY

The basic definitions and working principles used in fault-tolerant systems are summarized here. An extended description can be found in [8.1-8.4]. A fault-study is also given [8.4-8.6] since, to determine the effectiveness of fault-tolerance methods, it is very important to know which faults occur and what is their relative contribution to system failure. In this Chapter only hardware faults are considered.

8.2.1   Definitions

- Fault-Avoidance is any technique that is used to prevent faults.
- Fault-Tolerance (FT) is the ability of a system to perform a specified function even after the occurrence of a limited number of faults. It is used to improve reliability, safety and availability.
- Fault-Coverage is a measure of the effectiveness of fault-detection.
- Fault-Tolerance Degree is a measure that indicates which, and how many, faults can be tolerated without endangering safety or availability.
- Recovery Time specifies the time needed to restore correct operation.
- Fault-Tolerance Time is the time allowed for recovery. For process control, this has to be smaller than the time constant of the controlled process.

- Redundancy or Overhead is all the additional hardware, software, information, time and communication bandwidth which is not needed for normal operation, but which is necessary to make a system fault-tolerant. Redundancy is required both to detect and to correct faults.

8.2.2   Principles

A fault-tolerant system executes the following three steps to recover from a fault : fault-detection, fault-isolation (reconfiguration) and fault-correction (recovery). It is very important that a fault-tolerant system performs the above three steps within the fault-tolerance time. Notice that fault-detection is the corner-stone of a fault-tolerant system, as undetected faults will never be corrected. Fault-isolation is important to avoid a failed unit endangering the correct working of the remaining parts which have not failed.

8.2.3   Fault-Study

Two classes of hardware faults have to be distinguished. Short periods of faulty behaviour are referred to as transient faults. Due to the presence of memory elements however, they can cause permanent changes in the system. They cause 90% of all hardware failures [8.7]. Memories and communication paths are especially vulnerable to this kind of fault. A lot of trouble can be prevented by applying fault-avoidance techniques such as shielding and filtering which reduce the effects of electromagnetic interference, power problems, electrostatic discharge and radiation.

The second class of hardware faults contains the permanent faults which exhibit faulty behaviour until repaired. Power breakdowns occur most frequently and, therefore, an Uninterruptible Power Supply (UPS) is indispensable for critical applications. Experience shows that permanent component failures mostly appear at the beginning and the end of a device life so that burn-in and in-time replacement are recommended. Hardware design errors rarely appear due to modular design and extensive testing.

8.3   FAULT-TOLERANCE FOR UNIPROCESSOR APPLICATIONS

Many techniques exist to make a single processor application fault-tolerant. For each method, the possibilities and limitations offered by transputers are considered here. The methods are treated in a order of increasing hardware redundancy requirements.

8.3.1   Single Transputer Systems

The basic building blocks of a single transputer system are : the CPU, RAM, ROM and I/O-modules. Fault-detection and correction techniques for these components are now given in turn. Note that link-hardware is only needed for multiple-transputer architectures and therefore problems related to interconnection between processors will be discussed in Section 8.3.2.

A CPU can fail either transiently or permanently. To detect transient arithmetic errors, the internal error-logic of the transputer can be used but this only detects faults which cause overflow, divide by zero, array bound violation and floating point failures [8.8]. Higher fault-coverage is obtained by adding a timer process (watch-dog) in parallel with the user-application. All faults which obstruct normal program flow will fail to reset the timer in time, thus indicating an error-condition. The multi-tasking facilities offered by transputers, and the inherently available timers, make this very simple. To avoid false alarms due to scheduling delays however, sufficient margin has to be provided for the timeout. A better solution would be to put the timer process in the high priority queue but, even then, false alarms are possible if multiple processes are running in this priority, especially because no time-slicing is provided here. The ideal solution would be to have multiple priorities with the timer-process at the highest level. This can be achieved with real-time kernels such as, for example, Trans-RTXc [8.9]. To raise fault-coverage even further, time redundancy can be used : the program is executed twice and the results compared [8.10]. The transputer makes this method feasible for a wide range of applications thanks to its computational power. To detect permanent transputer faults, a processor self-test must be added. This test-program, running in parallel with the application and the above-mentioned timer process, will be triggered periodically. Its result will be compared with a value known in advance. A small program containing the most frequently used instructions will reveal most faults [8.11]. However, to detect all shortcomings, all functions and registers have to be tested exhaustively, which may cost a lot of time. It is clear that the test overhead also depends on the test-frequency. It may be intolerable when fault-tolerance time is small so that the test-frequency must be extremely high in order to detect faults in time. An exhaustive self-test is therefore seldomly used. To be practical, it should be integrated in the processor hardware, thereby improving fault-coverage without increasing testing overhead. However, a complete processor break-down will not be detected unless an external watch-dog is provided, which of course makes the internal timer process superfluous.

By adding extra redundant bits to the memory words, it is possible to detect both transient and permanent RAM faults, and possibly to correct them. A variety of coding techniques exist [8.1,8.3,8.12-8.13]. Many transputer vendors implement memory parity. A 7-bit Hamming code is realized on the MTM-EDC transputer board of Parsytec [8.14]. The latter configuration is especially interesting: it detects double bit errors and corrects single bit errors. To prohibit that a second error leads to an uncorrectable double error, faults have to be detected in time. Therefore, memory scrubbing is added : this ensures that also seldomly used words are tested and corrected in time. Overhead is minimized by integrating this facility into the memory controller hardware. The advantage of coding is its simplicity and efficiency but extra hardware is needed to do the coding/decoding and, of course, this hardware may fail as well, and should also be tested periodically. Besides, the coding/decoding also slows down the memory access time. For the Parsytec board for instance, one wait state has to be introduced for the read cycle and two for a byte-wise write operation. The latter is caused by the requirement that a full word, consisting of 4 bytes, is needed to generate the Hamming code, even if only one byte has to be written which necessitates a read-modify-write cycle. Only the 4 byte write cycle does not introduce an additional delay.

Because ROM faults are similar to RAM faults, the same fault-tolerance technique is applied but, thanks to the higher reliability of ROM storage, coding is often limited to a single checksum for the whole ROM [8.11]. Faults are detected by recomputing it periodically.

To extend the fault-tolerance boundary to the I/O-modules, additional measures are required. For example special read-back outputs have to be provided. Because these techniques are completely analogous to non-transputer systems, they are not covered in detail and a description can be found in [8.4].

Finally, it is possible to extend the fault-tolerance boundary into the controlled process itself by applying analytic redundancy where faults are detected by comparing the measured inputs with values that are computed by an analytic model of the process [8.15]. Defects in actuators, sensors etc. can then be detected without extra hardware. The only requirement is a good, robust model which matches real process behaviour. Of course sufficient computation power has to be available to evaluate the model in real-time, together with the normal processing.

The techniques listed above are simple and effective but fault-coverage is however not complete. It is therefore advisable to add Plausibility, Consistency and Evaluation Checks to the user software [8.3]. A Plausibility Check looks to see if the output is physically acceptable, Consistency Checking tests if the different outputs and inputs are consistent, while an Evaluation Check tests if the next value or state is possible with reference to the previous states. The most important limitation of these techniques is that faults not thought about are not covered.

A big disadvantage of a single transputer system is that no spare part is available to replace the failed processor. For high-safety systems, which may be stopped in case of a failure, this is not needed, at least when the fault-coverage provided by single transputer techniques is sufficient. It is however necessary to add an independent shut-down circuit to ensure that the system halts safely in case of an uncorrectable fault.

8.3.2   Dual Transputer Systems

When a back-up transputer is added, different configurations can be distinguished depending on their behaviour during normal, error-free processing. Cold, warm and hot back-up configurations use the second transputer as a spare part to take over control in case of an uncorrectable fault (high-availability), see later in Fig. 8.2. An active back-up configuration guarantees fast and almost perfect fault-coverage (high-safety), see later in Fig. 8.3. Before studying the different configurations in more detail, issues common to all kinds of back-ups are covered while a more general description is given in [8.4].

8.3.2.1   Generalities

All configurations require a high-speed communication link between the two processors. Thanks to the presence of four high-speed, serial links the transputer is very attractive for this kind of system. However, the inter-processor connection also introduces some problems.

The first problem is that data-transmission is susceptible to cross-talk and external noise, which may result in transient communication faults. Together with transient memory faults, they are the major cause of system failure as mentioned in the fault-study. Therefore fault-avoidance techniques should be used. The choice of the appropriate technique depends mainly on the length of the links [8.16]. A lot of trouble can be avoided by implementing the RS422 standard which uses differential line drivers/receivers. In harsh environments, however, optical fibres are preferable. To correct the remaining errors, fault-tolerance techniques have to be applied. Again coding is appropriate. To make efficient use of the communication bandwidth, only redundant bits for error-detection are added. Cyclic Redundancy Checks are especially interesting: with a limited number of redundant bits many errors can be detected, even if they occur in bursts [8.17]. Although this coding requires very little extra hardware, it is not provided on the transputer links and, since a software implementation costs too much processing power, another technique has to be looked for [8.18]. Sending the data twice and comparing afterwards is the best software alternative. Since this only provides error-detection, retransmission is then needed upon fault-detection. This is realized by returning the control message Data_Not_Correctly_Received to the sender, which triggers retransmission. This, of course, requires buffering of the data at the sender side until a Data_Correctly_Received message has been received. To maintain simplicity a second message is only transmitted as soon as the buffer becomes free, which implies that communication bandwidth is only efficiently utilized when acknowledges are generated fast. Software coding, therefore, not only requires a lot of computation power but also diminishes link bandwidth. However, the latter disadvantage is removed when a more complex, sliding window protocol is applied [8.19]. Another difficulty is that the control message itself can be corrupted. In this case, the data may also be retransmitted, which may result in the receiver accepting the same data twice. Such duplication can be intercepted by adding a sequence number to the message and by integrating a timeout in the protocol, it even becomes possible to recover messages which got lost. If an acknowledge is not received in time, a retransmission is triggered. The above algorithm belongs to the class of stop-and-wait protocols [8.19] and it in fact realizes the datalink layer (layer 2) of the OSI 7-layer model [8.19]. An efficient hardware implementation of such a protocol is offered by a Gate Array from Hema [8.20] which is designed for optical transputer interconnections.

A second problem is the avoidance of dead-lock due to a permanent or transient link fault. Because both transputers will run a uniprocessor application, this problem is limited to the system services which provide testing, checkpointing, synchronization and matching which will be explained further.

One final problem is that a link introduces an electrical coupling between the two transputers and fault-isolation is of vital importance, so that the failure of one transputer does not induce the failure of the second one. Optical fibres are therefore preferable. In fact this problem is not limited to link connections and all common circuitry, like for example clock and reset circuitry, has to be avoided while special attention has to be paid to power, grounding and links.

8.3.2.2   Cold back-up configuration

In a strict sense, cold back-up means that the spare transputer is not powered until it is needed for recovery, making it less sensitive to ageing. In a broader sense, the second transputer is powered but does not execute the critical program of the on-line transputer. Only upon fault-detection is it connected to the output and starts the back-up of the failed process. For fault-detection, single transputer techniques, like those discussed in Section 8.3.1, are used. External watch-dogs, however, are now no longer needed: correct working is verified by periodically sending the self-test results to the other transputer, as illustrated in Fig. 8.1. This even permits checking of self-test itself.

To reduce user-involvement, it is necessary to provide the self-test and neighbour-test described above as a system service, taking care that link or transputer failures do not result in deadlocks by starting a timer in parallel with the input or output command (Fig. 8.1). In occam, the OutputOrFail and InputOrFail routines can be used [8.16]. The problem with these, however, is that consistency is not guaranteed: one transputer may see a successful transmission while the other one sees a failed communication. The major difficulty is to avoid false timeouts due to (normal) process scheduling delays. A similar problem is met when implementing the internal watch-dog in single transputer system where, to avoid false alarms, all user processes had to be run in a lower priority than the testing service. A difference occurs when fast event processing is required due to the possibly long duration of the self-test where it must be possible to interrupt the testing so that the event can be serviced immediately. Of course, this processing must not take too long and it usually suffices to buffer events for subsequent processing so that this does not pose a real problem [8.21]. It is clear that multiple priorities are required to enable this interrupting.

```
PAR
   self-test :

      1.    execute test after period T
      2.    IF fault THEN set error flag and halt processor
      3.    start    time-out    and    output    test-results    to
            neighbour-test of the other node. Go to step 1 if
            either the communications succeeds in time or the
            time-out expires.

   neighbour-test

      1.    input test-results from self-test of other node. Go
            to next step if either the results arrive in time
            or the time-out expires.
      2.    IF either results are incorrect or time-out expired

            THEN stop neighbour-test and command switch-over if
            needed;
            ELSE go to step 1

   application processes
```

Fig. 8.1 Testing scheme in cold back-up configuration

High availability is achieved by using a cold back-up. Another advantage is that the back-up transputer can be used for non-critical tasks during normal error-free operation. When a fault occurs, however, priority has to be given to the "critical" process, with the non-critical tasks utilizing the remaining computer time. This graceful degradation requires a multiple priority scheduler, ideally assigning a priority to each process according to its importance. A disadvantage of cold back-up is that recovery is slow because the failed process is restarted from the beginning as there is no state information saved. This also implies that recovery is limited to applications where it is possible to recalculate the actual state. It is also clear that fault-coverage is limited to that of a single transputer system.

8.3.2.3 Warm back-up configuration

A warm back-up periodically receives the program state (checkpoint) of the controlling transputer. Upon fault-detection, the back-up restarts the computation beginning from the last received correct checkpoint. Hence recovery speed depends upon the frequency at which checkpoints are taken and, since saving the state costs time, a trade-off exists [8.22]. For cyclic programs it is obvious that the state must be saved periodically, at least when the cycle is not too long. Special measures have to be taken if some inputs and outputs appear only once in which case the back-up also has to track the I/O of the on-line unit [8.23].

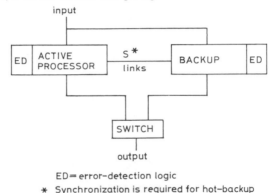

ED = error-detection logic

* Synchronization is required for hot-backup
  Matching is only needed when each unit has
  its own input module

Fig. 8.2 Basic dual transputer structure for cold, warm and hot back-up

A checkpoint exchange process has to be added to the system services already needed for cold back-up. This cannot be provided automatically, since the place of a checkpoint is application dependent. It is possible to limit user involvement by providing a service where the user only has to send a checkpoint-trigger, containing the start address and the length of the program state, to a higher priority checkpoint process. The state will then be sent to the back-up unit, taking into account link or processor failures and sharing of hardware channel(s) with the other services. As with cold back-up, optimum processing is achieved when multiple priorities are available.

Again high-availability is obtained and saving the state at particular points not only speeds up recovery, but also widens the application area. Graceful degradation is still possible. A disadvantage is that checkpointing not only increases overhead but also requires user-involvement. Again, fault-coverage is the same as in a single transputer system.

8.3.2.4   Hot back-up configuration

A hot back-up executes the control program in parallel with the on-line transputer (Fig. 8.2) and, when a fault is detected, switchover is accomplished. To reduce switchover bumps as much as possible, it is necessary to synchronize both transputers [8.4] otherwise both processors diverge due to small speed differences. A tight synchronization is however impossible since, even if both transputers use the same clock, they will not run in lock-step due to timing differences generated by their internal circuitry, as for example the PLL and DMA engines [8.24]. So only loose synchronization is possible. The advantage of this is that each transputer may have its own clock so that a common mode clock fault is avoided. The actual synchronization is mostly realized by software. Synchronization points, just like checkpoints, are inserted at particular places in the program. At these points, the two transputers wait for each other before continuing the program. A timeout has to be included to avoid obstruction by a single failure. Attempting to extend the fault-tolerance boundary, by providing each transputer with its own input-modules, poses another problem in that manufacturing, locality and sampling time differences may cause deviations in input values. To reduce bumping in case of a switchover, it is necessary that both units use the same input values. The action of producing a single, common value out of two received inputs is called matching [8.23,8.25]. The implementation differs from process to process and requires special software to be written by the application programmer.

Synchronization and matching services also have to be added to the system services. Both, however, are application dependent. The synchronization service is analogous to the checkpointing service where, after determining the synchronization points, the programmer only has to send a start-synchronization trigger and wait for an end-synchronization trigger from the synchronization process, which again runs in higher priority to minimize delay. In fact, the matching service is also similar. It realizes the input exchange between the two transputers. If a transputer is not responding in time, the matching program is informed and will take appropriate action. As already mentioned, the matching itself has to be realized in the user-software. Efficiency is maximized by integrating both these services. Synchronization is automatically obtained by waiting on the other input, which is only possible when matching is regularly executed.

At this point some remarks about occam have to be made. Because the ALT construct replaces the interrupt programming of conventional microprocessors, it has to be used with care, since, due to the indeterminacy of the ALT, divergence of identical programs is possible [8.8]. Therefore ALT's always have to be matched so that both transputers follow the same thread. It is advisable to prohibit the programmer to use the occam ALT and to replace it by a system service which provides a functionally identical, but matched ALT. This is, however, complex and time-consuming. To minimize scheduling delays it is also preferable to avoid the PAR construct in a uniprocessor application. This means that the efficient multi-tasking capability of the transputer is used solely to join easily the application program and the system services.

Again high availability is achieved and, thanks to the synchronization and matching services, a fast and smooth switchover is accomplished. However, graceful degradation is no longer possible. Another disadvantage is that fault-coverage is again limited to that of a single transputer system.

8.3.2.5   Active back-up configuration

Here again the two transputers execute the same program in parallel but this time the output of the back-up is used for comparison, making it completely active. Fast and thorough fault-detection is obtained and it is possible now to detect faults which cannot be detected in a single transputer system. To prohibit false alarms, due to program divergence, matching and (loose) synchronization are again required. This time the system is stopped when a message does not arrive in time. Loose synchronization has the additional advantage of reducing the probability of a common mode fault : because both units run asynchronously, it is less probable that a disturbance has the same effect in the two units (which would not be detected by the comparator). One disadvantage is that faults are only detected as soon as a result is calculated. This is in contrast with lock-step synchronization where immediate fault-detection is possible by comparing the system buses.

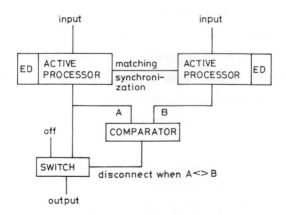

Fig. 8.3 Dual transputer system with active back-up

Besides synchronization and matching, a comparison service must also be provided now. Analogous to matching, synchronization can be integrated into the comparison.

The self-testing service remains useful since it detects faults in seldom   used parts and it makes fault-localization possible which can be used to increase availability [8.2]. Further, it allows for the detection of common mode errors which the comparator cannot detect.

In this case fast and thorough fault-detection is obtained and it is normally used to construct fail-stop systems. When the process can be stopped in a safe manner, this leads to a fail-safe controller. A drawback is that availability is lowered because the system is stopped as soon as one of the two units fails. However, by providing the above-mentioned self-testing services, availability can be improved because it becomes possible (in most cases) to determine the failed unit.

8.3.3   Triple Transputer System

Here again a lot of configurations are possible. This Chapter only discusses the one with two active back-ups because of its importance for hard, real-time systems. More generally this method is called Triple Modular Redundancy (TMR). Three transputers execute the same program in parallel and a 2-out-of-3 voting system is applied to determine the correct output. In this way faults are masked, leading to instantaneous and bumpless fault-correction. These two properties make TMR the appropriate method for hard, real-time systems which require both high availability and high safety.

Voting is very analogous to comparison but there are several important differences. The first difference is the timeout handling: the timer needed to avoid deadlocking due to faults has to be started as soon as two values are available. This is necessary to prevent a single faulty result coming too early and causing a premature expiry of the timeout. This would block fault-masking because it triggers voting at an instant where no, or a single, correct result is available [8.26]. A second difference lies in the network topology as there are different ways to interconnect the three transputers. A pipeline would require message passing through an intermediate node. This not only introduces an extra communication delay, slowing down synchronization and voting, but it also requires authentication techniques. The latter are needed to detect when an intermediate, failing node sends an incorrect message twice, which may cause incorrect voting. Such a failing node could also obstruct voting by absorbing messages. However, a transputer contains four links, so that direct communication paths between the different processors can be provided thus avoiding the above-mentioned problems. The final difference is that the matching module is more complicated in order to deal with Byzantine faults. Suppose, for example, that the matching consists of calculating the mean value of physically acceptable inputs. It is possible then that a failing module sends a different (physically acceptable) value to the correct transputers. Another possibility is that only one processor receives a value of the failing unit in time. A special "Byzantine agreement" protocol has to be applied, to assure that the correct transputers produce the same matched value which is required to reach agreement in the subsequent voting [8.25,8.27-8.29]. An additional round of message exchange is therefore needed, where the value a transputer receives from one transputer has to be sent to the other. This extra information makes it possible to reach agreement, at least when a failed unit cannot imitate a good processor. Hence authentication coding has also to be included in the protocol [8.30] since agreement without authentication is only possible in a 4-transputer configuration [8.27]. A transputer is very attractive for these kinds of protocol because it offers both high communication bandwidth for message exchange and high computation power for authentication and agreement processing. However, authentication has to be kept relatively simple because very secure methods, such as RSA, require too much overhead [8.31].

Thanks to its instantaneous and bumpless recovery, TMR is the ideal solution for hard, real-time systems. Concrete transputer based designs have been described in [8.32-8.34]. Hardware voting is worked out in Reference [8.32] based on a hardware link-synchronizer which makes it possible to obtain synchronization in a user-transparent way. However, extra (unreliable) hardware is needed and matching is not provided. Software voting is applied in References [8.33] and [8.34]. The former applies authentication and a Byzantine agreement protocol for guaranteeing that all transputers process the data in the same order, even when Byzantine faults occur (synchronization). The latter is a specific approach for a motor controller. By introducing analytic redundancy, the difficult and time-consuming matching process is avoided.

8.3.4   Unification Theory

In this Chapter four kinds of back-ups have been introduced: cold, warm, hot and active. The difference between them lies in their behaviour during normal error-free processing which is split up into three parts. Input processing includes the receipt of both input-data and state-information, control processing indicates normal program execution and output processing comprises the sending of the outputs.

From Table 8.1 it is obvious that the four back-ups cover all the significant combinations. An arbitrary degree of fault-tolerance can be realized by providing X cold, Y warm , Z hot and T active back-ups. Active back-ups always require voting. Note that comparison is a special case of voting. The ideal transputer kernel would support such an arbitrary combination of back-ups. By integrating all the above-described system services in one kernel, a framework is obtained which can be used for a wide range of applications and which reduces user-involvement to a minimum.

back-up	input processing	control processing	output processing
cold	no	no	no
warm	yes	no	no
hot	yes	yes	no
active	yes	yes	yes

Table 8.1 : Overview of input, control and output processing for the different kinds of back-up

8.4   FAULT-TOLERANCE FOR MULTIPROCESSOR APPLICATIONS

Until now, attention has been focused on uniprocessor applications. They are important because a lot of classical control algorithms can be implemented on a single transputer, so that a second or third processor is only added for fault-tolerance reasons. However modern, adaptive control algorithms are so compute-intensive that parallel processing on multiple processors is the only way to meet their real-time requirements [8.35]. The disadvantage of these multiprocessor applications is that the probability of a processor failure is significantly increased. However, enough processors are now inherently available to take over the tasks of a failed unit.

As with uniprocessor applications, fault-tolerance is still based on the use of back-ups. For each process of the parallel program, a cold, warm, hot or active back-up is provided. However, some additional problems arise. In the first place direct communication between all nodes is no longer possible due to physical limitations. So a message passing service has to be provided which takes into account link and node faults. A second difficulty is the processor testing: evaluation of a node by all its neighbours would introduce an intolerable testing overhead. Therefore, an intelligent test-strategy is necessary. Also the recovery control itself becomes more complex: it is no longer sufficient to start the cold, warm or hot back-up when a fault occurs; due to interaction between parallel processes, other nodes also have to take corrective actions; finally, when active back-ups are used, an additional problem is to determine where to vote or synchronize.

In the next paragraph, solutions are proposed which circumvent the above-mentioned problems by applying a specific transputer configuration. They have the disadvantage of realizing only a single degree of fault-tolerance, thus limiting the application area. The rest of the Chapter is devoted to the description of a flexible multiprocessor fault-tolerance kernel developed by the authors. As with the uniprocessor application kernel, it provides multiple levels of fault-tolerance making it suitable for a wide range of applications and does this in a user-transparent way. Its modular structure forms the ideal framework to introduce the different problems and solutions in obtaining multiprocessor fault-tolerance. At the same time the usefulness of the transputer is discussed.

8.4.1   Specific Transputer Configurations

A solution to obtain multiprocessor fault-tolerance consists of replacing each transputer by a fault-tolerant super-node. In [8.32] and [8.33], such a super-node consists of three transputers in a TMR configuration. The work in [8.32] implements a hardware solution which uses four of the already mentioned link-voters, one for each corresponding triple link. In this way fault-tolerance is automatically achieved. The user only has to realize the routing. Reference [8.33] describes a software solution based on building blocks consisting of three, fully interconnected transputers, each executing an authentication and Byzantine agreement protocol on every input. Although this results in a high overhead, it is needed because the ordering of arguments is more stringent here, due to the indeterminacy introduced by message passing. The message passing itself is based on sending authenticated data over three node-disjoint paths. A disadvantage of fully interconnecting the super-node is that only two links are left for interconnections with other super-nodes, so only a pipeline or ring is possible. The availability of more transputer links would remove this restriction. Both [8.32] and [8.33] avoid problems by keeping synchronization and voting local to the super-node. However, only a single degree of fault-tolerance, namely TMR, is possible, thereby introducing a lot of overhead.

Other solutions use a tailor-made implementation, thereby optimizing throughput. One example is the fault-tolerant aircraft controller designed in [8.36]. The drawback here, however, is that the design effort cannot be used directly for other applications.

8.4.2   Kernel for Multi-Level Fault-Tolerant Multiprocessing

The rest of this Chapter is devoted to the description of a modular multiprocessor kernel which provides multiple levels of fault-tolerance. It will be possible to adapt the degree of fault-tolerance to the application. TMR can, for example, be applied for critical applications with a small fault-tolerance time while, for a slow heating process, warm back-up can be realized. In this way no more redundancy is provided than required by the application. The kernel consists of two parts : a network module, which realizes fault-tolerant message passing, and a node module, which implements the test-strategy and the data and process management needed for multi-level node fault-tolerance. In fact this splitting is very natural as it corresponds to the twofold character of parallel processing since results not only have to be calculated, they also have to be communicated between nodes. The global structure corresponds very well to the OSI 7-layer model. Before elaborating both modules, it is necessary to look at the principles which have to be met to come to a successful design.

8.4.2.1   General principles

Multiprocessor utilization is largely influenced by the parallelism of the application and the Communication Computation Ratio [8.37]. Recovery methods must therefore neither lower the parallelism nor overload the communication network. The latter is especially important because the network is generally the bottle-neck of a multiprocessor. It also is clear that normal, error-free processing has to be optimized because faults rarely occur and an increase in recovery time is permitted as long as the time constant of the application is respected. In addition, the kernel has to be simple to avoid the introduction of new errors due to added complexity. This not only requires simple recovery mechanisms, but also a modular structure. A last, but important, requirement is that the kernel has to be distributed which ensures that a single failure will not shut-down the whole system.

8.4.2.2   The network module

The network module realizes fault-tolerant, inter-node message passing which recovers link faults. It receives data-packets from the node module of the source and routes them to the destination where they are again passed to the node module. This task is accomplished by the lower 3 levels of the OSI 7-layer model. The physical layer (layer 1) defines the electrical and mechanical interface of a link. The datalink layer (layer 2) realizes fault-tolerant node-to-node transmission. There is one datalink module per physical link, see later in Fig. 8.6. The routing layer (layer 3) forwards messages to the appropriate datalink module, or passes them to the node module when the destination node is reached. These layers are treated in more detail in the following.

The physical layer   This layer covers the mechanical and electrical interface embedded in the transputer link-hardware. In order to reduce noise and cross-talk, it is advisable to add either a RS422 or an optical interface [8.16].

The datalink layer   This layer realizes fault-tolerant, node-to-node transmission. Because the transputers have full-duplex links, it is obvious to realize this layer with two parallel modules, one a receiver and the other a sender module, see Fig. 8.6. The receiver accepts data transmitted by a sender-process of a connected transputer. A software node-to-node protocol is required to detect and correct transmission errors unless special link-hardware is used. This has already been described in Section 8.3.2.1, as it is completely analogous to fault-tolerant communication between the two processors of a dual transputer system. It was shown there that the absence of coding/decoding hardware not only introduces a high computation overhead, but also diminishes the communication bandwidth. The resultant global overhead, which depends on the communication load, is intolerable necessitating a simplification of the protocol [8.18]. Therefore, the coding and correlated acknowledge messages are no longer provided in this layer. The error-recovery of deformed and absorbed messages will be incorporated in the end-to-end protocol of the node module (see Section

8.4.2.3). This means that the fault-tolerance function of the datalink layer is reduced to the detection of link fractures and the timeout of the datalink protocol therefore is maintained. A disadvantage of this simplification is that an accumulation of faults generated on successive links may lead to an undetectable fault. For this reason hardware CRC-coding on each link is still advisable.

The routing layer   The routing layer receives messages from the node module or the datalink modules. It determines which link should be used to reach the destination node as fast as possible. The corresponding datalink module is used then to forward the data to the next node. If the destination node is reached, the message is passed to the node module. It is clear that in order to tolerate link faults, it must be possible to provide an alternative error-free path.

Different routing strategies exist but a routing header is needed in each case. The first class of methods puts only the number (address) of the destination node in the header. When the network is regular, the link to use in a particular intermediate node can be calculated with the aid of an algorithm. However, when faults occur, discontinuities are introduced making the algorithm useless or less efficient. Using a table, instead of an algorithm, has the advantage of being suitable for arbitrary networks. Such a routing table simply gives the link to use as a function of the destination node, and is stored in the routing layer. One drawback is the memory overhead which for practical configurations is limited. This table can easily be adapted in the case of a link or a node fault if a second table is available which contains the whole network configuration.

This approach has been realized in the first version of the network module [8.18]. A disadvantage is that node-disjoint paths cannot be forced. Node-disjoint paths are special in that they provide alternative paths which do not have any node in common, except the destination and source processor. So they are very useful if an intermittent communication fault cannot be localized. They also require less test-overhead as will be explained in the node module.

The second class of routing methods, implemented in the last version of the kernel, stores the complete communication path in the header. Because this only has to be done at the source node, it is obvious to move the routing table, which now contains multiple disjoint paths, to the node module. The table is calculated using a backtracking algorithm. The routing-task itself is extremely easy as it is limited to extracting, from the header, the number of the link that should be used to forward the message. In the header also the number of hops, which equals the number of intermediate nodes which are passed already, is stored. This allows a particular node to determine which linknumber must be used. For instance, when five nodes have been passed, the sixth linknumber must be extracted from the header and the message must be routed over this link. The number_of_hops in the header will be incremented next. To prevent perpetual cycling of messages, a threshold depending on the network size is introduced. When the number of hops exceeds this level, something has gone wrong and the message is thrown away.

After having determined the link to use, the routing layer links the message to the corresponding datalink queue. Because multiple messages intended for the same output link can arrive simultaneously, buffering is necessary. As the amount of buffer space is always finite, it is possible that a deadlock occurs. When for example the buffer space of two neighbour nodes is completely filled with messages intended for the other one, message exchange is no longer possible and the system deadlocks. A lot of methods have been designed to prevent those deadlocks [8.38-8.39]. Most of them only assure deadlock freedom as long as no link faults occur. A better solution is described in [8.19]. However, it inefficiently utilizes buffer space and complicates the design.

At present the kernel does not guarantee deadlock freedom. The available buffer space is used efficiently by sharing it between the node module and the different datalink lists. This guarantees that no deadlock will occur if the amount of buffer space exceeds the amount required to service traffic at every node [8.39]. The memory management is kept simple by providing buffers of a fixed length. A further simplification would be to adapt them to the largest possible message. This leads however to an intolerable waste of memory space. A trade-off has therefore to be made where the buffer size is large enough, so that assembly/disassembly of messages is only seldom needed, and small enough to minimize unoccupied buffer space. The optimal choice is application dependent [8.39]. The buffer exchange is managed by the central buffer manager of Fig. 8.6.

The final task of the routing layer is to provide a broadcast facility. This system service has to assure that a non-faulty node can correctly deliver its message to all other non-faulty nodes. It is used to trigger recovery by informing all processors of link and node faults. It is clear that this is not easy to achieve in the presence of faults since faulty nodes can omit, reroute or alter information passing through them [8.40-8.41]. This can be solved by sending multiple copies of the broadcast message over node-disjoint paths to the other non-faulty units [8.40]. At the receiving node majority voting is applied.

In our kernel a simpler solution is implemented, based on the assumption that corrupted messages can be detected with the aid of coding techniques. When a node sends a broadcast to all its neighbours, these check the redundant bits to look if the message is corrupted or not. If not, they forward the broadcast via all links except the one which originally received it. In this way corrupted messages are thrown away. Omitting or rerouting does not pose a problem as transmission takes place over all network links.

One problem is to stop the broadcast in an orderly manner. For this the following rule is applied: a message must not be forwarded when it already has been received correctly. To check this, a broadcast list is added which temporarily buffers the received broadcast messages (see Fig. 8.6). The disadvantage of the method is that the degree of fault-tolerance is limited to the error-detection capabilities of the coding technique. In our kernel a simple checksum is applied. Authentication coding would be ideal but imposes an intolerable overhead as already mentioned in Section 8.3.3.

Note that message diffusion is speeded up by placing a broadcast message at the head of a datalinklist.

8.4.2.3   Node module

The node module has to realize node fault-tolerance. This consists of recovery of transmission errors caused by node faults and recovery of computation errors in the user processes. The first task is implemented by the transport layer which corresponds to layer 4 of the OSI 7-layer model. The second task is accomplished by the fault-tolerance layer. This layer is not provided in the OSI model. In fact it replaces layers 5 and 6 which are not needed in a multiprocessor system.

The transport layer   This layer corrects transmission errors caused by node faults. Examples are errors introduced by incorrect storage, or copying, in an intermediate node or by the complete absorption of a message. An end-to-end protocol, analogous to the node-to-node protocol (datalink layer), is needed. Again coding techniques, a software acknowledge and a timeout are used. One difference is that, in our kernel, the message is retransmitted over an alternative node-disjoint path instead of using the same link. In this way message exchange is not blocked by a difficult to detect communication fault, as explained in the routing layer. A difficulty common to all node-to-node protocols is the determination of the timeout. Because the destination is no longer the neighbour node, it is very difficult to estimate a reasonable value for the timeout. It depends on the distance between source and destination and, even more important, on the network load. A trade-off has to be made. A long timeout reduces the number of false retransmissions, while a short timeout guarantees fast recovery. A heavily loaded network will trigger a lot of unnecessary retransmissions which burden the network even more, worsening the problem. This situation is called congestion, and congestion control methods are described in [8.19]. At present no special measures are provided in our kernel. However, fast message passing and retransmission over node-disjoint paths postpone congestion to higher communication loads.

Much current research is directed at producing methods which make the end-to-end timeout superfluous, by detecting message absorption on a more local basis. In contrast with the datalink layer, the end-to-end protocol is not simplified in the kernel. Because it only has to be executed at the source and destination processor, the overhead is acceptable. For coding a checksum is applied. The importance of the end-to-end protocol is strengthened by the above-mentioned simplification of the datalink layer.

Another task of the transport layer is the assembly/disassembly of application messages into packets of constant length. This can cause reassembly deadlock when memory space is completely filled with incomplete messages. Solutions are described in [8.39]. As it is analogous to routing deadlock, the kernel again applies the above-mentioned sharing of memory buffers. Note that such a deadlock can also be caused by a faulty node. By sending huge amounts of false messages, it can fill the buffers of non-faulty nodes quickly and it is therefore necessary to detect and isolate failed processors fast. This, however, requires an intolerable testing overhead. A practical alternative is to check if a message is sent by the correct source process which allows most false messages to be intercepted. This approach is realized in our kernel and it requires the addition of an extra identification in the header. Again authentication coding would be ideal to be secure.

A final task of the transport layer is the management of the routing table and the addition of the routing header to the messages. More details have been given in the routing layer.

The fault-tolerance layer   This layer controls the application processes in such a way that computation faults can be recovered. Therefore, a rather complicated management of back-up processes is necessary. Because multiple levels of fault-tolerance are provided, cold, warm, hot and active back-ups are supported. As already mentioned, the implementation is complicated by the need of a special test-strategy to reduce testing overhead and the necessity of a special recovery control service to make fault-correction possible despite the interdependency of the user-processes. The test-strategy is realized by the testing module. The recovery control service is implemented in the data and process manager module. This module also provides the checkpointing, synchronization, matching and voting services.

The testing module   This module realizes the testing service. Processor-testing is required to trigger recovery in case of cold, warm and hot back-ups. For active back-ups, it is necessary to detect latent (hidden) faults. The module consists of the self-test and neighbour-test processes, similar to those in dual transputer systems. To avoid false alarms it is again necessary to put them at a high priority. Minimum testing overhead is obtained by assuring that each processor is tested by one neighbour. However, some difficulties may rise. The first problem is to guarantee that all non-faulty nodes are still tested when multiple units have failed. A second problem is that a faulty node can generate false error-messages. Special measures have to be taken to avoid this leading to the shut-down of non-faulty processors.

Algorithms which solve these problems, as in [8.42-8.43], are quite complex. In our kernel a simplified solution is implemented. The first problem was solved as follows. Each node contains a self-test which is triggered each period T. The different non-faulty neighbours check these test-results in turn. The timeout in those nodes is adapted to this number of correct neighbours. Under the assumption of a single fault and complete fault-coverage, the failure will be detected within a time, T, even in the presence of already failed nodes. Using the transmission of the test-results as a link test, it is clear that a link is only checked each 4T. However, this does not pose a problem thanks to the retransmission over node-disjoint paths and the detection of linkfractures by the datalink layers. To solve the second problem an error-message is passed to the broadcast module of the routing layer upon fault-detection. To avoid incorrect shut-down, recovery is only started upon receipt of a confirmation generated by another neighbour. This is speeded up by doing an extra test as soon as a broadcast is accepted. A limitation of our implementation is that recovery can only be started when two non-faulty neighbours exist. A lot of refinements are however possible. The most interesting one is to store the number of transient faults and false messages in the neighbour nodes [8.35]. By starting recovery as soon as a threshold is exceeded, faults not covered by the periodic self-test can be corrected.

The data and process manager This module realizes the recovery control, checkpointing, synchronization, matching and voting services but only the recovery control and synchronization services are treated here. The other topics are not described since checkpointing and matching do not differ from uniprocessor applications and voting is related to synchronization.

The recovery control service is necessary for cold, warm and hot back-ups to avoid the necessity of all processes having to start from the beginning in case of a fault. To illustrate the problem, consider Fig. 8.4 where cold back-up is used. Suppose that process Z, running on node 1, fails. This is detected in the subsequent periodic test. Starting the cold back-up of process Z is not sufficient to correct the fault. Indeed, it is possible that process Z has sent incorrect data to process U after the fault has occurred and before the fault was detected. This implies that also process U has to be restarted. Even worse, U may have produced incorrect results due to the acceptance of incorrect data, so that also process V has to roll-back. All these processes can only be re-evaluated if all the input-data are regenerated, necessitating the restart (roll-back) of the processes X and Y . The phenomenon described above is called the domino-effect [8.44-8.45].

To avoid this, recovery points are needed where the state of the program is saved. Inputs received after a recovery point are preserved until the next correct recovery point. In this way, roll-back is limited to the last correct state and to the processes which have received an incorrect input. For a cold back-up also, the outputs have to be preserved because a cold back-up does not contain the input arguments needed for recovery. They have to be re-sent by the processes which have generated them. It is clear that an intelligent data and process management is required to determine which inputs, outputs and recovery points are no longer needed. To avoid the user himself having to do this complex management, it has to be provided by the recovery control process. This requires the automatic determination of the recovery points in the first place. Because roll-back is always caused by the receipt of an incorrect input, it would be logical to save the state just before using the input. For most applications this would lead to an intolerable overhead if done for each input individually. A significant improvement is obtained by grouping the inputs and providing a single recovery point in front of it.

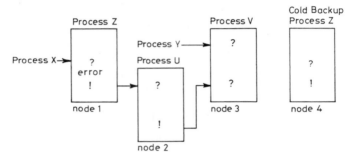

Fig. 8.4 The domino effect

This brings us to a programming style in which a program is split in large sequential processes which only input at the beginning. In the kernel this is obtained by implementing the Argument Flow operating principle [8.46]. Argument Flow combines the computation efficiency of Control Flow with the automatic employment of parallelism and automatic recovery point determination of Data Flow. The program is divided in routines each consisting of several high level instructions. Communication is limited to the transmission of arguments from producing to consuming routines. A routine is fired as soon as all inputs are arrived as illustrated in Fig. 8.5. A special programming environment has been designed which makes Argument Flow programming very simple [8.47].

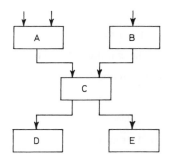

Fig. 8.5   Argument flow

Using Argument Flow it is not only possible to automatically determine the recovery points, but it also permits realization of the data and process management, described above, by utilizing a simple 3-phase handshake. This handshake is based on two control messages, namely input_is_correct and output_may_be_removed. Consider routine C (Fig. 8.5). The first phase consists of sending the results of C to D and E, without waiting for the test-results. When the subsequent test is positive, input_is_correct's are sent from C to D and E, at least when input_is_correct's have also been received for all the inputs of C. This is phase 2. After this phase both C and D + E contain correct arguments. So the data in A + B are no longer needed for recovery of a single failure. C knows this and sends an output_may_be_removed to A and B. When A and B have received output_may_be_removed's, from all consuming routines, removal is started of both the input and output data of that instance. This clarifies the data and process management during error-free processing. Now suppose that the processor fails during the execution of C. A C_is_failed broadcast is sent then to all nodes. As a consequence, the back-up process of C is started and the required inputs, which are still available thanks to the 3-phase handshake, are re-sent by the routines A and B. Of course this is only needed for a cold back-up, because the other back-ups have received them during normal processing, as explained in the unification theory. The nodes D and E are restarted too. Also, if needed, the consuming routines of D and E are re-initialised. To do the handshake, a firing and routine table are used (Fig. 8.6) with an extended description of the algorithm given in [8.46].

The synchronization service is required for hot and active back-ups. In a multiprocessor system program, divergence is not only introduced by internal timing differences or ALT's, as discussed in Section 8.3.2.4, but also by the communication network. Messages are not guaranteed to arrive in the same order at both the on-line and active back-up transputer. In this way processes may be started in a different sequence at both units. This does not pose a problem when the processes are time-sliced. The synchronization timeout only has to take into account an extra safety margin for network and scheduler delays. Of course, the task queues which contain the hot and active back-up processes always have to be equally loaded. Because synchronization point determination is quite complex, it has again to be automated. This time the outputs are the most obvious place to do the synchronization. In this way, it can be combined with voting. This again would lead to an intolerable overhead, if done for each output individually. The application therefore has to be split in large sequential processes which group the outputs at the end. By implementing the above-mentioned Argument Flow operating principle, this is automatically obtained in our kernel. At the moment research is being done to relieve the synchronization requirement further. In fact "strong" synchronization is only necessary for the I/O-processes, for the intermediate processes it is only necessary to match ALT's, to avoid buffer overflow and to detect faults in time.

Because all the system services described above depend on the same information, they have been integrated in a single data and process manager module which also realizes the firing of Argument Flow routines. The kernel also executes the 3-phase handshake for the active back-up processes. The only difference is that input_is_correct's are generated upon a successful voting instead of a successful self-test. The resultant uniformity not only simplifies the kernel, but it also permits adaption of the degree of fault-tolerance to a lower granularity, where the kind of back-up can be chosen individually for each process of the application instead of for the whole application. It is even possible to simultaneously provide different kinds of back-up for a process. Providing both a cold and active back-up, for example, makes it possible to recover a failed comparison because a cold back-up is available to generate a third output. An extended description is given in [8.46]. It is clear that a considerable communication overhead is unavoidable unless the execution time of all processes is predetermined [8.48]. This emphasizes the importance of a high speed network. However, simplicity and parallelism are maintained as required by the general requirements of Section 8.4.2.1.

8.4.2.4 Implementation aspects of the kernel

All the layers have to run in parallel which can easily be realized thanks to the hardware scheduler of the transputer. To avoid false alarms, however, the testing module has to run in highest priority. The datalink and routing layers are put at the next level. This is necessary to minimize communication delay, which is essential for high parallelism and small fault-tolerance time. The transport and fault-tolerance layer may be put at a lower priority because they are not needed to pass messages between nodes. They have however to run at higher priority than the application processes. The user processes themselves have also to be ordered according to their importance. This clearly shows that multiple priorities are required and because the transputer only provides two priorities, a real-time kernel such as Trans-RTX has to be used.

Another point to consider is the interconnection between the different layers. In a first implementation, this was done by using software channels. This realizes a clear interface as required by the OSI 7-layer model. However, the resultant copying introduced an intolerable time overhead. A significant speed-up is obtained by only passing pointers instead of complete messages. For this, C is preferred to occam. Overhead can be further decreased by integrating different layers in one module. Strictly speaking, this is not allowed by the OSI 7-layer model, as it decreases modularity, but in this way it is possible to minimize performance degradation. In our actual implementation, the routing and datalink layer have been merged (Fig. 8.6)

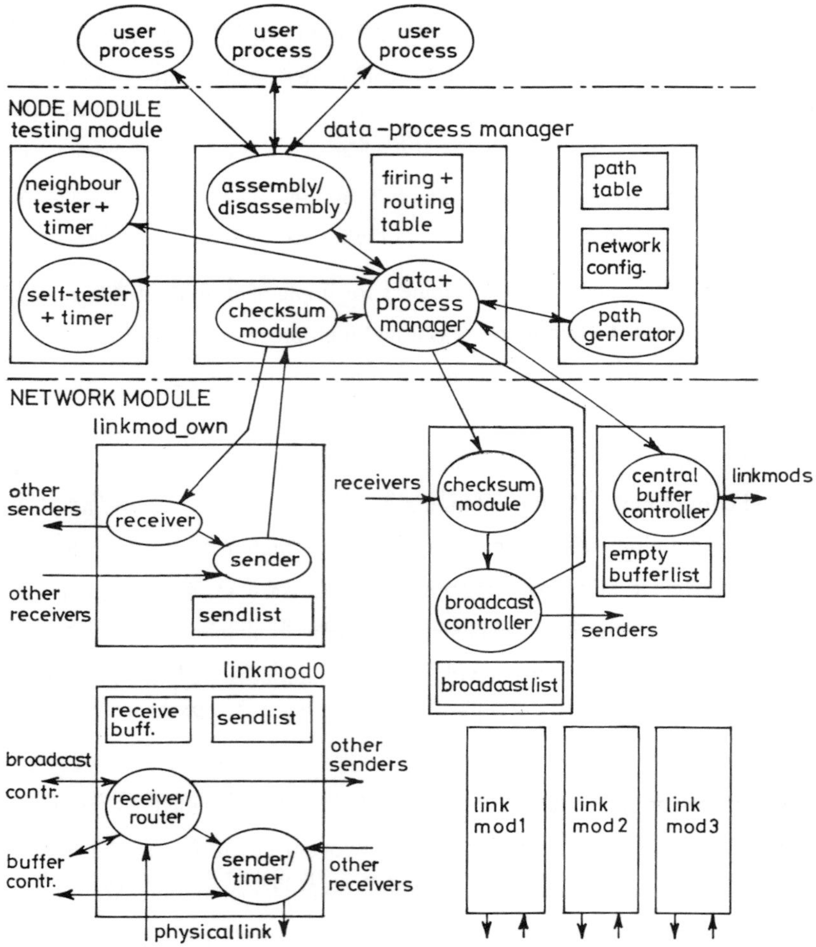

Fig. 8.6 Global structure of the kernel

which, thanks to the simplicity of the router, does not pose a problem. The transport layer is combined with the fault-tolerance layer because they use the same data tables. The interface between the two remaining system layers, the network and node module, is accomplished by providing a special datalink module (linkmod_own in Fig. 8.6) which is analogous to the other datalink modules.

The buffering, data and process management is significantly simplified by the use of extended data structures which is a second reason why C is preferred. However, optimum efficiency would be obtained if occam were extended with pointer primitives and extended data structures.

8.5   CONCLUSIONS

In this Chapter, the suitability of transputers for implementing fault-tolerant systems has been demonstrated. Both uniprocessor and multiprocessor applications have been discussed, showing that they use similar fault-tolerance techniques.

When only a single processor is available, coding and extensive testing are applied to detect and correct faults. Adding additional transputers in a cold, warm, hot or active back-up configuration makes it possible to achieve high-availability or high-safety even if a transputer fails. By integrating the necessary services, such as testing, checkpointing, synchronization, matching and voting in a single kernel, a framework is obtained which can be used for a wide range of uniprocessor applications and which minimizes user-effort.

For multiprocessor applications, the kernel has to be extended. A fault-tolerant message passing service, a test-strategy and recovery controller service have to be added. Simplicity and efficiency are maintained by implementing the Argument Flow operating principle. The kernel described makes it possible for the user to provide fault-tolerance in a way that is transparent for the user. A distinctive feature is that it allows a different degree of fault-tolerance to be assigned to each process instead of assigning a global fault-tolerance degree. In this way the amount of redundancy can be kept to a minimum.

The suitability of the transputer stems from its high speed, point-to-point links and its fast hardwired two priority scheduler. The former is necessary because the system services require a lot of communication between the nodes while the latter is needed to easily join the system services and application processes. An efficient implementation is however only possible when multiple priorities are available which also permit the realization of ideal graceful degradation. Until it is embedded in the transputer hardware, such multiple priority scheduling has to be provided by a software kernel.

ACKNOWLEDGEMENTS

The research reported here has been supported in part by the Belgian National Fund for Scientific Research and by the European Community under Esprit Parallel Computing Action project 4043.R

REFERENCES

[8.1]   Johnson BW: *Design and analysis of fault-tolerant digital systems*, Addison-Wesley Publishing Company, Amsterdam, 1989.

[8.2]   Faller R: Type approval of fault-tolerant systems, *BIRA Seminar on TUV-approved safety-oriented programmable controllers*, Antwerp, Belgium, 1990.

[8.3]   Pradhan DK: *Fault-tolerant computing*, Prentice-Hall, Englewood Cliffs NJ, 1986.

[8.4]   Cuyvers R, Lauwereins R, Peperstraete JA: Fault-tolerance in process control: possibilities, limitations and trends, *Journal A*, **31**, 4, 1990, pp33-40.

[8.5]   Cuyvers R: Why does a computer fail and how to prevent it?, *Internal Report*, KUL-ESAT, Belgium, 1988 (Dutch).

[8.6]   Russell D, et al: Tolerant to a fault, *Systems International*, June 1987, pp96-100.

[8.7]   Kirrmann HD: Fault tolerance in process control: an overview and examples of European products, *IEEE Micro*, 1987, pp27-50.

[8.8]   *The transputer data book*, INMOS Limited, 1989.

[8.9]   Verhulst E: Trans-RTX, *Internal Report*, Intelligent Systems International, Leuven, Belgium, 1990.

[8.10]   Marshall WG, Forsythe W: Self-checking multiprocessor module for train control applications, *Electronics Letters*, **17**, 12, 1981, pp408-410.

[8.11]   Peperstraete JA: Autonomous and non-autonomous testing, *Course on Microcomputer systems*, KUL-ESAT, Belgium, 1990.

[8.12]   Peterson WW: *Error correcting codes*, MIT Press, 1981.

[8.13]   Derycke G, Feryn P: Design of a fault-tolerant transputer board, *MSc diss*, KUL-ESAT, Belgium, 1990 (in Dutch).

[8.14]   Wassmann L: *MTM-EDC multiple transputer module with error detection and correction*, Technical Documentation Version 1.2, Parsytec Gmb H, Dec 1989.

[8.15]   Frank PM: Advanced fault-diagnosis techniques in aerospace systems, *Proc of the 3rd Annual European Computer Conference on VLSI and Computer Peripherals*, Hamburg, Germany, 1989.

[8.16] *The transputer applications notebook: systems and performance*, INMOS Limited, 1989.

[8.17] Ramabadran TV, Guitonde SS: A tutorial on CRC computations, *IEEE Micro*, 1988, pp62-73.

[8.18] Bettens S, Caerts C: Design and realization of a fault-tolerant transputer network, *MSc Dissertation*, KUL-ESAT, 1989 (in Dutch).

[8.19] Tanenbaum AS: *Computer networks*, Prentice Hall, Englewood Cliffs NJ,1981.

[8.20] Helze M: Neural networks in industrial applications on Inmos transputers, *Proc of 3th Int Transputer Conf and Exhibition: Transputers for industrial applications*, Antwerp, Belgium, 1990.

[8.21] Welch PH: Managing hard real-time demands on transputers, *7th Occam Users Group and Int Workshop on Parallel programming of transputer-based machines*, Grenoble, France, 1987.

[8.22] Chandy KM, Ramamoorthy CV: Rollback and recovery strategies for computer programs, *IEEE Trans on Computers*, **21**, 6, 1972, pp546-556.

[8.23] Kirrmann HD: Fault-tolerance in process control: an overview and examples of European products, *IEEE Micro*, 1987, pp27-50.

[8.24] Standeven J, Colley MJ: Performance aspects of transputers in fault-tolerant systems, *Workshop on Real-time systems: theory and applications*, University of York, UK, 1989.

[8.25] Moore WR, et al: A review of synchronization and matching in fault-tolerant systems, *IEE Proc Pt E*, **131**, 4, 1984, pp119-124.

[8.26] Standeven J et al: Hardware voting of transputers in real-time NMR fault-tolerant systems, *Proc of the 3rd Conf of the North American Transputer Users Group*, Sunnyvale CA, 1990.

[8.27] Lamport L, et al: The Byzantine generals problem, *ACM Trans on Programming Languages and Systems*, **4**, 3, 1982, pp382-401.

[8.28] Dolev D, Strong HR: Authenticated algorithms for Byzantine agreement, *SIAM J Comput*, **12**, 4, 1983, pp656-666.

[8.29] Infis AH, Moore WR: Economic approach to fault-tolerant synchronization, *IEE Proc Pt E*, **135**, 2, 1988, pp82-86.

[8.30] Rivest RL, Shamir A, Alleman L: A method for obtaining digital signatures in public key cryptosystems, *Comm ACM 21*, 1978, pp120-126.

[8.31] Blommaert M, Boelanders J: Implementation of cryptographic methods in distributed systems, *MSc Diss*, KUL-ESAT, 1990 (in Dutch).

[8.32] Standeven J, et al: Hardware voter for fault-tolerant transputer systems, *Microprocessors and Microsystems*, **13**, 9, 1989, pp588-596.

[8.33] Ezhilchelvan PD, et al: Constructing replicated systems using processors with point-to-point communication links, *Proc 16th Int Conf on Computer Architecture*, Jeruzalem, Israel, 1989, pp177-184.

[8.34] Adriaensen D, Schrooten J: Realization of fault-tolerant motor controller using a parallel computer, *MSc Dissertation*, KUL-ESAT, 1991 (in Dutch).

[8.35] Kopetz H, et al: Distributed Fault-tolerant real-time systems: the Mars approach, *IEEE Micro*, 1989, pp26-40.

[8.36] Thompson HA et al: Implementation of a fault-tolerant transputer-based gas turbine engine controller, *Proc for the Workshop on Real-Time Systems: Theory and Applications*, University of York, UK, 1989.

[8.37] Lauwereins R: Design of an argument flow parallel computer: from program organization to multiprocessor architecture, *PhD Dissertation*, KUL-ESAT, Belgium, 1989.

[8.38] Gallizi E: A deadlock-free communication system for a transputer network, *Proc of the 12th Occam User Group*, Technical Meeting, Exeter, England, 1990, pp11-21.

[8.39] Shumway M: Deadlock-free packet networks, *Proc 2nd Conf North American Transputer Users Group*, Durham, NC, 1989, pp139-177.

[8.40] Ramanathan P, Shin KG: Reliable broadcast in hypercube multiprocessors, *IEEE Trans on Computers*, **37**, 12, 1988, pp1654-1657.

[8.41] Dolev D, et al: Atomic broadcast: from simple message diffusion to Byzantine agreement, *Proc 15th Int Symposium on Fault-Tolerant Computing*, 1985, pp200-206.

[8.42] Meyer FJ, Pradhan DK: Dynamic testing strategy for distributed systems, *IEEE Trans on Computers*, **38**, 3, 1989, pp356-365.

[8.43] Kuhl JG, Reddy SM: Fault-diagnosis in fully distributed systems, *Proc 11th Int Symposium on Fault-Tolerant Computing*, 1981, pp101-105.

[8.44] Wood WG: Decentralized recovery control protocol, *Proc 11th Int Symposium on Fault-Tolerant Computing*, 1981, pp159-164.

[8.45] Barigazzi G, Stugini L: Application transparent setting of recovery points, *13th Int Symposium on Fault-Tolerant Computing*, 1983, pp48-45.

[8.46] Cuyvers R, et al: A kernel for multi-level fault-tolerant multiprocessing, *Proc of the IEEE Southeastcon '91*, Williamsburg, 1991, pp248-252.

[8.47] Lauwereins R, et al: GRAPE: A Case tool for digital signal parallel processing, *IEEE ASSP Magazine*, Special Issue, 1990, pp32-43.

[8.48] Cuyvers R, et al: Argument flow: an ideal principle for fault-tolerant multiprocessing, *Int Symposium on Mini and Microcomputers and their Applications (MIMI '88)*, Gerona, Spain, 1988, pp120-123.

Chapter 9

A Formal Approach to the Software Control of High-Speed Machinery

DJ Holding and JS Sagoo

9.1 INTRODUCTION

Complex high-speed machines, such as packaging machines, comprise a series of actuators which are used to process a product as it is moved through the machine. Major advances in flexible machine design can be achieved by replacing the mechanical transmissions used to synchronise actuator motions by sets of independent, software-controlled, electro-mechanical drives which deliver energy direct to the point of use. The benefit to be derived from such an approach is that mechanical constraints are removed and flexibility in machine layout is obtained in which a range of control and drive modules may be used to create a new generation of machines, with mechanical complexity being traded for sophistication in control.

This Chapter describes the development of systematic methods for the design of real-time control software for flexible, modular, high-speed machines comprising multiple, independent drives. The rôle of such software is to enforce system-critical synchronisation between concurrent systems under normal and abnormal conditions. The approach adopted is a "systems approach" in which the software is regarded as a component of a system with safety-related implications.

The research described in this Chapter includes work on the specification, design, and verification of synchronisation logic using semi-formal methods, and on the implementation of the control software using concurrent programming languages and transputers. It also describes how the implementation software can be ruggedised using software fault-tolerance techniques. These are illustrated by considering the design of real-time control software for two independently-driven, interacting mechanisms for a high-speed packaging machine.

9.2   THE DESIGN OF FLEXIBLE HIGH-SPEED MACHINES

Complex high-speed machines, such as packaging machines, typically comprise multiple, cam-actuated mechanisms which process and combine materials as they move through the machine to produce a finished product. The mechanisms can have complex motion requirements and are traditionally driven from a central prime mover via mechanical-linkages such as shafts, gears or pulleys, which deliver energy to the point of use or re-distribute energy during braking. In such machines, control is implemented in an efficient but inflexible manner by the cams which provide tight control of the actuator functions and the mechanical linkages which coordinate and synchronise the actuator motions. However, the traditional philosophy of using mechanically-linked sub-systems limits the extent to which conventional systems can be adapted to meet new requirements for higher-speed, more flexible designs.

The trend in high-speed machine development is towards flexible designs for short production run applications, in which the machine functions are reconfigured between runs to accommodate changes in product specification. Major advances in flexible machine design can be achieved by replacing the traditional centralised prime mover and power transmission system by independent drives which supply energy direct to the point of use. However, when each actuator is driven independently, the total energy demands of the actuator must be supplied by its driver. Careful consideration has to be given to the selection of appropriate drives. The use of independent drives allows flexibility to be extended into the actuator function. For example, cam-driven actuators can be replaced by software-controlled, electro-mechanical actuators, in which the actuator function is defined by software and can be readily modified or reprogrammed.

9.2.1 Introducing Flexibility using Multiple Independent Drives

Flexibility can be introduced into the design of high-speed machines through the use of independent drives. This requires the identification of suitable drives and controllers for each independent machine function. The criteria used when selecting drives depends on the particular class of motion. In the case of continuous drives, where the primary requirement is to regulate a continuous motion which may be subject to large disturbances, emphasis is placed on the torque-speed characteristic (to ensure that the necessary acceleration can be obtained) and the power-rate rating (as a measure of the ability of the motor to deliver power and produce a stiff system which can respond quickly to disturbance loads) [9.1]. In the case of intermittent motions, the primary requirement is to accelerate and decelerate the load through the motion profile, and the principal criteria used are the torque-speed characteristic, the power-rate rating, and inertia matching (to ensure maximum energy transfer from the motor to the load) [9.2].

In both intermittent and continuous drive applications the feasibility of using independent drives has been significantly increased by the availability of modern large power-rate drivers, such as brushless d.c. motors having neodymium-iron-boron magnet rotors which have power-rate ratings that are approximately twenty times greater than those of conventional d.c. motors of similar power ratings. Modelling and simulation are commonly used to ensure that a drive has the dynamic performance and accuracy required to drive a particular actuator.

Control is typically implemented using complex feedback and feedforward control for each independent drive [9.3]. Careful design is necessary to achieve a stiff profile-following characteristic and a high degree of point-to-point accuracy. The use of dedicated digital controllers, some of which are based on high speed digital signal processing (DSP) devices, has led to significant increases in the bandwidths of such systems. Distinct trends include the use of dedicated controllers with phase-locked loop techniques for high speed, continuously synchronised systems and the use of software-based, discrete-event logic for intermittently synchronised systems.

9.2.2 Software Control of Independent Drives

The flexibility of independent drives can be realised only if each independently driven actuator is properly controlled and the complete set of independent drives is properly coordinated and synchronised. In traditional machines, the mechanical linkages automatically maintain synchronisation. However, when the mechanical linkages are replaced by independent software-controlled drives, the drives must be coordinated and forced into synchronisation by appropriate synchronisation logic which will be implemented in software. Careful consideration has to be given to the specification and design of such software to ensure that the synchronisation is correct and is implemented in a reliable and safe manner. In addition, if the synchronisation logic or software is system-critical, or has safety-related implications, then it must be designed to appropriate standards to ensure the safe operation of the system under both normal and abnormal conditions.

The development of software engineering methods for the specification, design, implementation and verification of real-time concurrent software is a current area of research. This Chapter describes an integrated approach to the design of such systems and identifies notations and techniques which can be used at various parts of the design cycle. Emphasis is placed on the design of synchronisation and control software for intermittently synchronised systems. Section 9.3 provides an overview of formal methods for the design of real-time concurrent software and Section 9.4 presents an integrated approach to the design of time-critical and system-critical systems using Petri nets and Temporal Logic. To implement such designs, the Petri net models must be translated into a software implementation using property preserving transformations. Section 9.5 describes Petri net models of the software constructs found in concurrent programming languages such as occam. These models form the basis for the translation of Petri net designs into executable occam code. Section 9.6 explains how software fault tolerance techniques can be used to ruggedise the implementation software and describes how Petri nets can be used in the systematic design of fault tolerant mechanisms for concurrent real-time software.

The application of these techniques to a research-demonstrator system, comprising a high-speed manufacturing system with time-critical and system-critical attributes, is considered in Sections 9.7 and 9.8. The development of mature design techniques, based on such methods, will be a pre-requisite for the use of software-controlled, independent drives in multiple drive systems with safety implications.

9.3   SOFTWARE ENGINEERING TECHNIQUES FOR CONCURRENT REAL-TIME SYSTEMS

The software for a real-time programmable system will typically comprise a set of interacting processes which are distributed over a suitable processing architecture. The starting point for the design of such software is the system requirements specification which states what the system should do in a clear and precise manner. The requirements specification is normally translated into a design by a process of elaboration, in which the description of what the system should do is elaborated until the description comprises a set of easily implemented activities. The design will describe how each activity or task should be carried out and how it should be implemented.

In applications which involve safety functions or have implications for safety, the system must perform in a reliable and safe manner. Ideally, the requirement specification should be subject to detailed investigation to ensure that the proposed system has the desired functionality and safety. Considerable research has been conducted into the design of software-based, real-time systems for use in system-critical or safety-critical applications and this has led to the development of standards and guidelines for the design of software for these types of system [9.4],[9.5].

The proposed guidelines for industrial applications [9.6] attach considerable importance to the use of formal methods in the specification, design and verification of systems. The aim of these methods is to provide a notation, which enables the system requirements to be expressed precisely, and an underlying mathematical framework that allows analysis and reasoning about a systems properties and performance. Formal methods should allow a specification to be translated into a design using property preserving transformations. The preservation of such properties is necessary to ensure that the design and implementation satisfy the specification. The designer also may consider using software fault tolerance to provide robustness in the design of a system.

The various phases of the software design cycle for such systems is shown in Fig. 9.1. These phases can be integrated only if the output of each phase can be used as the input to the next phase. This requires the selection of a formal method with the scope to encompass all phases of the design cycle, from specification capture to software implementation and ruggedisation.

9.3.1   Overview of Formal Methods

Numerous formal specification techniques have been proposed [9.7],[9.8]. The following presents a brief survey of relevant techniques and considers the use of formal methods for the development of functional specifications and designs for real-time distributed systems. To describe such systems, the formal notation must include constructs for the description of sequential and concurrent behaviour and the notion of time. In addition, the design of time-critical (or hard) real-time systems requires sophisticated reasoning about whether a system can satisfy real-time

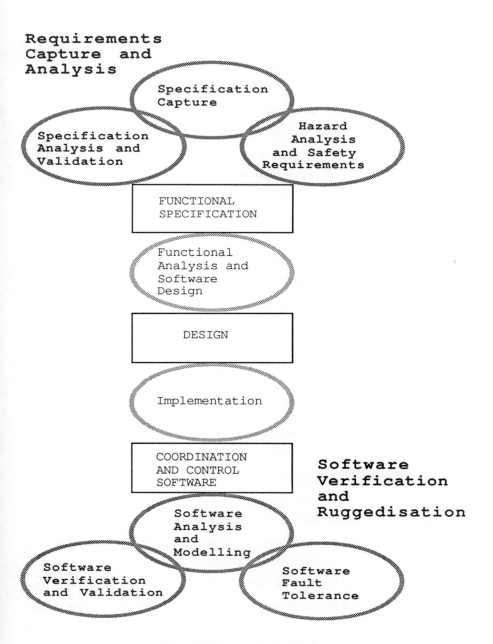

Fig.9.1 Software design cycle

constraints (the timeliness of actions) and this necessitates the use of formal methods with a quantitative notion of time.

Various approaches have been proposed for the formal specification of systems. Some techniques, such as VDM [9.9] and Z [9.10], share a common computational model and mathematical structure and are increasingly being applied in industry. However, they do not address concurrency and the notion of time. Other techniques, such as CSP [9.11], do allow the specification and verification of concurrent systems. For real-time applications, a timed version of CSP has been proposed which allows reasoning about real-time systems [9.12]. Unfortunately, both Z and CSP lack a tangible user interface.

Temporal logic [9.13],[9.14] is an alternative technique which can be used to specify and verify concurrent systems and reason about their temporal behaviour [9.15],[9.16]. Temporal logic embraces two notions of time; branching time, which has a tree-like nature, can be used to represent different possible futures, and linear time which views systems as having only one possible future. Most research uses linear-time temporal logic. Temporal logic further subdivides the notion of time into qualitative-time, which is used to make temporal statements such as "eventually", "henceforth", "until" [9.17], and quantitative-time in which explicit time values are used to constrain temporal operators, such as "eventually within 5 time units". Examples of quantitative or real-time temporal logic are RTTL [9.18], ESM/RTTL [9.19], RTL [9.20], and MODECHART [9.21].

The notion of using semi-formal and formal methods, based on Petri nets and temporal logic, in the specification and verification of real-time systems is attractive because Petri nets can be used to capture the causal aspects of a system and to validate system properties, and temporal logic can be used to reason about the temporal aspect of the system's behaviour and prove properties such as liveness (whether a state can be reached eventually) and freedom from deadlock. However, the formalisms of Petri nets and temporal logic are dissimilar. Initial attempts at combining the formalisms involved writing separate specifications in each formalism, although there is no way of checking the consistency of these specifications [9.22],[9.23],[9.24]. For example, interpreted Petri nets (IPN's) and branching time temporal logic have been used in an interactive design tool for specifying and verifying distributed systems [9.23]; predicate-action nets and a branching-time temporal logic have been used in a formal study of communication protocols [9.22]; and condition event (CE) nets and temporal logic have been used in the formal development of a Petri net analyser [9.24].

The problem of combining the two formalisms [9.25] has been addressed by a number of research workers. Suzuki [9.26] combined Petri nets and temporal logic and introduced it as a new class of Petri nets known as temporal Petri nets, with a view to making them applicable to both design and verification. Temporal Petri nets have been applied to the formal analysis of a daisy chain arbiter [9.27], where it was shown that the process of verification, using an axiomatic proof technique, was much simpler than the traditional approach. They have also been used in the formal analysis of the alternating bit communication protocol [9.28] and in the specification of synchronisation logic for a real-time control system [9.29].

Suzuki's method is useful for proving that a controller will correctly carry out specified functions, i.e. those functions which are defined explicitly in a specification, through the proof of liveness properties. This is somewhat different from showing that a system will not cause a hazardous event. Therefore, work has continued on the development of formalisms and proof systems which will allow the proof of safety properties for systems modelled by temporal Petri nets.

He and Lee [9.30] have adopted a somewhat different approach that uses a state-based logic to relate the computational models of Predicate Transition (PrT) nets and linear first order temporal logic. Their approach maintains consistency between the formalisms and they have developed an algorithm which translates PrT nets into temporal logic and a proof system which combines the strength of the Petri net and temporal logic approaches. This method, which provides a unified approach for verifying liveness and safety properties, has distinct advantages over conventional temporal Petri net techniques (which can be used to verify liveness properties but cannot be used to prove safety properties, which have to be inferred from a reachability graph). This method is described in detail in Section 9.4 and is applied to the design of logic for the intermittent synchronisation of two independent drives which form part of a flexible machine system in Section 9.7.

9.4   PETRI NETS

Petri nets are a powerful modelling technique that captures the causal relationships between events and conditions [9.31]. They are commonly used to model concurrent processes such as the flow of information and control in programmable systems. A Petri net comprises two types of nodes, places representing conditions (or states) and transitions representing events, which are interconnected by directed arcs. Tokens, which reside at the places, are used to indicate the instantiation of a state. The current state of a net is represented by the distribution of tokens in the net. A simple Petri net is shown in Fig. 9.2 in which the places, transitions and tokens are represented by the circles, bars and dots respectively.

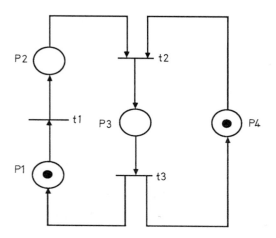

Fig.9.2 A simple Petri net

There are many forms of Petri net. The type considered below is the condition event (CE) net in which each place can contain not more that one token. This allows a one-to-one semantic correspondence between places and conditions. The attributes of CE nets have been described in detail by Peterson [9.31].

9.4.1   Petri Nets and Condition Event Nets

The basic structure of a Petri net [9.31] can be represented by the tuple:

$$C = \{P,T,I(t),O(t),M\}.$$

Here

P is a set of finite places, $P = \{p_1,p_2,..,p_n\}$, where $n>0$.
T is a set of finite transitions, $T = \{t_1,t_2,..,t_m\}$, where $m>0$.
I is the input function that maps transitions to places, $I: T \rightarrow P$, where a place p_i is an input place of transition t_j if $p_i \in I(t_j)$.
O is the output function that maps transitions to places, $O: T \rightarrow P$, where a place p_i is an output place of transition t_j if $p_i \in O(t_j)$.

The distribution of tokens in a net is represented by the marking M which maps places to the number of tokens in each place, (in CE nets M is restricted to a binary mapping). The marking can be represented formally as:

$$M: P \rightarrow \{0,1,2,..,k\}, \quad \text{where} \quad k>0$$

A marking that is of particular interest is the initial marking M_0. The tokenised input places of a marked Petri net $C = \{P,T,I(t),O(t),M_0\}$ with a particular marking M is:

$$M(p_i) \geq \#[p_i,I(t_j)]$$

where $\#[p_i, I(t_j)]$ represents the number of tokens in the input place p_i, for all $p_i \in P$.

The marking of a Petri net changes from M to M' when a transition, which is enabled, eventually fires. The enabling and firing rules of Petri nets are:

(i)   a transition is enabled, if and only if, each of its input places has at least one token,

(ii)   a transition can fire only if it is enabled,

(iii) when a transition fires, a token is removed from each of its input places and a token is deposited into each of its output places.

Thus, an enabled transition $t_j \in T$, with marking M, may fire to yield a new marking M' defined by:

$$M'(p_i) = M(p_i) - \#(p_i, I(t_j)) + \#(p_i, O(t_j))$$

where $\#(p_i, O(t_j))$ represents the number of tokens deposited in the output places by the firing of transition t_j.

It follows that the distribution of tokens in a net (the marking) is changed by the firing of transitions, and the dynamic behaviour of a system can be represented as the sequence of state changes caused by the "firing" of the corresponding transitions.

Petri nets can be analysed to determine the state reachability and the existence of undesirable or unsafe states. The nets can also be simulated to investigate state activity and the occurrence of deadlock. However, they are not a formal method in the sense that Petri nets alone cannot be used to prove the liveness and safety properties of a net, nor can they be used to prove that the modelled system will not enter an unsafe state.

9.4.2   State Reachability, State Activity and Deadlock

Deterministic concurrent systems, including fault tolerant systems, can be modelled using Petri nets [9.32]. The dynamic behaviour of such systems is defined by the sequence of state transitions which take place from a given initial state, or marking of the net, and the behaviour of the system can be analysed by tracing tokens as they flow through the net.

This analysis is usually carried out using reachability sets, which comprise those markings which are potentially reachable from a given initial marking. The reachability set can be represented conventionally as a graph or tree, where the nodes of the graph are markings and the arcs of the graph are transitions which must fire to arrive at the given marking. In simple cases, the reachability graph can be analysed by inspection. In general, the number of reachable markings can be very large and the analysis of the reachability set is usually performed by computer. Analysis of the reachability set allows the designer to determine which transition sequences are live, whether any given marking is reachable, and whether the Petri net is prone to deadlock. To keep the analysis manageable it is often necessary to attempt to bound the Petri net or to reduce the complexity of the net by applying net-reduction techniques. However, the analysis is still subject to the problem of combinatorial explosion.

9.4.3   Timed Petri Nets

The real-time performance of systems can be studied by adding time to the basic Petri net. In the time Petri net [9.33] a minimum and a maximum time delay are associated with each transition; this has proved useful for modelling timeouts in communication protocols and the technique has been developed for proving the correctness of protocols [9.34]. An alternative approach, known as the timed Petri net [9.35], associates a discrete time parameter "τ" with each transition "τ" such that, once the transition is enabled, it will fire after the period τ. There are a number of variants of timed Petri nets. For example, time values may be associated with places, rather than transitions, in order to maintain the instantaneous firing rule for transitions [9.36]. Alternatively, a value can be placed on the length of time a transition is enabled and on its firing time [9.37]. More recently, timed Petri nets have been used in the development of techniques for analysing the safety aspects of hard real-time systems [9.38].

Timed Petri nets lack satisfactory methods for verifying the liveness properties of the nets [9.39]. Also, the representation of time, in both time Petri nets and timed Petri nets, is not powerful enough to represent fundamental temporal properties of concurrent systems such as liveness and fairness [9.27]. Therefore, the use of these Petri nets has been confined to the area of performance evaluation. In the design of safety-related systems, timed Petri net techniques are used only for the preliminary assessment of the safety aspects of a systems [9.29].

9.4.4   Temporal Petri Nets

Since timed Petri nets can not represent the fundamental temporal properties of concurrent systems, research has been conducted into other methods of incorporating the notion of time into Petri nets. Suzuki has combined CE nets and temporal logic to form temporal Petri nets by considering the transition firing sequence generated from a particular net marking [9.26],[9.27]. Specifically, the places, transitions and marking of a temporal Petri net can be described in the notation:

```
p = (p has a token),   where   p ∈ P   and   t ∈ T
t = (t fires)
t(ok) = (t is firable)
t(¬ok) = (t is not firable)
¬p = (p has no token)
```

Consider the possibly infinite transition firing sequence represented as (M, α), where M is the marking and α is the firing sequence. To reason about this firing sequence, temporal formulae can be written using the atomic temporal operators:

O next,   □ henceforth,   ◊ eventually,   U until,

•   and,   + or,   ¬ not,   → implication.

Using the above notation, the following propositions can be made which form the basis for the proof of liveness properties [9.27]:

Let the temporal Petri net be given by

   TN = (C, f)

where, C   represents the structure of the CE net defined in Section 9.4.1,

    f   is the set of temporal formulae,

    M_0 represents the initial marking.

If for any CE net, propositions (i) and (ii) are true, then proposition (iii) follows:

(i)   for any marking M, reachable from M_0, by a firing sequence α, if transition
    t ∈ T is firable at M, then t remains firable until t fires

    $(M_0, \alpha) \models □ [t(ok) → t(ok)Ut]$

    where $\models$ is known as the semantic turnstile and has the meaning that, for
    (M_0, α) in the semantic domain, it is true that □ [t(ok) →
    t(ok)Ut] .

(ii)   whenever t becomes firable, then it will eventually become disabled

    f implies   □ [t(ok) → ◊t(¬ok)]

(iii) $(M_0, \alpha) \quad |= \quad \Box \ [t(ok) \rightarrow \Diamond t]$,   for any t within the sequence α.

Proposition (i) can be checked by observing the structure of the net or the reachability graph. The use of these propositions in the proof of liveness properties is as follows. Knowledge of the reachability graph generated using Proposition (i) can be used with Proposition (ii) and (iii) to specify and verify the desired properties of a system in an axiomatic manner. The crux of the argument is that the net must satisfy Proposition (i). The use of these methods is demonstrated in Section 9.7.3.2.

9.4.5   Extended Temporal Petri Nets

The work of He and Lee [9.30] integrated the computational models of PrT nets and first order temporal logic. In order to specify and verify concurrent systems, an algorithm was developed for translating PrT nets into temporal logic and a proof system was developed to assist in the verification of both safety and liveness properties. A formal derivation of the algorithm for PrT nets may be obtained from [9.30].

Since transformations exist between PrT nets and CE nets, and they share the same computational model [9.25], it is assumed that the translation algorithm and the proof system developed for PrT nets [9.30] can be used for CE nets. The adaptation of this algorithm to CE nets will yield a technique referred to as extended temporal Petri nets [9.40].

Thus for CE nets, for every tokenised place $p \in P$ in the CE net, the initial marking M_0 can be represented by:

$$M_0 = \{p_1, \ \ldots \ , p_n\}$$

and a propositional formula characterising the initial marking M_0 can be expressed as the conjunction of the places in M_0:

$p_1 \bullet p_2 \bullet \ \ldots \ \bullet p_n \, .$

This is referred to as the domain-dependent axiom.

Also, for every transition in the net, an inference rule can be written which defines the firing of the transition in terms of system-dependent pre-conditions, X, and post-conditions, Y:

$$X \ \Rightarrow \ OY$$

For each transition under consideration, X contains a formula comprising the conjunction of all the tokenised places of the pre-conditions of the transition and the conjunction of the negation of the places that form the post-conditions. Y contains a formula comprising the conjunction of all the tokenised places that form the post conditions of the transition and the conjunction of the negation of the places that form the pre-conditions.

The proof system comprises the domain independent axioms and inference rules for temporal logic, as described in [9.13], and the domain dependent axioms and inference rules described above. The use of this technique is demonstrated in Section 9.7.3.3.

9.5   PETRI NET MODELLING OF CONCURRENT SOFTWARE

Imperative programming languages provide notations for the expression of algorithms. Programs written in such languages prescribe what has to be done and the sequence in which the task is to be carried out. Careful consideration should be given to determining when to take decisions which bind or constrain the design, such as the choice of programming notation or processing architecture. It is desirable that the process of analysis is not subject to implementation constraints before the analysis has revealed the characteristics of the problem. This is particularly important if the designer is to exploit fully the advantages which can be obtained by using modern concurrent programming notations and processing hardware, such as occam [9.41] and the transputer [9.42].

In the design process for a sequential system, the problem is analysed and a sequential order is imposed on the problem to yield a sequential design that is compatible with the proposed implementation. The solution will comprise six primitive constructs which are to be found in all sequential programming languages [9.43]:

sequence,
input ,
output,
assignment,
selection (decision),
repetition (iteration).

These constructs correspond to the six sequential constructs in occam,

```
( SEQ, ?, ! , := , IF, WHILE )
```

with the proviso that input and output comprise synchronous communications to other (external) processes. Petri nets can be used to model sequential constructs [9.31] and Petri net models of the above occam sequential constructs are shown in Fig. 9.3.

In the design process, concurrency can be included at both the software and hardware level. Concurrent imperative programming languages, such as Modula-2, Concurrent Pascal, Ada and occam, provide notations for the expression of concurrency. Programming notations for the description of loosely-coupled, real-time concurrent systems normally provide two additional primitive constructs for describing concurrency [9.43]. The simplest concurrent construct is that which initiates a number of processes in parallel, such as the occam PAR construct. Each parallel process runs asynchronously and then terminates. The construct does not terminate until all the parallel processes have terminated.

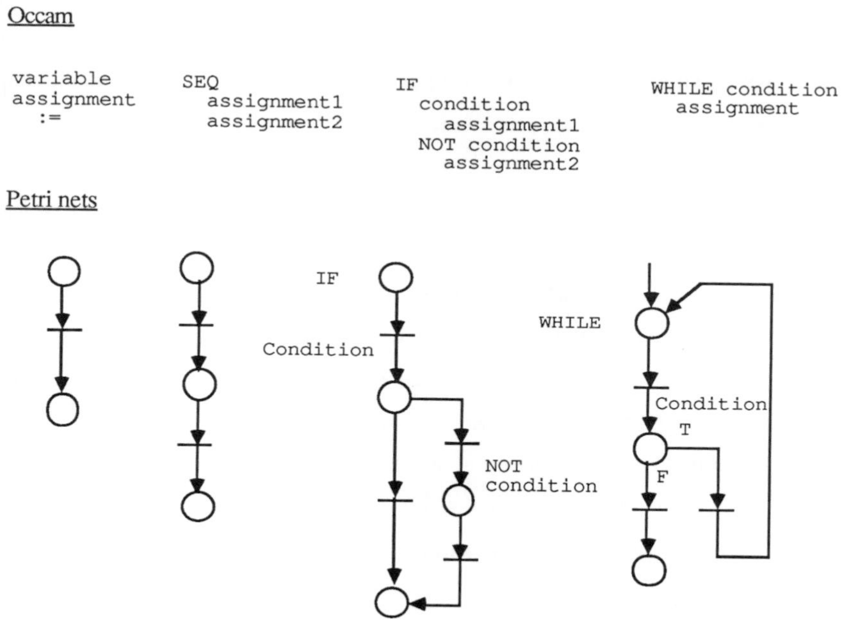
Occam
variable
assignment
:=
SEQ
assignment1
assignment2
IF
condition
assignment1
NOT condition
assignment2
WHILE condition
assignment
Petri nets
IF
Condition
NOT
condition
WHILE
Condition
T
F

Fig.9.3 Petri net models of occam sequential constructs

All concurrent programming languages provide facilities for defining inter-process actions. These typically include communications via shared variables and/or communications by message passing. The inter-process actions are asynchronous if the read and write operations on shared variables are asynchronous, if the inter-process action comprises separate one-way communications such as send and receive messages, or if a single inter-process message may be left in a message buffer such that the sender does not need to wait for the receiving process. Asynchronous communications are not supported in occam at the primitive level.

Alternatively, the communicating processes will be forced into mutual synchronisation if the action of communication is an atomic, two-way action. Synchronisation by message passing enforces a strict discipline on the designer because errors in the synchronisation logic will lead to deadlock. The more flexible constraints associated with asynchronous communications would appear to offer a design advantage. However, the synchronous system is more amenable to analysis. Such synchronisation by message passing is supported in occam by the pair of synchronous input and output primitives (? !).

Non-deterministic selective communications, such as those which occur when a number of processes compete for access to a non-pre-emptive resource, are normally accommodated by use of guarded processes [9.44]. For example, occam makes use of synchronous communications between processes to support guarded alternative processes (the ALT construct). This construct offers a set of alternative processes for execution, each guarded by a synchronous input (or a synchronous input in conjunction with a boolean expression, or the special SKIP primitive which is always ready). The first guard to be satisfied enables its protected process for execution; the other processes are not enabled and will not be executed.

Petri nets can also be used to model concurrent constructs [9.45] and Petri net models of the occam concurrent constructs [9.46] are shown in Fig. 9.4.

Many engineering systems, such as embedded computer real-time systems, are required to maintain synchronism with an asynchronous external system, or to respond to stimuli from such a system, within a finite and specified delay. In real-time programming there is a primary need for a mechanism for handling the concept of time. Real-time sequential programming languages include an additional primitive construct which allows the formal inclusion of time.

Occam provides a local sense of time by means of a real-time time-counter. A process may read the current value of the counter (clock ? time) or wait until the counter exceeds a given value (clock ? AFTER timenow PLUS interval). Petri nets models of the occam real-time constructs [9.46] are shown in Fig. 9.5.

Occam

```
PAR                chan ? x   chan ! y              ALT
   p1                                                  chan1 ? a
   p2                                                     p1
   p3                                                  chan2 ? b
                                                          p2
```

Petri nets

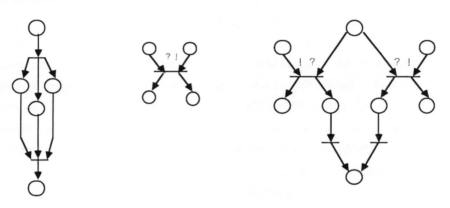

Fig.9.4 Petri net models of occam concurrent constructs

Occam

```
        clock ? time           clock ? AFTER timenow PLUS interval
```

Petri Nets

Fig.9.5 Petri net models of occam time constructs

9.6   THE DESIGN OF SOFTWARE FAULT TOLERANCE MECHANISMS USING PETRI NET TECHNIQUES

The use of formal methods in software design aims to produce correct design through fault prevention methods. However, it is probable that faults will still be introduced into a design, either explicitly, as part of a particular component, or implicitly, through the omission of a particular feature or attribute. Faults in a specification or design will lie hidden within the system and will only become apparent if a particular instantiation of the system state activates the fault and generates an error.

Fault tolerance can be used to limit the scope of faults or to mask errors so that they do not lead to failure. Fault tolerance involves the use of redundancy to give the system resilience [9.47],[9.48],[9.49],[9.50]. The most common fault tolerant technique, N-modular redundancy [9.47], involves the N-fold replication of processes or systems. The replicated processes are operated in parallel and the results computed by the variant paths are compared. If an error is generated by any one path, it will be detected and the erroneous result will be suppressed, thus masking the fault. N-modular redundancy is characterised by the massive redundancy of software and often of hardware; the usual replication factor is three and diverse techniques are used in the programming of the triplicated paths.

Error detection and recovery techniques provide an alternative approach to software fault tolerance. The aim of the method is to detect an error, to assess the damage caused by the error, and to initiate an error recovery mechanism in order to compute an error-free result. The method is characterised by the economical use of redundant software. Two recovery techniques are commonly used. The forward error recovery method [9.51],[9.52] aims to minimise delay by transforming the erroneous state directly into a correct or acceptable state. In the alternative method, backward error recovery [9.53],[9.54], the system backtracks through previous states until it can restore a previously computed correct state and restart processing in the forward direction. Following the restart, a diverse forward path is often used to save time or to avoid a common mode error in the forward path.

The recovery block is a fundamental backward error recovery structure for fault tolerance in sequential systems [9.53],[9.54]. A design notation for the recovery block scheme is given below [9.54]:

```
ensure acceptance test AT
  by process P
  else by process Q
  else by default;
```

The recovery block technique requires considerable modification if it is to be applied to networks of communicating sequential processes, because errors can propagate between processes through inter-process interactions which cannot be revoked. Error detection mechanisms for distributed systems must take into account the promulgation of errors in their assessment of error damage. Also, the error recovery scheme must involve all processes which may have been affected by the error. It follows that the structure of the inter-process actions in a distributed system is central to the design of the fault tolerant mechanism.

The conversation mechanism proposed by Randell [9.54] uses a coordinated set of recovery blocks to implement a distributed error detection and recovery mechanism. The method involves partitioning the set of concurrent processes into groups of processes which will cooperate in error detection and recovery. However, the partitioning must not be performed arbitrarily because the backtracking recovery operation must be a properly coordinated procedure, involving all the concurrent processes which are party to an error. The boundary of the conversation consists of a recovery line, a test line and two side walls, which enclose the set of interacting processes that are party to the conversation. Thus, the conversation forms a recovery block for a general set of distributed processes.

Identifying the boundary is not a trivial task because the state of each asynchronous process is independent of the state of other processes, except when the processes are forced into synchronism by inter-process communications. In general, it is not possible to determine *a priori* the particular sequence of states which will be instantiated when the software is executed. Therefore, the boundary must be identified dynamically or must be independent of the sequence of occurrence of the independent states. The problem of the dynamic identification of conversation boundaries has been the subject of much research [9.55],[9.56] and considerable care is necessary in the design of such systems because, unless the recovery is carefully controlled and its scope bounded, dynamic recovery techniques may exhibit the domino effect [9.54]. The alternative approach, which requires the analysis of the structure of the interacting processes, results in a general or *static* solution which is valid for all possible sequences of occurrences of states [9.57].

A method has been developed [9.57] which allows the systematic placement of conversations to protect specific processes or functions. The technique is based on the analysis of the inter-process actions associated with a specified process or function, because these provide the mechanism for the migration of errors. Specifically, the method has been developed for systems which communicate using synchronous communications, as in CSP and occam, and involves the use of Petri net models and state reachability graphs to identify those state changes which are caused by inter-process communications. The extent of allowable error migrations for the protection of a specific process or function can be determined by tracing the inter-process communications following the error. The aim is to identify proper conversation boundaries which bound the extent of error migration.

Consider the Petri net represented by the tuple,

$$C = \{P, T, I(t), O(t), M\} \text{ defined in Section 9.4.1 .}$$

For a given transition $t_j \in T$, the next state function $\delta(M, t_j)$ defines the effect of the transition from the present state M to the next state M' [9.31]:

$$\delta(M, t_j) = M'(p_i) = M(p_i) - \#(p_i, I(t_j)) + \#(p_i, O(t_j)),$$
$$\text{for all} \quad p_i \in P.$$

The reachability set $R(C, M_0)$ defines all possible markings reachable from M_0 in Petri net C. The reachability graph can be constructed from $R(C, M_0)$ by forming the set of next state functions for all $\delta(M, t_j) \in R(C, M_0)$

The system dynamics can be defined through a state-change table which lists the state changes for each transition in the reachability graph [9.57]. The elements of the state-change table are defined by the input and output functions, I and O, which comprise the relative components of the present state M and the next-state M' (the subset of the initial-state, which is terminated by the transition, and the subset of the next-state, which is generated by the transition). Therefore, for each transition t_j :

$$I(t_j) = M - M'$$
$$O(t_j) = M' - M$$

Because the reachability graph defines all process interactions, no interactions can take place between different branches of the graph. Therefore, any closed partition of the graph can be considered to be the boundary of a conversation [9.57]. For such a boundary, it is possible to define two sets, S and F, which are formed by the union of input and output functions for all traces within the boundary:

$$S = \{I(1) \cup I(2) \cup ..I(r)\}$$
$$F = \{O(1) \cup O(2) \cup ..O(q)\}$$

The entry and exit states of a conversation K and J can be identified by taking the relative complements of these two sets:

$$J = F - S$$
$$K = S - F$$

These sets of states, K and J, form the recovery line and test-line states of the conversation respectively. In effect, the conversation is defined by a closed boundary drawn on the reachability graph and its physical implementation is identified by deriving the corresponding recovery-line and test-line states. The technique, which is known as boundary placement, can be used to determine boundaries which protect a specific process or to protect all the processes associated with a particular function [9.57]. The method can be automated (using the underlying set theory) and provides a systematic method for the placement of conversations, or properly nested sets of conversations.

In practice, it is usual to design conversations to protect a particular function or process. The transitions t_i and places p_i associated with such a process or function can be identified if each transition or place is assigned the attributes of a process (or function) identifier $PROC_k$:

$$PROC_k = \{t_k, p_k\}, \quad \text{where } t_k \in T \text{ and } p_k \in P$$

When protecting such a process, the rôle of the conversation is to prevent inward or outward error migration for the duration of the conversation. Such migrations can take place only through inter-process or inter-function communications. The inter-process communications can be identified by examining the attributes of the elements of the state-change table. The state-change table can then be reduced to a communications state-change table by removing all intra-process transitions and forming equivalence relationships between all substates created by intra-process actions. This considerably reduces the complexity of the state-change table and allows ready identification of conversation boundaries and the associated recovery-line states and test-line states [9.57].

A conversation mechanism normally comprises a coordinated set of recovery points, a coordinated set of acceptance tests, the protected process, an alternative process, and a "default" or forward recovery process. In concurrent systems, the structure of the fault tolerant system can be simplified by computing the primary and alternative processes in parallel. The recovery line processes are used to save the system state on entry to the conversation; this state is assumed to be error free. In general, the acceptance test can be performed in two phases. In the first phase, local tests are carried out as each constituent process in the conversation produces partial results. If any local test indicates a fault then the whole set of processes in the conversation must be decreed faulty. However, local tests are not sufficient for an acceptance test of the whole conversation, and the local tests must be followed by a second phase of tests which assess the complete set of results. This requirement can be achieved by a centralised global acceptance test which assesses the complete set of results from the conversation. Naturally, the conversation will be implemented properly only if these processes are controlled and coordinated such that the "ensure" notation is implemented correctly and without deadlock. Methods for implementing conversation mechanisms using occam are detailed in [9.58].

9.7   CONTROL APPLICATION

The above techniques have been applied to specification, design and verification of the synchronisation logic for a time-critical real-time system which consists of an incremental arbor drum and an intermittent transfer slider as shown in Fig. 9.6. The drum is required to increment in 22.5° steps and to dwell between increments with tight constraints on angular position. The slider is required to move into an arbor following a tightly constrained motion profile. In addition, each interacting mechanism has to meet tight constraints on positional accuracy or velocity and, at the normal operating speed of 450 cycles per minute, the peak velocities and accelerations of the drum and arbor are 14 rad s^{-1}, 800 rad s^{-2} and 8 ms^{-1} and 680 ms^{-2}. The motion profiles of the arbor drum and transfer slider are shown in Fig. 9.7. To meet these demanding requirements, each axis is independently driven by a high-performance brushless d.c.

motor. Extensive simulation was used to ensure drive compatibility and performance [9.1, 9.59].

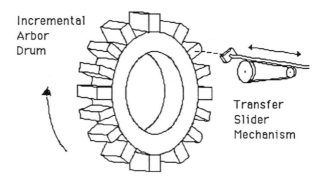

Fig.9.6 Arbor drum and transfer slider

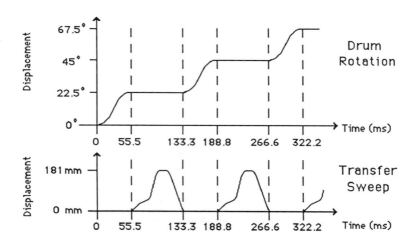

Fig.9.7 Arbor drum and transfer slider motion profiles

9.7.1 Requirement Specification

The principal rôle of the control system is to ensure the intermittent synchronisation of the transfer slider and the drum. The asynchronous concurrent motion of the arbor drum and transfer slider is permitted. Clearly, the drum must be at rest and in position before the slider is inserted into the arbor. Similarly, the slider must be withdrawn from the arbor before the drum can rotate. The critical point in the slider's motion occurs when the slider is moving towards the drum, and a decision has to be taken either to continue moving and insert in the arbor (if the drum is stationary and in position), or to decelerate and stop (if the drum is rotating or not in position). This system critical decision must be computed in a timely manner, as shown in Fig. 9.8.

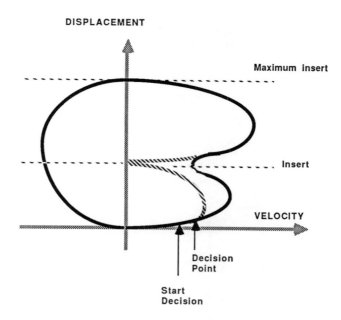

Fig. 9.8 Motion profile and time-critical decision

9.7.2 Design of Synchronisation Logic

The motion of the drum and slider can be modelled as two simple asynchronous cyclic concurrent processes [9.29, 9.60] as shown in the Petri net model Fig. 9.9. The places model the system states which are crucial to the correct and safe operation of the system. Since the physical system has inertia, the model includes implicit information about the position and velocity control of the system. For example, at the point at which the safety-critical decision is taken, the slider is still moving towards the arbor at considerable velocity and the decision must be computed and implemented in a time-critical manner.

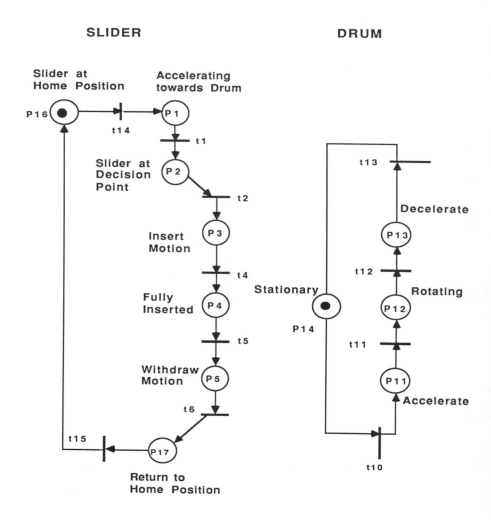

Fig.9.9 Petri net model of arbor drum and transfer slider

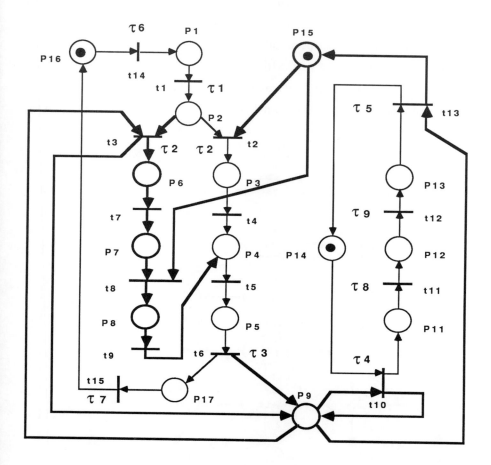

Fig. 9.10 Petri net model of synchronisation logic

The proposed synchronisation logic for the system [9.29], comprising interlocks, decision and abort mechanisms, is shown superimposed on the model of arbor drum and transfer slider in Fig. 9.10. Timings $\tau_1 - \tau_9$ are applied to those transitions which are central to reasoning about the timeliness T_2 of computing the decision at place p_2. The state reachability graph for all proper markings is shown in Fig. 9.11. Static analysis shows that all combinations of places correspond to safe markings [9.29]. The states S1 - S34 shown in the figure can be generated from the initial marking p_{14}, p_{15}, p_{16} of state S1. However, static analysis alone is not sufficient to show that time-critical control decisions, such as those associated with place p_2, will be taken in a timely manner. Specifically, analysis shows that critical timing problems affect the transitions between states S16, S20, S23 and S26. Therefore, these states are associated with a timing hazard and are denoted by shading in Fig. 9.11. The problem of analysing and verifying the proposed design is addressed in the following sections.

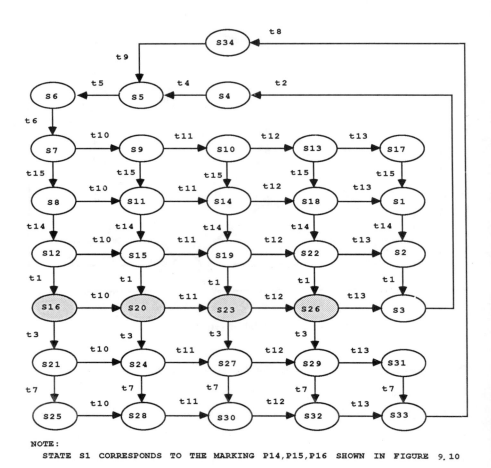

NOTE:
STATE S1 CORRESPONDS TO THE MARKING P14,P15,P16 SHOWN IN FIGURE 9.10

Fig.9.11 State reachability graph for timed Petri net

9.7.3 Verification of the Synchronisation Logic

To verify the synchronisation logic, timed Petri nets were used to evaluate the system performance, to identify time-critical sections and determine their timing requirements, and to derive the corresponding performance constraints on the control system. Temporal Petri nets were used to verify the liveness properties of the synchronisation logic in order to show that it will carry out the required function. Extended temporal Petri nets are used to proof safety properties for the synchronisation logic.

9.7.3.1 Performance analysis using timed Petri nets

A timed Petri net for this problem is derived by assigning variable time parameters, $(\tau 1 - \tau 9)$, to those transitions which play an important role in the motion, as shown in Fig. 9.10. System performance can be explored by forming relational expressions of relative timing [9.29].

For example, if it is required to ensure that the slider makes a decision to insert, then, from the marking (p_9, p_{14}, p_{17}), place p_{15} must be reached before place p_2 (i.e. it must be guaranteed that when state (p_9, p_{14}, p_{17}) is reached, state (p_1, p_{14}, p_{17}) must eventually follow). This can be expressed in terms of timing requirements as:

$$\tau 4 + \tau 5 + \tau 8 + \tau 9 \leq \tau 6 + \tau 7$$

If it is assumed that $\tau 7$ and $\tau 5$, $\tau 8$, $\tau 9$ are constant for the slider and drum respectively, the above can be simplified:

$$\tau 4 + K1 \leq \tau 6 + K2$$

where $K1 = \tau 5 + \tau 8 + \tau 9$ and $K2 = \tau 7$.

It follows that the main design parameters are $\tau 4$, the drum enable time, and $\tau 6$, the slider rest period. Consideration can then be given to determining timing requirements for the desired motion given various system constraints. Thus:

(i)   if $\tau 7 < \tau 4$, then t_{15} fires before t_{10} and the timing requirement becomes:

$\tau 6 \geq \tau 9 + \tau 8 + \tau 5 + \tau 4*$

where $\tau 4*$ is the remaining time of $\tau 4$.

(ii)   if $\tau 7 > \tau 4$, then t_{10} fires before t_{15} and the timing requirement becomes:

$\tau 7* + \tau 6 \geq \tau 9 + \tau 8 + \tau 5$

where $\tau 7* =$ the remaining time of $\tau 7$.

In both cases, (i) and (ii), time parameter $\tau 6$ can be varied to produce the desired motion.

A further condition may arise if the system reaches state (p_2, p_9, p_{13}), in this case it must be ensured that $\tau 5 > \tau 2$ so that the desired motion is achieved.

9.7.3.2   Analysis of system and liveness properties using temporal Petri nets

Following Suzuki's method [9.27], the initial marking of the net, M_0, can be represented as:

$M_0 = \{p_{14}, p_{15}, p_{16}\}$

Analysis of the net shows that for this initial marking, Proposition (i) holds for all transitions in the net.

Using proposition (ii) of Section 9.4.4 it can be seen that:

$\square$ [$t_n(ok)$ $\rightarrow$ $\lozenge t_n(\neg ok)$],   where $n = \{ 1, \; .. \; ,15 \}$.

This will result in 15 temporal formulae, one for each transition denoted (1 - 15).

Since Proposition (i) is valid, it is possible to infer using proposition (iii) that:

$\square$ [$t_m(ok)$ $\rightarrow$ $\lozenge t_m$],   where $m = \{ 1, \; .. \; ,15 \}$.

This will result in a further 15 temporal formulae, denoted (16 - 30).

The above formulae 1-30 form the basic axioms of the Petri net, and are essential for formulating proofs of liveness properties. To illustrate the proof technique, consider the proof of the important property that, whenever the slider reaches the decision point, then, eventually, a decision is made about whether the slider continues moving or stops:

Lemma 1

    $\square$ $[t_1 \rightarrow \lozenge(t_2 + t_3)]$

Proof:

1. $t_1 \rightarrow O(t_2(ok) + t_3(ok))$,   from Petri net
2. $t_1 \bullet t_{13}(\neg ok) \rightarrow O t_3(ok)$,   from Petri net
3. $t_1 \bullet t_{13}(\neg ok) \rightarrow \lozenge t_3(ok)$,   weakening 2 by temp. logic
4. $t_1 \bullet t_{13}(ok) \;\; \rightarrow O t_2(ok)$,   from Petri net
5. $t_1 \bullet t_{13}(ok) \;\; \rightarrow \lozenge t_2(ok)$, weakening 4 by temp. logic
6. $(t_1 \bullet t_{13}(\neg ok) \rightarrow \lozenge t_3(ok))$ + $(t_1 \bullet t_{13}(ok) \rightarrow \lozenge t_2(ok))$, from 3 or 5
7. $(t_1 \rightarrow (t_{13}(\neg ok) \rightarrow \lozenge t_3(ok))$ + $(t_1 \rightarrow (t_{13}(ok) \rightarrow \lozenge t_2(ok))$
8. $t_1 \rightarrow (t_{13}(\neg ok) \rightarrow \lozenge t_3 + t_{13}(ok) \rightarrow \lozenge t_2)$
9. $t_1 \rightarrow \lozenge(t_3 + t_2)$, from 8 by tautology
10 $\square$ $[t_1 \rightarrow \lozenge(t_2 + t_3)]$,   from 10 by temp. reasoning

Similarly, proofs may be constructed for other liveness properties which are essential to the correct function and safe operation of the system. For example:

Lemma 2

Whenever the drum stops, then, eventually, the slider must proceed to insert into the drum.

$$\square \ [\ t_{13} \rightarrow \Diamond (t_2 + t_8) \ ]$$

Lemma 3

Whenever the slider starts to accelerate, then, eventually, it will insert into the drum.

a) $t_{14} \rightarrow \Diamond t_5$

b) $t_{14} \rightarrow \Diamond (p_{14} \cdot p_4)$

Lemma 4

Whenever the slider clears the drum, then, eventually, the slider will insert into the drum and the drum will come to a stop after rotating.

$$\square \ [\ t_6 \rightarrow \Diamond (t_1 \cdot t_{13}) \ ]$$

However, it should be noted that liveness proofs are restricted to showing that certain sequences of events will occur. They can *not* be used to show that certain events will not occur. For example, liveness proofs can not be used to show that the slider will not insert in the arbor drum while it is moving. This safety-critical result must be inferred from the reachability graph.

9.7.3.3   Analysis of safety properties using extended temporal Petri nets

Following He's method [9.30], inference rules of the Petri net can be set up, based on the firing conditions (post and preconditions) of each transition:

Derived domain-dependent axiom:

$$p_{14} \bullet p_{15} \bullet p_{16} \qquad\qquad (9.1)$$

Domain-dependent Inference Rules (IR):

1 $p_{16} \bullet \neg p_1 \Rightarrow O(p_1 \bullet \neg p_{16})$

2 $p_1 \bullet \neg p_2 \Rightarrow O(p_2 \bullet \neg p_1)$

3 $p_{15} \bullet p_2 \bullet \neg p_3 \Rightarrow O(\neg p_2 \bullet \neg p_{15} \bullet p_3)$

4 $p_3 \bullet \neg p_4 \Rightarrow O(p_4 \bullet \neg p_3)$

5 $p_4 \bullet \neg p_5 \Rightarrow O(p_5 \bullet \neg p_4)$

6 $p_5 \bullet \neg p_9 \bullet \neg p_{17} \Rightarrow O(\neg p_5 \bullet p_9 \bullet p_{17})$

7 $p_2 \bullet p_9 \bullet \neg p_6 \Rightarrow O(\neg p_2 \bullet p_9) \bullet p_6$

8 $p_6 \bullet \neg p_7 \Rightarrow O(p_7 \bullet \neg p_6)$

9 $p_{15} \bullet p_7 \bullet \neg p_8 \Rightarrow O(p_8 \bullet \neg p_7 \bullet \neg p_{15})$

10 $p_8 \bullet \neg p_4 \Rightarrow O(p_4 \bullet \neg p_8)$

11 $p_{14} \bullet p_9 \bullet \neg p_{11} \Rightarrow O(\neg p_{14} \bullet p_9) \bullet p_{11}$

12 $p_{11} \bullet \neg p_{12} \Rightarrow O(p_{12} \bullet \neg p_{11})$

13 $p_{12} \bullet \neg p_{13} \Rightarrow O(p_{13} \bullet \neg p_{12})$

14 $p_{13} \bullet p_9 \bullet (\neg p_{14} \bullet \neg p_{15}) \Rightarrow O(\neg p_{13} \bullet \neg p_9) \bullet p_{14} \bullet p_{15}$

15 $p_{17} \bullet \neg p_{16} \Rightarrow O(p_{16} \bullet \neg p_{17})$

He's inference rules and proof technique can be used to prove both liveness and safety properties. The following examples illustrate the use of the technique to prove safety properties for the arbor drum and transfer slider system. Consider the important properties:

1 A situation will never occur when the slider has taken a decision to insert and the drum is rotating

   $\square \ \neg [p_4 \bullet p_9]$

2 A situation will never occur when the slider is at the decision point and no decision is made.

$$\square \; \neg [p_2 \bullet \neg (p_9 + p_{15})]$$

The proof of the first property $\square \; \neg [p_4 \bullet p_9]$ is by contradiction:

1   $\neg \; \square \; \neg [p_4 \bullet p_9]$ to prove negation of the above

2   $\lozenge \; [p_4 \bullet p_9]$ equivalent by def. of $\lozenge$ and n

3   $\neg [p_4 \bullet p_9]$ Assume derivable from eqn.(9.1); for this to be a valid state it must satisfy the following temporal axiom, where w is any propositional formula.

4   $w \bullet \lozenge \neg w \rightarrow \lozenge (w \bullet O \neg w)$

5   $\lozenge (\neg [p_4 \bullet p_9] \bullet O [p_4 \bullet p_9])$ substituting 3 for w

6   $\lozenge ([\neg p_4 + \neg p_9] \bullet O [p_4 \bullet p_9])$ from 5 by De Morgan

7   $\lozenge ([\neg p_4 \bullet O [p_4 \bullet p_9] + [\neg p_9 \bullet O [p_4 \bullet p_9])$ from 6 by expansion

Examining each disjunct of 7 and simplifying using propositional logic:

8   $[\neg p_4 \bullet O [p_4 \bullet p_9]$ first disjunct of 7.

9   $\neg p_4 \bullet O p_4$ weakening 8 by temporal logic.

10   $O p_9$ weakening 8 by temporal logic.

However, the inference rules that will yield 9 are IR 10 and IR 4

$$p_8 \bullet \neg p_4 \; \Rightarrow \; O (p_4 \bullet \neg p_8)$$
$$p_3 \bullet \neg p_4 \; \Rightarrow \; O (p_4 \bullet \neg p_3)$$

In both cases, the conclusion 10 is not obtained. A similar analysis can be done for the second disjunct of 7, which will also yield a contradiction. Thus, both disjuncts of 7 are proved false, proving that the assumed state $\neg [p_4 \bullet p_9]$ is false. Thus, statement 2, that $\lozenge \; [p_4 \bullet p_9]$ is false, and the desired Property 1 is proved by contradiction. A similar procedure can be used to prove Property 2.

It is of note that these results could have been deduced by inspection of the reachability graph, Fig. 9.11, which has no state $s = \{p_4, p_9\}$. However, the use of extended temporal Petri nets has allowed the *proof* of important safety properties. This gives a considerable advantage over previous methods in which such properties could only be inferred.

9.8   CONTROLLER DESIGN

The Petri net model of the design has been verified by proving *both* liveness and safety conditions. The design, shown in Fig. 9.10, comprises models of the arbor drum and transfer slider (referred to as the physical system) and the interlock logic necessary to coordinate and synchronise their motion. However, the correct operation of the interlock requires knowledge of the current state of the interlock and the state of each actuator (drum and slider). Therefore, any implementation must include a data acquisition interface with the physical system to ascertain the state of the arbor drum and slider. Thus, the controller will comprise the coordination and synchronisation logic, a detailed motion generation subsystem for each axis (drum and slider), and the interfaces to the independently-driven arbor drum and slider.

The design and implementation of the full coordination and synchronisation logic present an interesting problem. The primary requirement is to translate the model of the specification into a design in such a manner that the desirable and proven properties of the specification are invariants of the translation. This can be achieved by embedding the reference-model of the physical system, as shown in Fig. 9.9, within the controller. Careful design of the interfaces is necessary to ensure the proofs, reachability graphs etc. of the embedded model are inherited by the overall Petri net and can be used for analysis purposes. Fig. 9.12 shows the Petri net of the design of the embedded controller.

A preliminary analysis of the full design shows that those properties essential to correct operation are inherited by the controller. Work is continuing on the analysis

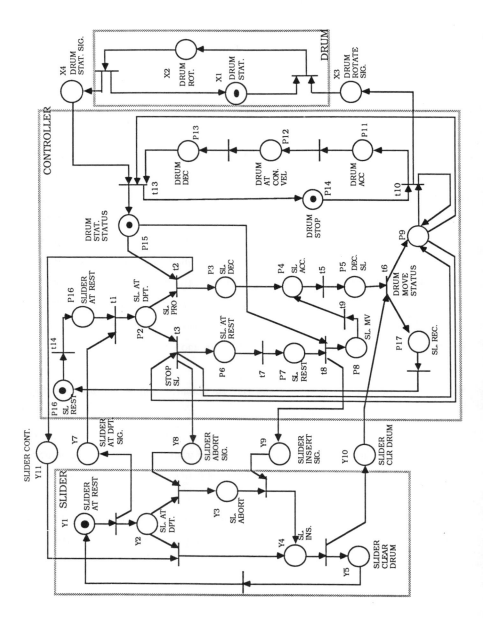

Fig.9.12 Petri net of controller and controlled system

of the design and on deriving rules for the design and modelling of interfaces. Fundamental work is also being undertaken on analysis methods and tools. The designs described above are being implemented on a laboratory scale demonstration rig of the arbor drum and transfer slider.

9.9   CONCLUSIONS

The use of independent software-controlled drives allows flexibility to be introduced into high-speed machine design. In such applications, the software becomes a key component of the system and may control system-critical or safety-critical machine functions. The use of formal methods for the design of such software is recommended. This Chapter has explored the use of formal methods in the design of concurrent real-time software. A systematic approach based on temporal Petri nets has been presented and it has been shown that these techniques can be used to *prove* system and safety properties. This provides a distinct advantage over previous methods in which safety properties could only be inferred. An extension of these techniques to the design of fault tolerant software has also been presented.

The application of these techniques requires a design to be translated into software using property preserving transformations. Petri net models of occam constructs have been described and can be used to draw a correspondence between the Petri net design and an occam implementation. A control implementation has been presented in which a form of model reference technique is used to embed proven synchronisation logic in a controller.

Many of these techniques are being implemented on a research demonstration system comprising multiple, independent drives. The performance of a controller in a time-critical application will be explored using "hardware-in-the-loop", real-time simulation. Further research is also being conducted into temporal Petri nets and the design of software tools to support the underlying analysis and design techniques.

ACKNOWLEDGEMENTS

The authors wish to acknowledge of the support of the SERC for various aspects of this research. In particular, work on the independent software control of machinery was carried out under SERC Grant GR/D/69358; work on the development of formal methods and software fault tolerance is being carried out under SERC Grant GR/F/26584; and work on the development of software tools for the formal design of synchronisation logic is being conducted under SERC/DTI Grant GR/G 60666.

REFERENCES

[9.1]   Fenney L, Draper CM, Foster K and Holding DJ: Modular machine systems, *Proc IMechE/SERC Conf on High Speed Machinery*, pp19-27, IMechE, London, Nov 1988.

[9.2]   Seaward DR and Johnson RC: Selecting electric servo systems for a dynamic accuracy rather than a power/torque specification, *Proc Eurotech Direct Conference*, Birmingham, UK, Pub IMechE, July 1991.

[9.3]   Seaward DR and Johnson RC: Considerations for directly coupled phase synchronised drives, *Proc UPEC*, C4, Sept 1988.

[9.4]   MOD (UK) Interim Defence Standards 00-55 and 00-56, Issue 1, April 1991.

[9.5]   Software considerations in airborne systems and equipment certification, RTCA/D, 178A, RTCA, Washington DC, 1985.

[9.6]   Software for computers in the application of industrial safety-related systems, IEC draft standard 65A (Secretariat) 94, and draft British Standard, Document 89/33006, BSI, 1989.

[9.7]   Pnueli A: Applications of temporal logic to the specification and verification of reactive systems: a survey of current trends, *Lecture Notes in CS*, 224, pp510-584, Springer-Verlag, 1986.

[9.8]   Joseph M and Goswammi A: Formal description of real-time systems: a review, *Information and Software Technology*, **31**, 2, pp67-76, 1989.

[9.9]   Jones CB: *Software development: a rigorous approach*, Prentice Hall, 1980.

[9.10]   Spivey JM: *The Z notation: a reference manual*, Prentice Hall, 1989.

[9.11]   Hoare CAR: *Communicating Sequential Processes*, Comm ACM, **21**, 8, pp666-677, 1978.

[9.12]   Reed GM and Roscoe AW: A timed model for CSP, *Theoretical Computer Science*, **58**, pp249-261, 1987.

[9.13]   Pneuli A: The temporal logic of programs, *Proc 18th Symp Foundations of Computer Science*, IEEE, Providence, pp46-57, 1977.

[9.14]   Gabbay D, Pneuli A, Shelah S and Stavi J: The temporal analysis of fairness, *7th Ann Symp. on Principles of Prog Lang*, Las Vegas, 1980.

[9.15]   Lamport L: Proving liveness properties of concurrent programs, *ACM Trans Prog Lang Systems (ACM TOPLAS)*, **4**, 3, pp455-495, 1982.

[9.16]   Alpern B and Schneider FB: Defining liveness, *Inf Process Lett*, **21**, 4, pp181-185, 1985.

[9.17] Lamport L: A simple approach to specifying concurrent systems, *Comm ACM*, **32**, 1, pp32-45, 1989.

[9.18] Bernstein A and Harter P: Proving real-time properties of programs with temporal logic, *Proc of ACM SIGOPS 8th Ann ACM Symp on Operating Syst*, Prin, pp187-197, 1983.

[9.19] Ostroff JS: Modelling, specifying and verifying real-time embedded computer systems, *Proc Real-time Systems Symp*, IEEE, pp124-132, 1987.

[9.20] Jahanian F and Mok AK: Safety analysis of timing properties in real-time systems, *IEEE Trans Software Eng*, **SE-12**, 9, pp890-904, 1986.

[9.21] Jahanian F and Stuart DA: A method of verifying properties of modechart specifications, *Proc Real-Time Sys Symp*, pp12-21, 1988.

[9.22] Diaz M and Guidacci Da Silverira G: Specification and validation of protocols by temporal logic, in Ed REA Mason, *Information Processing 83*, Elsevier Science Pub BV (North Holland), pp47-52, 1983.

[9.23] Queille JP and Sifakis J: Specification and verification of concurrent systems in CESAR, *LNCS 224*, Springer-Verlag, pp510-584, 1982.

[9.24] Anttila Matti, Erikson H and Ikonen J: Tools and studies of formal techniques - Petri nets and temporal logic, in Eds: Rudin H and West CH, *Protocol specification testing and verification III*, Elsevier Science Pub BV (North Holland), pp139-148, 1983.

[9.25] Genrich HJ, Lautenbach K and Thiagarajan PS: Elements of general net theory, in Ed: Brauer W, *LNCS 84*, Springer-Verlag, 1980.

[9.26] Suzuki I: Fundamental properties and application of temporal Petri nets, *Proc 9th Annual Conf Inform Sci Syst*, John Hopkins Univ, Baltimore, MD, pp641-646, March 1985.

[9.27] Suzuki I and Lu H: Temporal Petri nets and their application to modelling and analysis of a handshake daisy chain arbiter, *IEEE Trans Computers*, **38**, 5, pp696-704, May 1989.

[9.28] Suzuki I: Formal analysis of the alternating bit protocol temporal Petri nets, *IEEE Trans Software Eng*, **16**, 11, pp1273-1281, Nov. 1990.

[9.29] Sagoo JS and Holding DJ: The specification and design of hard real-time systems using timed and temporal Petri nets, *Microprocessing and Microprogramming*, 30, pp389-396, 1990.

[9.30] He Xudong and Lee JAN: Integrating predicate transition nets with first order temporal logic in the specification and verification of concurrent systems, *Formal Aspects of Computing*, **2**, pp226-246, 1990.

[9.31] Peterson JL: *Petri net theory and the modelling of systems*, Prentice Hall, 1981.

[9.32] Carpenter GF, Holding DJ and Tyrrell AM: Design and simulation of a software fault tolerant mechanism for application in distributed processing systems, *Microprocessors and Microprogramming*, **22**, pp175-185, 1988.

[9.33] Merlin PM and Farber DJ: Recoverability of communication protocols, implications of a theoretical study, *IEEE Trans Comms*, **COM-24**, 9, pp1036-1043, 1976.

[9.34] Berthomieu B and Menascre M: An enumeration approach for analysing time Petri nets, *Proc IFIP Congress*, Paris, pp41-46, 1983.

[9.35] Ramachandani C: Analysis of asynchronous concurrent systems by Petri nets, *Project MAC*, TR-120, MIT, Cambridge, 1974.

[9.36] Sirfakis J: Use of Petri nets for performance evaluation, *3rd Int Symp on Modelling and performance of computer systems*, pp75-93, 1977.

[9.37] Razouk RR: The derivation of performance expressions for comm protocols from timed Petri nets, *Computer Comm Review (USA)*, **14**, 2, pp210-217, 1984.

[9.38] Levenson NG and Stolzy JL: Safety analysis using Petri nets, *IEEE Trans Eng*, **SE-13,** 3, pp386-397, 1987.

[9.39] Koymans R, Shyamasundar R, W de Roever, Gerth R and Arun-Kumar S: Compositional semantics for real-time distributed computing, *Lecture Notes in CS*, 193, Springer Verlag, 1985.

[9.40] Sagoo JS and Holding DJ: A comparison of temporal Petri net techniques in the specification and design of hard real-time systems, *Proc Euromicro 91*, Vienna, Pub: Microprocessors and Microprogramming, Sept 1991.

[9.41] Inmos: *Occam 2 Programming Manual*, Prentice Hall, 1988.

[9.42] Inmos: *The Transputer Databook*, 2nd Ed, Inmos, 1989.

[9.43] May D: Occam, *Sigplan Notices*, **18,** 4, pp67-79, 1983.

[9.44] Hoare CAR: *Communicating sequential processes*, Prentice Hall, 1985.

[9.45] Mekly LJ and Yau SS: Software design representation using abstract process networks, *IEEE Trans Software Engineering*, SE-6, pp420-434, 1980.

[9.46] Carpenter GF: The use of Occam and Petri Nets in the simulation of logic structures for the control of loosely coupled distributed systems, *Proc UKSC Conf on Computer Simulation*, (UKSC 1987), pp30-35, 1987.

[9.47] Avienzis A: The N version approach to fault tolerant software, *IEEE Trans SE*, **SE-11,** 12, pp1491-1501, 1985.

[9.48] Hecht H: Fault tolerant software, *IEEE Trans on Reliability*, R-28, pp227-232, 1979.

[9.49] Anderson T and Lee PA: *Fault Tolerance, Principles and Practice*, Prentice Hall, 1981.

[9.50] Anderson T (ed): *Resilient Computing Systems*, Collins Professional and Technical Books, 1987.

[9.51] Levenson NG: Software Fault Tolerance; the case for forward error recovery, *Proc AIAA Conf on Computers in Aerospace*, pp50-54, 1983.

[9.52] Campbell RH and Randell B: Error recovery in asynchronous systems, *IEEE Trans Software Engineering*, SE-12, pp811-826, 1986.

[9.53] Horning JJ, Lauer HC, Melliar-Smith PM, and Randell B: A program structure for error detection and recovery in *Lecture Notes in Computer Science*, **16,** Springer Verlag, pp171-187, 1974.

[9.54] Randell B: System structure for software fault tolerance, *IEEE Trans SE*, **SE-1,** pp220-232, 1975

[9.55] Merlin PM and Randell B: State restoration in distributed systems, *Proc 8th Int Symp on Fault Tolerant Computers*, pp129-134, 1978.

[9.56] Russell DL: State restoration in systems of communicating processes *IEEE Trans Software Engineering*, **SE-6,** pp183-194, 1980.

[9.57] Tyrrell AM and Holding DJ: Design of reliable software in distributed systems using the conversation scheme, *IEEE Trans on Software Engineering*, **SE-12,** pp921-928, 1986.

[9.58] Holding DJ and Carpenter GF: Software fault tolerance, Chapter 8 in Ed: Fleming PJ *Parallel processing in control - the Transputer and other architectures*, Peter Peregrinus, 1988.

[9.59] Seaward DR and Johnson RC: On the simulation of brushless drives, *Proc UPEC*, B5, Sept 1988.

[9.60] Holding DJ, Fenney L and Foster K: The use of Occam in the specification, simulation, synchronisation and control of high-speed intermittent drives, *Proc UKSC Conf on Computer Simulation (UKSC 87)*, Bangor, Pub: Soc Computer Simulation, pp108-113, Sept 1987.

Chapter 10

Real-Time Control and Simulation

Performance Analysis Tools

PJ Fleming and DF Garcia Nocetti

10.1   INTRODUCTION

There are three fundamental problems to be solved when considering the implementation of a control algorithm on parallel processing systems:

- identifying parallelism in the algorithm,
- partitioning the algorithm into tasks,
- allocation of tasks to processors.

This Chapter describes a suite of CAD tools to automate the parallelisation of a class of algorithms and to permit performance assessment. These tools are applied to a test case and the results are analyzed.

In Chapter 1, we have seen how parallelism can be expressed in a variety of ways. Here we are concerned, principally, with the identification of algorithmic parallelism. Having identified tasks to be executed in parallel, careful task allocation is necessary to achieve good processor utilisation and to optimise inter-processor communication in the target system.

There is a number of parameters which have a significant influence on the performance of multi-processor systems. These include the amount of parallelism inherent in the problem, the method for decomposing a problem into smaller modules or tasks, the method applied to allocate these tasks to processors, the grain size of the tasks, sequential execution times, communication overheads, scheduling overheads, the number of processors, the speed of processors and memories, and the topology adopted [10.1-10.6]. Analyzing the performance of multi-processor systems is thus a very complex task, since many factors jointly determine system performance and these factors are inter-related.

The granularity issue, for example, has already been cited in Chapter 1. When the grain size of computations executed is reduced, in order to better exploit the parallelism available in the application, processors complete the computation more rapidly. As a result communication over the interconnection network is more frequent and the communication overhead is increased thus slowing down processors. Since the interaction among these various performance factors is very complex and involves many tradeoffs, it is necessary to tune system parameters such that the whole system achieves its peak performance at minimum cost.

To support the application of parallelism in this way we have developed tools to automate this process on transputer-based systems. These tools assist the control engineer in the determination of the likely speedup, the number of processors to be used, and in experimentation with alternative system topologies.

The control system design package, MATLAB, has been integrated with the Transputer Development System (TDS), to generate an **E**nvironment for **P**arallel **I**mplementation of **C**ontrol **A**lgorithms and **S**imulation (**EPICAS**). This environment offers the control engineer a suite of software tools to automate the implementation of control algorithms and simulation systems on transputer-based architectures. The tools are used to map systems onto transputer architectures of different sizes and topologies, and to evaluate strategies, by displaying, **on-line,** task allocation, processor activity and execution time data.

An overview of EPICAS is provided in Section 10.2. A flight control law (VAP) is described next in Section 10.3. This is used as a representative example in succeeding Sections to illustrate how EPICAS works. The mapping strategy implemented in EPICAS is described in Section 10.4 and applied to this theme example. Task allocation methods and transputer network topologies are covered in Section 10.5. Performance analysis tools are applied in Section 10.6 and prompt a discussion of the merits or otherwise of alternative task allocation strategies and topologies. The granularity issue, in particular, is explored in some depth. The Chapter concludes with a review of the tools developed and the approaches adopted, and suggestions for new tools to support the implementation of transputer-based simulation and control.

10.2   EPICAS

EPICAS integrates the control system design package, MATLAB [10.7,10,8], with the Transputer Development System (TDS). It has been developed originally to run on a PC-based system, but a SUN-based version of this system using the Occam Toolset is currently under development.

This environment offers the control engineer a number of software tools to automate the implementation of control algorithms on transputer-based systems. The need for such an environment arose out of our previous work on mapping strategies for implementing controllers on transputer networks [10.9]. The effort involved in human-engineered implementations stimulated research into the development of software tools to automate the implementation process.

The tools within the environment, see Fig. 10.1, are grouped in two sets: MATLAB tools for parallel partitioning, and occam tools for task allocation.

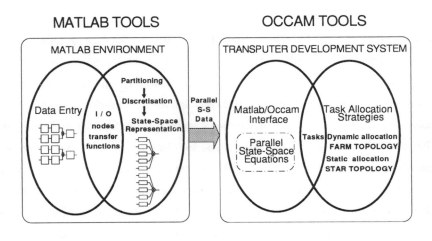

Fig. 10.1 EPICAS - an environment for mapping systems on transputers

The tools for parallel partitioning, based on MATLAB, generate a parallel representation of a system (e.g. a control law) as a number of independent tasks. A continuous-time system description in block diagram form may be input. The software performs the partitioning, discretisation and parallel representation of the system as a number of state-space equations.

The occam tools for task allocation, developed in TDS, automate the mapping of the tasks (state-space equations) onto a number of transputer-based topologies, using either static or dynamic allocation strategies. These tools permit the evaluation of both types of strategies, by displaying on-line task allocation, processor activity and execution times on the target hardware.

10.3   FLIGHT CONTROL LAW EXAMPLE

The Versatile Auto-Pilot (VAP) control law is described briefly in this Section. This law is one (the more complex) of two control laws for approach and landing developed in theoretical studies at Royal Aerospace Establishment, Bedford, [10.10,10.11]. The control law had previously been flown on the Civil Avionics Section's BAC 1-11 using a single-processor (M68000) implementation. A 4-transputer implementation has subsequently been flown as part of a Demonstrator project. It is a 4-input, 2-output control algorithm and is presented in block diagram form in Fig. 10.2.

The inputs are pitch rate (q), barometric height error (h_B), vertical acceleration (d^2h/dt^2) and airspeed error (u_a); the outputs are elevator rate demand ($d\eta/dt$) and throttle demand (v_d). The diagram notation follows the convention that the gain between the elevator position and an aircraft state error input is denoted by **G** with the error variable as a subscript. Similarly, **A** is used to denote the gain associated with throttle position. The throttle position control law consists of a smoothing lag on the airspeed error input together with the **A** gains. As the elevator servo-system is a rate demand servo, the elevator control law demand is of derivative type. The first component of the elevator control law comprises **G** gains together with a 0.1s lag. In the second component of the law, the height error inputs from several sources are mixed in complementary filters with normal acceleration information. These signals are further transformed by lag terms and **G** gains.

The VAP control law is not particularly demanding for implementation on a transputer array. However, it is of sufficient complexity, possessing significant cross-coupling terms, to be a non-trivial exercise for parallelisation. A variety of parallelisation approaches are described in [10.12]. The preferred approach is described in the next Section.

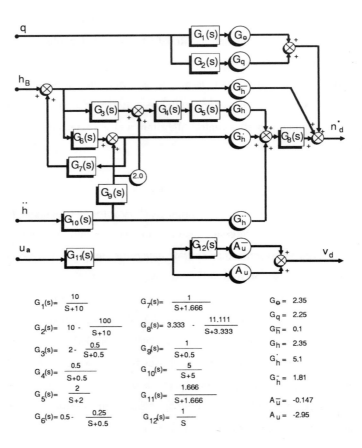

$G_1(s) = \dfrac{10}{S+10}$

$G_2(s) = 10 - \dfrac{100}{S+10}$

$G_3(s) = 2 - \dfrac{0.5}{S+0.5}$

$G_4(s) = \dfrac{0.5}{S+0.5}$

$G_5(s) = \dfrac{2}{S+2}$

$G_6(s) = 0.5 - \dfrac{0.25}{S+0.5}$

$G_7(s) = \dfrac{1}{S+1.666}$

$G_8(s) = 3.333 - \dfrac{11.111}{S+3.333}$

$G_9(s) = \dfrac{1}{S+0.5}$

$G_{10}(s) = \dfrac{5}{S+5}$

$G_{11}(s) = \dfrac{1.666}{S+1.666}$

$G_{12}(s) = \dfrac{1}{S}$

$G_e = 2.35$

$G_q = 2.25$

$G_{\bar{h}} = 0.1$

$G_h = 2.35$

$G_{\dot{h}} = 5.1$

$G_{\bar{h}}^{\cdot} = 1.81$

$A_{\bar{u}} = -0.147$

$A_u = -2.95$

Fig. 10.2 VAP control law block diagram

10.4   MAPPING STRATEGY

The **Parallel State-Space** strategy seeks to maximise the parallelism available by modifying the algorithm into a set of independent tasks, using a state-space model of the system. The input-output relationship, for each input-output pair, is obtained and expressed in block-diagonal, state-space form. This is reduced to a set of low-order, state-space equations which may executed concurrently. Parallelisation tools have been developed in MATLAB.

10.4.1 MATLAB Overview

MATLAB (**Mat**rix **Lab**oratory) [10.7] was first released in 1980 as a collection of software tools of linear algebra, matrix computation and numerical analysis to assist scientists and engineers with their numerical calculations. Complex arithmetic, eigenvalues, root-finding, matrix inversion, and FFT's are examples of these tools. Elementary matrix commands for data analysis and statistical tools are also provided. The present version of MATLAB, written in C, was designed as an integrated system, including graphics, programmable macros, IEEE arithmetic, a fast interpreter and many analytical commands. The implementation used here is PC-MATLAB [10.8] and runs on IBM PC-compatible machines which can also host the Transputer Development System.

MATLAB essentially provides the user with a set of low-level commands and the capability to define new commands through the creation of m-files (files containing a sequence of MATLAB statements distinguished by having the extension ".m"). M-files are a means of automating long sequences of commands. The new files are subsequently added to the set of available commands. Through the use of m-files, MATLAB has been extended by the provision of Toolboxes. Toolboxes, specialising in control engineering applications, include Control System Design [10.13], Robust-Control [10.14], Multivariable Frequency-Domain [10.15], Signal Processing [10.16], System Identification [10.17] and State-Space Identification [10.18]. MATLAB has thus become a de facto industry standard for control systems research and design. A number of m-files have been developed for this work and are described in detail in [10.12].

10.4.2 Parallel Partitioning MATLAB Toolbox

The MATLAB tools, developed for partitioning of control algorithms, are a collection of customised m-files. This Toolbox includes utilities for data entry, block partitioning, and parallel representation, which are called *blkentry.m*, *blkpart.m* and *paradata.m* respectively, see Fig. 10.3. The toolset enables the user to perform automatic partitioning of the control algorithms into a number of independent tasks.

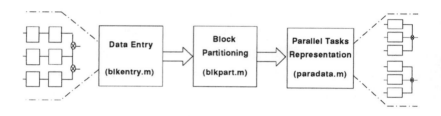

Fig. 10.3 MATLAB tools for parallel partitioning of systems

As practical controllers are often described in block form, block diagram entry facilities are provided to accept this type of system description. The MATLAB tool, *blkentry.m,* provides a means of inputting system information from, say, a block diagram representation such as that given in Fig. 10.2.

The MATLAB tool, *blkpart.m*, transforms the control law into a number of independent tasks, by obtaining each input-output relationship and reducing the control algorithm to a set of independent path transfer functions. The utility accepts the block description produced by the data entry tool outlined above and generates a state-space model of the familiar form:

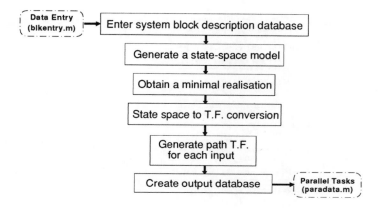

Fig. 10.4 Overview of partitioning process

$$\dot{x} = Ax + Bu \qquad (10.1)$$
$$y = Cx + Du \qquad (10.2)$$

If a state-space model is already available as the original system representation, this model is, of course, supplied directly to the partitioning software tool, and the block data entry tool is not required. When the system description is in the form of a transfer function block diagram, program **blkpart.m** generates a block diagonal state-space model consisting of the unconnected transfer functions. Using the interconnection data, the program connects up the block diagonal model and returns a state-space model (see Fig. 10.4).

Redundant or unnecessary states, introduced by constant gain blocks in the block diagram, are removed by transforming the matrices A, B and C to controllability and observability staircase forms using available MATLAB functions. This transformation isolates the uncontrollable and unobservable states, which are then removed from the

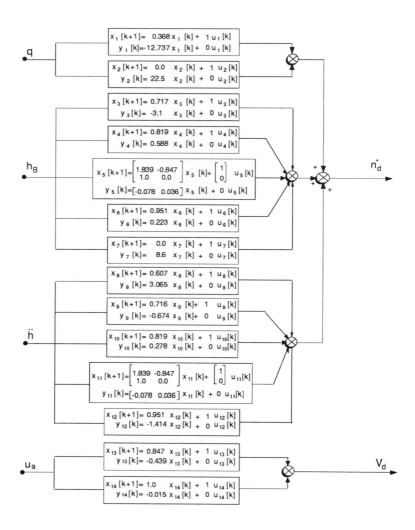

Fig. 10.5 VAP control law: parallel tasks representation

model, thus eliminating redundancy in the representation.

A parallel representation of the system is obtained using the new function, **paradata.m**. This tool essentially decomposes the block diagonal, state-space model into a parallel connection structure of low-order (first- and second-order), state-space models which are subsequently discretised using the pole-zero mapping method and finally represented as a parallel connection of discrete-time, state-space equations. In Fig. 10.5, the VAP control law is reconfigured as a parallel connection of state space equations, for T = 0.1s. Note that x_1, x_2, ... , x_{14} represent vectors of dimension 1 or 2. This tool also produces an output database which includes the coefficients of the state-space equations and their association to form the controller outputs. The output database is ported to the Transputer Development System, where a set of occam-based tools has been written to map this partitioned representation of a system, using alternative strategies of task allocation, onto a parallel processing transputer-based network.

10.5 TASK ALLOCATION METHODS AND TRANSPUTER NETWORK TOPOLOGIES

10.5.1 Task allocation tools

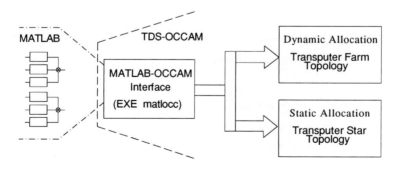

Fig. 10.6 Occam tools for task allocation

A set of tools for the allocation of tasks onto transputer-based systems has been developed using the Transputer Development System. The toolset, depicted in Fig. 10.6, has been written in occam2 and is used to automate the mapping of control algorithms onto a number of transputer topologies, using both static and dynamic task allocation strategies.

A control algorithm, partitioned by the MATLAB tools into a set of independent state-space equations, is imported into TDS using a MATLAB-Occam interface tool and mapped onto a parallel processing, transputer-based network. The mapping of the control algorithm is achieved using tools that implement either dynamic or static task allocation strategies. The dynamic allocation tools are based on a Processor Farm computational model while the static allocation toolset is based on a Processor Star topology. The toolset permits the evaluation of both approaches, by displaying processor activity and performance. The tools are described in detail in [10.12].

In the following sub-Sections, the partitioned version of the VAP control law is used to illustrate the application of the task allocation tools to a working example of digital flight control. In order to map the control algorithms considered onto a transputer network, a purpose-built Eurocard transputer system [10.19], developed in-house for real-time control applications, has been used. This system includes a number of single-transputer boards as basic building blocks, accommodated in a Eurorack, along with a variety of support boards. These include a crossbar switch, system reset/analyze, ADC/DAC and digital I/O cards. This modular system is portable and customisable allowing the user to select only the modules of direct use, in order to distribute the limited transputer resources as efficiently as possible.

10.5.2 Processor Farm Topology

The dynamic task allocation tools are a number of occam programs based on a Processor Farm computational structure. Processor farming is a conceptually simple method of utilising multiple processors. The operation of the farm is based around the ability to dynamically schedule tasks onto a collection of processing elements. The scheduling action must occur very frequently, and, as a worst case, will equal the number of tasks in the partition. It must be simple, so that it does not present too large an overhead.

The most typical version of the processor farm model (see Fig.10.7) uses a single master processor for scheduling tasks to one or more worker processors connected in a line.

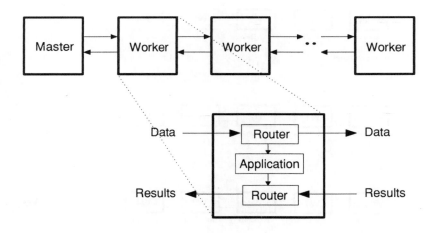

Fig. 10.7 Processor farm model

The application code or computational task (in our case, a first- or second-order, state-space model plus all the coefficients of the partitioned control algorithm to form the state-space equations) runs on each of the worker processors and routers are used to route data and results through the network. Task identifiers, to define which tasks must be executed, and input data are passed to the network as required, in order to utilise the full processing potential of the system. This provides an automatic mechanism for dynamic load balancing. Results are collected by the master as they are calculated by the workers. Finally, these results are used to compute the system outputs.

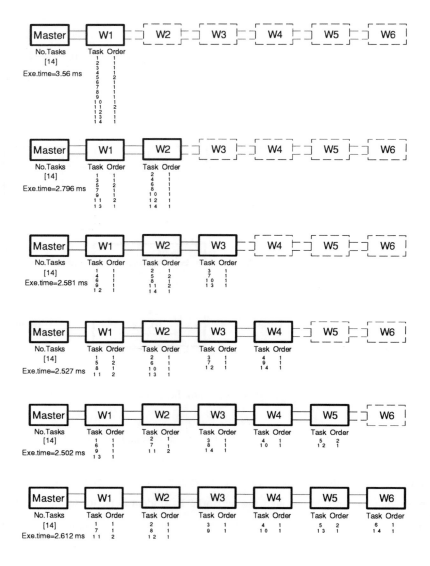

Fig. 10.8 Processor farm activity for 1 to 6 workers (T414-15 processors)

Fig. 10.8 illustrates typical output from the system when investigating farm performance of different numbers of transputers executing the VAP control law. Data in the figure indicates the total execution time for the 14 tasks, which processor they were executed on, and the associated order (1 or 2) of each task. In view of the potential bottleneck experienced by flow of data between the Master processor and W1, a processor farm topology consisting of three lanes of workers emanating from the Master processor can also be assessed.

10.5.3 Processor Star Topology

Tools for static task allocation are based on a Processor Star model as the computational structure. This model employs a central process for distributing a package of fixed tasks to a number of worker processes arranged around the central node. The tasks are allocated to the workers and bound to them for their lifetime. Each worker executes a fragment of the application code (in our case, a sub-set of the state-space equations of the model). Communications between task groups take place during the initial distribution of data and the final computation to form the output values.

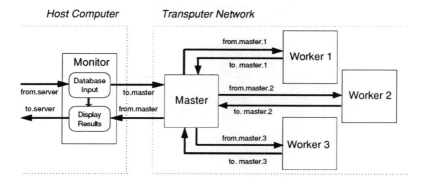

Fig. 10.9 Transputer implementation of a processor star array

The transputer implementation of this topology, recognising the 4-link limitation, is given in Fig. 10.9. The application code resides on the workers. The master sends an identifier to each available worker to indicate which component of the application is to be executed. The master also executes a portion of the computational task. When the workers complete their job, partial results are sent back to the master which in turn calculates a final computation. Typical output from such an exercise is depicted in Fig. 10.10, where, again, the example application is the VAP control law consisting of 14 tasks.

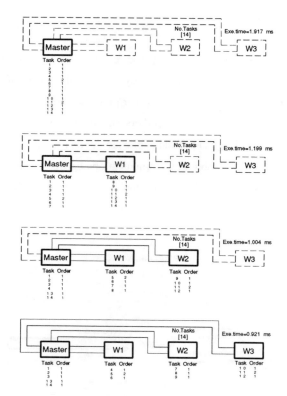

Fig. 10.10 Processor star activity for 0 to 3 workers (T414-15 processors)

10.6 PERFORMANCE ANALYSIS

10.6.1 Performance Metrics

There are many ways of measuring the performance of parallel algorithms running on parallel processing systems. However there is no single suitable metric for absolute performance estimation [10.20]. A variety are used in reference [10.12], of which one, speedup, S (see Chapter 1, Section 1.6.3), is given special prominence here.

10.6.2 Processor Farm Performance

Measurements were carried out for varying the number of workers in the farm, from 1 up to 6 workers, in the test case presented. Figure 10.11 shows the resulting execution time performance of this array for two types of transputers: T414-15 (T4) and T800-20 (T8). The total execution time, in each case, is the interval in which the master executes a complete iteration (allocates tasks, receives results of each task and computes the global system outputs). Two sets of results are given in each graph: for a linear farm arrangement and an extended version of the farm.

Considering first the linear farm results, it is clear that the benefits of parallel processing are not convincing for either set of processors. The reduction in execution time for multiple processors is greater for the T4 implementation than for the T8 case. The linear farm of T4 transputers shows a modest reduction in execution time from 1.273 to 1.422ms, as additional processing power is introduced. However, no extra improvement can be realised for more than 5 workers. An explanation for this latter result is simply that the extra communication overheads involved in extending the farm length are not offset by the corresponding additional computing power provision. Also, in general, the R/C ratio is unacceptably low for this implementation, i.e. there is a granularity mismatch and the algorithm parallelisation is too fine for this hardware implementation. This is compounded for the T8 case where the R/C ratio is further eroded since the increased processing power of the T8 is not matched by a corresponding improvement in its communication speed.

In this processor farm realisation, the scheduling action performed by the master is simple (a list scheduling of independent tasks) and thus does not present a significant overhead to the performance. Overhead due to communications is thus the important component and is exacerbated when the linear array is long. This contrasts somewhat with the findings of related research which applied process farming to the calculation of the inverse dynamics for a robot manipulator [10.21]. Here the scheduling operation took almost 70 % of the total execution time. However, the two schemes differ in respect of their required scheduling algorithms.

In the light of these results, therefore, the linear farm arrangement may be unsuitable for more than a small number of processors due to its limited throughput. (A message may require $O(N)$ propagations to reach its destination in a network of N processors and each must route $O(N)$ messages.) Researchers have investigated schemes for scheduling tasks to the processors in the farm which keep the overhead of communicating data to a minimum [10.22,10.23]. One of these schemes is to increase the effective throughput by adopting different topologies of processors (e.g. tree, star, etc.).

Based on these strategies, the original linear farm model here has been extended by configuring the system as three chains of worker processors arranged around a central master. This approach required a more sophisticated task allocation strategy. However, a reduction in communication overhead was expected, because in this extended approach there is a shorter path between the controller and any worker. This is borne out by the results illustrated in Fig. 10.11, where execution times for the extended case represent a marked improvement on the linear arrangement. Again we note (Fig. 10.11(b)) that for this particular problem size there is a point at which adding processors serves no useful purpose.

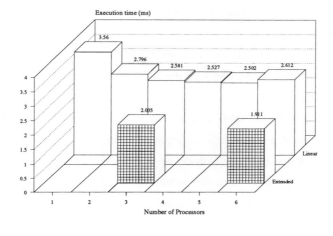

(a)

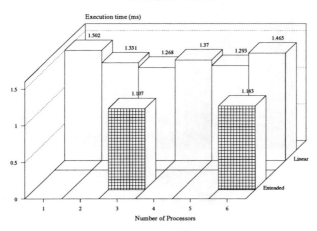

(b)

Fig. 10.11 Performance of the processor farm topology: (a) T414-15 implementation; (b) T800-20 implementation

10.6.3 Processor Star Performance

In a similar way to that of the Processor Farm, measurements were carried out for different numbers of processors in the Processor Star configuration for which tasks are allocated statically. Fig. 10.12 shows the resulting execution time performance using T4 and T8 transputers. Compared with the farm approach, it is clear that the static allocation strategy is more appropriate in this particular application. There is a significant reduction in execution time as additional processing power is introduced but at the expense of a reduction in efficiency. Investigation revealed that this loss of efficiency was due to a combination of load imbalance of tasks coupled with communication overheads. Nevertheless this approach performs better than other implementations (using dynamic allocation) for the same number of processors.

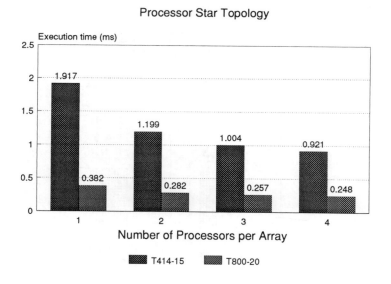

Fig. 10.12 Performance of the processor star topology

The use of T8 transputers exhibited a considerable improvement in execution time when compared with the T4 implementation; however, smaller values of efficiency can be noted. Again the less favourable R/C ratio associated with the T8 contributes to these results.

10.6.4 Effects of Increasing Task Granularity

Having noted in 10.6.2 and 10.6.3 that the task granularity arising from the parallelisation exercise may lead to an unfavourable R/C ratio for transputer implementation, this sub-Section investigates the effect of increasing task granularity for the topologies under consideration. This is achieved by increasing the order of complexity of the tasks, by means of aggregating small grains together on single processors (thus augmenting the grain size). This evaluation is undertaken to provide better estimates of speed improvements for future, much larger problems.

The resulting size of the task models ranged from *size 2* to *size 8*. A *size 2* task model, for example, will execute twice as much processing as the reference model, which has *size 1*. A *size 3* task will execute three times as much, and so on. Fig. 10.13 depicts the execution time performance and its associated speedup using T4 transputers for the eight different sizes of the task models. Fig. 10.13(a) shows the variation of execution time as the size of a fixed number of tasks (14 tasks) is increased. As would be expected, there is an increase in algorithm execution time over the size 1 case (Fig. 10.11), roughly proportional to the size of the tasks performed. However, the relatively small amount of communication of the coarser granularity (higher R/C) reduces overheads, and consequently a better performance is achieved. The improved speedup (Fig. 10.13(b)) for coarser grain tasks is significant.

A similar approach was used to evaluate the performance of static allocation strategies on models of coarser granularity. Fig. 10.14 depicts the execution time performance and associated speedup of this approach using T4 transputers. Again the improved speedup for the coarser grain tasks is important.

Execution time (ms)

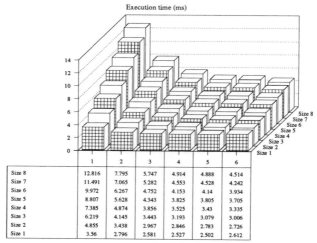

	1	2	3	4	5	6
Size 8	12.816	7.795	5.747	4.914	4.888	4.514
Size 7	11.491	7.065	5.282	4.553	4.528	4.242
Size 6	9.972	6.267	4.752	4.153	4.14	3.934
Size 5	8.807	5.628	4.343	3.825	3.805	3.705
Size 4	7.385	4.874	3.856	3.525	3.43	3.335
Size 3	6.219	4.145	3.443	3.193	3.079	3.006
Size 2	4.855	3.438	2.967	2.846	2.783	2.726
Size 1	3.56	2.796	2.581	2.527	2.502	2.612

Number of Processors per Farm

(a)

Speedup

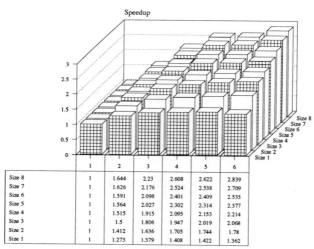

	1	2	3	4	5	6
Size 8	1	1.644	2.23	2.608	2.622	2.839
Size 7	1	1.626	2.176	2.524	2.538	2.709
Size 6	1	1.591	2.098	2.401	2.409	2.535
Size 5	1	1.564	2.027	2.302	2.314	2.377
Size 4	1	1.515	1.915	2.095	2.153	2.214
Size 3	1	1.5	1.806	1.947	2.019	2.068
Size 2	1	1.412	1.636	1.705	1.744	1.78
Size 1	1	1.273	1.379	1.408	1.422	1.362

Number of Processors per Farm

(b)

Fig.10.13 Performance of processor farm topology for different task sizes:

(a) Execution time; (b) Speedup

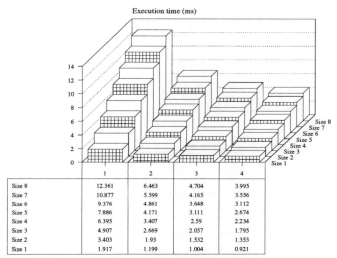

Execution time (ms)

	1	2	3	4
Size 8	12.361	6.463	4.704	3.995
Size 7	10.877	5.599	4.165	3.556
Size 6	9.376	4.861	3.648	3.112
Size 5	7.886	4.171	3.111	2.674
Size 4	6.395	3.407	2.59	2.234
Size 3	4.907	2.669	2.057	1.795
Size 2	3.403	1.93	1.532	1.353
Size 1	1.917	1.199	1.004	0.921

Number of Processors per Array

(a)

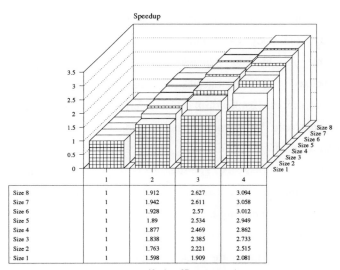

Speedup

	1	2	3	4
Size 8	1	1.912	2.627	3.094
Size 7	1	1.942	2.611	3.058
Size 6	1	1.928	2.57	3.012
Size 5	1	1.89	2.534	2.949
Size 4	1	1.877	2.469	2.862
Size 3	1	1.838	2.385	2.733
Size 2	1	1.763	2.221	2.515
Size 1	1	1.598	1.909	2.081

Number of Processors per Array

(b)

Fig.10.14 Performance of processor star topology for different task sizes:

(a) Execution time; (b) Speedup

This study of the effect of task granularity on parallel processing performance emphasises the importance of matching task size to processor characteristics and clearly demonstrates that an effective parallel processing implementation will be the reward for the designer who pays attention to this issue.

10.7   CONCLUDING REMARKS

This Chapter has presented a software approach for the automation and evaluation of parallel processing implementation of control laws on transputer-based systems. A suite of tools, **EPICAS,** has been described which integrates a respected and widely-used control system CAD software package, MATLAB, with a transputer development system. This suite of tools has been used to analyze the performance of dynamic and static task allocation schemes on systems of varying size.

A parallel version of a digital flight control law has been mapped, using both types of task allocation strategy, onto a number of parallel processing, transputer-based systems. Although the study was limited to a single control algorithm, this has provided valuable insight into the potential performance, improvements and bottlenecks associated with these strategies. In its basic realisation, for this particular controller example, process farming displayed an inferior performance when compared with the static approach. An extended version, using the triple chain of workers, offered an improvement in performance, significantly reducing communication overheads and, thus, execution time. The static task allocation approach, using a star topology, exhibited the best performance, having the advantage that there was no overhead associated with allocating tasks in real-time.

Granularity issues received much attention. Through experiments in varying the size of task granularity in a controlled manner, it was confirmed that appropriate matching of task size to parallel processor architecture resulted in effective implementations of parallel processing systems for control.

Recently, Maguire [10.24] has devised a scheme to measure processor granularity and obtained the following results:

T414	0.005
T800	0.075
T9000	0.3125 (estimated).

These measures support the observations that larger task sizes are required to realise efficient performance on T800 series processors and serve to indicate the mapping changes which must be anticipated for the T9000 series.

Of course, these measures do not convey the whole story. For example, inter-transputer communication is more efficient when longer messages are sent rather than a large number of small messages. Having introduced, then, the notions of task granularity and processor granularity it is further worth investigating "communications granularity" [10.25], where communications speed and the handling of message size varies from processor to processor.

The EPICAS environment is already being extended in a variety of ways. It is being ported to new platforms (Sun/SparcStations and the Occam Toolset) and new implementation language alternatives are being provided. It is also being used as a vehicle for the testing of fault-tolerant strategies. It is recognised that the approach thus far has concentrated on the parallelisation of the control algorithm. Of course control software contains many algorithms: for control, simulation, optimisation, filtering and identification, in addition to simpler practical tasks such as event logging and data checking. It is envisaged that EPICAS may eventually form part of a more comprehensive scheme, perhaps based on a software engineering CASE tool, to assist control engineers in the mapping of control software onto a parallel processing system.

REFERENCES

[10.1] Sarkar V: *Partitioning and scheduling parallel programs for multiprocessors,* Pitman Publishing, London, 1989.

[10.2] Cvetanovic Z: The effects of problem partitioning, allocation, and granularity on the performance of multiple-processor systems, *IEEE Transactions on Computers,* **C-36,** 4, pp421-432, 1987.

[10.3] Shaffer P: Experience with implementation of a turbojet engine control program on a multiprocessor, *Proc 1989 American Control Conference,* pp2715-2720, 1989.

[10.4] Kasahara H and Narita S: Practical multiprocessor scheduling algorithms for efficient parallel processing, *IEEE Transactions on Computers,* **C-33,** 11, pp1023-1029, 1984.

[10.5] Lee SY and Aggarwal JK: A mapping strategy for parallel processing, *IEEE Transactions on Computers,* **C-36,** 4, pp433-441, 1987.

[10.6] Berger M and Bokhari S: A partitioning strategy for nonuniform problems on multiprocessors, *IEEE Transactions on Computers,* **C-36,** 5, pp570-580, 1987.

[10.7] Moler C: *MATLAB user's guide,* Department of Computer Science, University of New Mexico, Albuquerque, USA, 1980.

[10.8] Moler C, Little J, Bangert S and Kleinman S: *PC-MATLAB user's guide,* The MathWorks Inc. 1987.

[10.9] Garcia Nocetti F, Thompson HA, De Oliveira MCF and Fleming PJ: Implementation of a transputer-based flight controller, *Proc IEE,* Part D, **137,** 3, pp130-136, 1990.

[10.10] Goddard KF: Theoretical studies of automatic control laws for a BAC 1-11 aircraft utilising the wing spoilers for direct lift control, *Technical Report 79034,* Royal Aircraft Establishment, 1979.

[10.11] Goddard KF and Cooke N: Flight trials of an automatic control law for a BAC 1-11 Aircraft, *Technical Report 80003,* Royal Aircraft Establishment, 1980.

[10.12] Garcia Nocetti DF and Fleming PJ: *Parallel processing in digital control,* Springer Verlag, 1992.

[10.13] Laub A, Little J: *Control systems toolbox for use with MATLAB,* User's Guide, The MathWorks Inc. August, 1986.

[10.14] Chiang R, Safonov M: *Robust-control toolbox for use with MATLAB,* User's Guide, The MathWorks Inc. June, 1988.

[10.15] Boyle JM, Ford MP, Maciejowski JM: *Multivariable frequency domain toolbox for use with MATLAB,* User's Guide, GEC Eng Research Centre and Cambridge Control Ltd. April, 1988.

[10.16] Little J, Shure L: *Signal processing toolbox for use with MATLAB,* User's Guide, The MathWorks Inc. August, 1988.

[10.17] Ljung L: *System identification toolbox for use with MATLAB,* User's Guide, The MathWorks Inc. April, 1988.

[10.18] Milne G: *State-space identification toolbox for use with MATLAB,* User's Guide, The MathWorks Inc. March, 1988.

[10.19] Entwistle P, Lawrie DI, Thompson HA and Jones DI: A Eurocard computer using transputers for control systems applications, *IEE Colloquium on Eurocard computers - a solution to low-cost control,* September, 1989.

[10.20] Parkinson D and Liddell HM: The measurement of performance on a highly parallel system, *IEEE Transactions on Computers,* **C-32,** 1, 1983.

[10.21] Entwistle PM: *Parallel processing for real-time control,* PhD dissertation, University of Wales, Bangor, 1990.

[10.22] Jones DI and Entwistle PM: Parallel computation of an algorithm in robotic control, *Proc IEE Control 88 Conference,* Oxford, pp438-443, 1988.

[10.23] Green SA, Paddon DJ: An extension of the processor farm using a tree architecture, *Proc 9th OUG Technical Meeting,* Southampton, UK, September 1988.

[10.24] Maguire LP: *Parallel architectures for Kalman filtering and self-tuning control,* PhD dissertation, The Queen's University of Belfast, 1991.

[10.25] Dodds GI: *Personal communication,* 1991.

Index